HEALTHCARE GENDER AND CONFLICT IN KASHMIR

HEALTHCARE GENDER AND CONFLICT IN KASHMIR

Dr B A Dabla

ISBN: 978-93-5128-105-4

Price : ₹ 990

First Published, 2015

Published by

Kalpaz Publications
C-30, Satyawati Nagar
Delhi-110052, Ph. : 9212142040
E-mail: kalpaz@hotmail.com

Laser Typesetting: Future Computer, Delhi
***Printed** at:* G. Print Process, Delhi

Cataloging in Publication Data-DK

Courtesy: D.K. Agencies (P) Ltd. <docinfo@dkagencies.com>

Dabla, Bashir A., **author.**

Healthcare gender and conflict in Kashmir / Dr BA Dabla.

pages cm

Includes index.

ISBN 9789351281054

1. Women's health services-India-Jammu and Kashmir. 2. Rural health services-India-Jammu and Kashmir. 3. Political violence-Health aspects-India-Jammu and Kashmir. 1. Title.

DDC 362.108209546 23

Contents

Acknowledgement

I am extremely grateful to the **Indian Council of Medical Research, New Delhi** for sponsoring this research project on the very crucial topic of medical sociology. I am particularly grateful to Dr Bontha A. Babu who helped at every stage of this research from sponsorship to the conclusion.

I am thankful to the University of Kashmir, Srinagar for providing every facility available. to complete the research work in time.

I am equally and personally grateful to all respondents (General and Professional) for giving us patient hearing and enough time for discussing the themes related to this study. Without their help and co-operation, all the valuable data in this study couldn't have been incorporated.

I am equally thankful to the following research staff members of the project for working with academic commitment and in professional manner:

- Dr Ali Mohammad Rather, Senior Research Fellow;
- Ms Sabah Jan, Research Investigator;
- Ms Sumeera Nazir, Research Investigator;
- Mr Shamasul Haque, Research Investigator;
- Mr Aftab Ahamd Bhat, Research Investigator.

Finally, I thank my staff members in the Department of Sociology of Kashmir University for giving all help for successful completion of this research project.

DR B A DABLA
Principal Investigator

Foreword

As the fact stands, the gender health and its long-term care has got basic and primary importance, because of which the reproductive process is maintained and continued. Though this healthcare is crucial for human survival, it has not been provided as per their needs and requirements, especially in the past. Thus, it may be argued that women in general have suffered in their health in the past. In reality, every woman on an average had to face various health problems in their life span. This situation was caused because of biological and social-cultural factors. There was also no organised effort for providing treatment and facilities. This situation of gender healthcare prevailed in Kashmir when the conflict partly collapsed the then existing healthcare system. This added more problems to the existing gender healthcare. A local most popular English daily newspaper, *Greater Kashmir*, commented in its editorial that:

> *Not just the neo-natal segment, the entire healthcare sector in the state has been in a shambles due to a composite set of factors that over the years have gone unattended by the successive governments. While the infrastructure deficit has a major role in retarding the progress in the state's health sector, factors like casual administrative handling, tardy political approach, weak peripheral support and massive corruption within, have exacerbated the situation.*

(27th June, 2012)

These negative features of the gender healthcare system are the focus of this study. This academic study is bi-dimensional: it intends to study the negative aspects of this system and, at the same time, to highlight positive aspects of this system.

This report, based on the sociological-empirical study, is composed of three sections. The first section deals with the conceptual dimensions of gender healthcare, cultural basis of this healthcare system, and role of conflict in the deterioration of this system. This section also includes the mention of methodology adopted during the course of study.

The second section is devoted to the explanation of findings of this study. This sociological explanation in five chapters has focussed on gender healthcare areas, needs and facilities in Kashmir. It has also presented the views about gender healthcare and health administration [put forth by medicos, para-medicos and administrators], and problems related to gender healthcare in Kashmir. This section presents several case studies about facilities, programmes and problems of gender healthcare institutions as follows:

Four case studies of PHCs

- Hazratbal [Srinagar] PHC
- Hardpanzu [Buclgam] PHC
- Achabal [Anantnag] PHC
- Delina [Baramulla] PHC

Two case studies of Health Care

- I. C. D. S. in Kashmir
- N. R. H. M. in Kashmir

Two case studies of

- Lal Ded Maternity Hospital, Srinagar
- G. B. Pant Children Hospital, Srinagar

The third section of this report explains the perceptions, opinions and suggestions presented by the respondents during field investigation. Issues like family planning, gender sex ratio, female foeticide, maternal mortality, and cultural restrictions on health have been analysed in this connection. Moreover, some crucial questions such as what is exactly lacking in the present gender healthcare system? What has to be done to make it a positive system? And what role government and private sectors have in developing-promoting gender healthcare in Kashmir? In addition, the suggestions presented by respondents about an ideal gender healthcare system and all concerned themes have been explained. Finally, this section gives the author's objective views and conclusions about the topic of this research, i.e., positive gender healthcare system in Kashmir.

This report has also got the summary of the findings [which gives a brief 'mirror look' of the findings], foreword, acknowledgements, and list of tables.

Dr B A Dabla
Principal Investigator
Department of Sociology
University of Kashmir
Srinagar

Summary of The Findings

In the following, we present the brief summary of the findings of this empirical study on Gender Healthcare (GHC) in Kashmir during 2012-2013.

1. Gender Healthcare and Conflict

(i) Loss of Healthcare Infrastructure

(a) 292/600 [48.66 per cent] respondents felt that, due to conflict situation in Kashmir, local healthcare infrastructure collapsed. It could not stop its deterioration. This response was shared by 115/200 [57.50 per cent] professional and 177/400 [44.25 per cent] general respondents. The 106/600 [17.66 per cent] respondents opined that the gender healthcare facilities and services collapsed more in rural than urban areas after 1990. This response was conveyed by 33/200 [16.50 per cent] professional and 73/400 [18.25 per cent] general respondents.

(b) The 76/600 [12.66 per cent] respondents upheld the view that since government was extremely busy in countering militancy, it had no time to plan and subsequently construct new hospitals. This view was shared by 23/200 [11.50 per cent] professional and 53/400 [13.25 per cent] general respondents.

(c) The 71/600 [11.83 per cent] respondents said that healthcare system lost the professional and trained manpower from different centres after 1990. This was shared by 24/200 [12.00 per cent] professional and 47/400 [11.75 per cent] general respondents.

(ii) Areas of Women's Suffering Due to Conflict

(a) The 551/600 [91.83 per cent] respondents responded by saying the conflict situation in Kashmir had collapsed the entire system of facilities-services which led to many serious hardships for women during emergency times, especially in rural and hilly areas. This response was shared by 146/200 [73.00 per cent] professional and 84/400 [21.00 per cent] general respondents.

(b) Increase in the mental health cases among women due to conflict was conveyed by 230/600 [38.33 per cent] respondents who belonged to professional 146/200, [73.00 per cent] and general 84/400, [21.00 per cent] respondents.

(c) During conflict period in Kashmir women experienced lot of impact in terms of rise of women specific diseases/problems among them. This was revealed by 132/600 [22.00 per cent] respondents who included 87/200 [43.50 per cent] and 45/400 [11.25 per cent] professional and general respondents respectively.

(d) Violence against women started in an organised way after the conflict started in Kashmir. While criminal violence took place outside family, domestic violence took place inside family. This was conveyed by 03/600 [00.50 per cent] respondents, who were all 03/200 [01.50 per cent] from professional category.

(e) Constant situation of conflict over two long decades gave rise to the trends of MMR and IMR in Kashmir as per professional's observation. This was confirmed by the decadal census reports.

(iii) Other Gender Healthcare Related Problems

(a) The 72/600 [12.00 per cent] respondents said that the continuous armed conflict between the militants and security forces led to over-crowding and over-burdening in all hospitals because a large number of people were injured during the attacks. This had negative effect on the gender healthcare facilities. These respondents belonged to professional 45/200 [22.50 per cent] and general 27/400 [06.75 per cent] categories.

(b) The 66/600 [11.00 per cent] respondents reported that the funds meant for local gender healthcare facilities and services could not be utilised in the abnormal conditions of conflict. This information was revealed by 55/200 [27.50 per cent] professional and 11/400 [02.75 per cent] general respondents.

(iv) Fulfilment of Medical Losses

(a) The 106/600 [17.66 per cent] respondents maintained that in order to overcome the medical losses during the conflict, the government has to initiate and present all gender health facilities and services as early as possible. If people get medical facilities fast again, they may forget the medical losses. This response was shared by 73/200 [36.50 per cent] professional and 33/400 [08.25 per cent] general respondents. The government should immediately recruit female medicos and para-medicos in all hospitals and health centres. This was conveyed by 74/600 [12.33 per cent] respondents who belonged to professional 55/200 [27.50 per cent] and general 19/400 [04.75 per cent] categories.

(b) The number of hospitals which remained static in Kashmir for past many years needs to be increased. This was revealed by 63/600 [11.50 per cent] respondents who composed of 35/200 [17.50 per cent] professional and 28/400 [07.00 per cent] general respondents. In the opinion of 43/600 [07.16 per cent] respondents, the government must formulate many pro-gender health schemes and implement those seriously, it was shared by 24/200 [12.00 per cent] professional and 19/400 [04.75 per cent] general respondents.

(c) In the post-conflict period, there must be complete co-operation between government and private sector in the field of gender healthcare facilities and services. This will prove highly purposeful and will fulfil all requirements. These views were expressed by 25/600 [04.16 per cent] respondents who composed of 17/200 [08.50 per cent] professional and 08/400 [02.00 per cent] general categories.

(d) There must be separate hospitals and health centres at all levels in order to help the women in totality. That was suggested by 40/600 [06.66 per cent] respondents who composed of 21/200 [10.50 per cent] professional and 19/400 [04.75 per cent] general categories.

2. Gender Healthcare Areas and Needs

(i) Gender Healthcare Areas

(a) Gynaecology as a major gender healthcare field was reported by 321/400 (80.25 per cent) respondents from the general category and 147/200 (73.50 per cent) respondents from the professional category. A total of 468/600 (78.00 per cent) respondents reported it as the major gender healthcare field.

(b) Reproductive and child health and maternal and child health as a gender healthcare field was reported by 141/400 (35.20 per cent) respondents from the general category and 64/200 (32.00 per cent) respondents from the professional category.

(c) Reproductive endocrinology as a gender healthcare field was reported by 29/400 (07.25 per cent) respondents from the general category and 35/200 (17.50 per cent) respondents from the professional category. A total of 64/600 (10.66 per cent) respondents reported it as an important health field.

(d) Issues pertaining to adolescent healthcare as a gender healthcare field were reported by 25/400 (06.25 per cent) respondents from the general category and 20/200 (10.00 per cent) respondents from the professional category. A total of 45/600 (07.50 per cent) respondents reported it as important health field.

(e) Pre/post-delivery and natal care was reported by 30/400 (07.50 per cent) respondents from the general category and 17/200 (08.50 per cent) respondents from the professional category. A total of 47/600 (07.83 per cent) respondents reported these as important gender health field.

(f) Mental health as a gender healthcare field was reported by 19/400 (04.70 per cent) respondents from the general category and 18/200 (09.00 per cent) respondents from the professional category. A total of 37/600 (06.16 per cent) respondents reported it as important gender healthcare field.

(g) Social and preventive medicine (SPM) as a gender healthcare field was reported by 5/400 (01.25 per cent) respondents from the general category and 17/200 (08.50 per cent) respondents from the professional category. A total of 22/600 (03.66 per cent) respondents reported it as an important health field.

(h) Oncology as a gender health care field was reported by 18/400 (04.50 per cent) respondents from the general category and 20/200 (10.00 per cent) respondents from the professional category. A total of 38/600 (06.33 per cent) respondents reported it as important gender health field.

(ii) Gender Healthcare Needs

(a) In the background of CMC areas and the loss these suffered recently, the GHC needs required for women were identified as follows:

S.No.	Needed Area	Total	Responses (No.) Prof	Gen
1.	Separate Hospitals for Woman	72	33	39
2.	Specialised Female Staff	91	70	21
3.	Health Education	162	57	105
4.	Well-Equipped Referral Transport	50	19	31
5.	Awareness Programmes about GHC	158	79	79
6.	Improved Facilities and Infrastructure	62	14	48
7.	Immunisation	59	12	47
8.	Remove Gender Disparity	12	05	07
9.	Pre- and Post-marital counselling	17	04	13
10.	Special Maternity Healthcare	04	03	01
11.	Establish Blood Banks	10	07	03
12.	Pre- and Post-delivery Care	31	21	10
13.	Health Services during nights	02	01	01

3. GHC, Government Policy, Programmes and Health Administrators

(i) Though there exists general policy towards GHC, a significant number of respondents, 89/600 (14.83 per cent), felt that there exists no health policy for women in J&K. While 36/200 (18.00 per cent) among them belonged to professional category, 53/400 (13.25 per cent) respondents were of general category.

(ii) In this regard, they refer to the delivery related services. It means that these services must be provided in time necessarily. 09/600 (01.50 per cent) respondents in total who expressed this opinion belonged to 04/200 (1.20 per cent) professional and 05/400 (1.25 per cent) to general category.

(iii) The 577/600 (96.16 per cent) respondents conveyed that governments concern regarding gender healthcare reflects in its planning and programmes. They belonged to 188/200 (94.50 per cent) professional category and 368/400 (92.00 per cent) general respondents. But, at the same time, 23/600 (3.83 per cent) respondents have no idea about any gender healthcare policy of the government. They belonged to 09/200 (2.25 per cent) professionals and 14/400 (7.00 per cent) general respondents.

(iv) The health administrators, who included doctors, para-medical and health administrators revealed that they often follow gender health guidelines in related documents. Study revealed that there were 49/600 (08.16 per cent) respondents who thought a positive gender health attitude and follow seriously the policy guidelines. While 18/400 (04.50 per cent) were general, 31/200 (15.50 per cent) were professional respondents.

4. Problems of Gender Healthcare in Kashmir

(i) Major Gender Health Diseases

(a) Anaemia as gender health disease was reported by 217/400 (54.25 per cent) respondents from the general category and 132/200 (66.00 per cent) respondents from the professional category. A total of 349/600 (58.16 per cent) respondents reported it as an important gender health problem.

(b) Urinary Tract Infection and Sexually Transmitted Disease as gender healthcare diseases were reported by 102/400 (25.50 per cent) respondents from the general category and 96/200 (48.00 per cent) respondents from the professional category. A total of 198/600 (33.00 per cent) respondents reported these as important health problems.

(c) Thyroid as gender healthcare disease was reported by 91/400 (22.75 per cent) respondents from the general category and 79/200 (39.50 per cent) respondents from the professional category. A total of 170/600 (28.33 per cent) respondents reported it as an important health problem.

(d) Menstrual disorders as gender healthcare disease were reported by 91/400 (22.75 per cent) respondents from the general category and 79/200 (39.50 per cent) respondents from the professional category. A total of 170/600 (28.33 per cent) respondents reported it as an important gender health problem.

(e) Menorrhagia as gender healthcare disease was reported by 09/400 (22.75 per cent) respondents from the general category and 03/200 (39.50 per cent) respondents from the professional category. A total of 12/600 (28.33 per cent) respondents reported it as crucial disease.

(f) Jaundice as gender healthcare disease was reported by 91/400 (22.75 per cent) respondents from the general category and 79/200 (39.50 per cent) respondents from the professional category. A total of 170/600 (28.33 per cent) respondents reported it as an important health problem.

(g) Leucorrhoea and other infections as gender health care disease were reported by 74/400 (18.50 per cent) respondents from the general category and 36/200 (18.00 per cent) respondents from the professional category. A total of 110/600 (18.33 per cent) respondents reported it as an important health disease.

(h) Malnutrition as gender health disease was reported by 39/400 (09.75 per cent) respondents from the general category and 12/200 (06.00

per cent) respondents from the professional category. A total of 51/600 (08.50 per cent) respondents reported it as an important health disease.

(i) UTI as gender health disease was reported by 36/400 (09.00 per cent) respondents from the general category and 17/200 (08.50 per cent) respondents from the professional category. A total of 53/600 (08.38 per cent) respondents reported it as an important health disease.

(j) Heart problem as gender health disease was reported by 27/400 (06.75 per cent) respondents from the general category and 18/200 (09.00 per cent) respondents from the professional category. A total of 45/600 (07.50 per cent) respondents reported it as an important health problem.

(ii) Other Problems of Gender Healthcare

(a) Cultural restrictions as gender healthcare problem was reported by 99/400 (24.75 per cent) respondents from the general category and 51/200 (25.50 per cent) respondents from the professional category. A total of 150/600 (25.00 per cent) respondents reported it as an important health problem.

(b) Accessibility to modern healthcare as gender healthcare problem was reported by 44/400 (11.00 per cent) respondents from the general category and 27/200 (13.50 per cent) respondents from professionals reported it. A total of 71/600 (11.83 per cent) respondents reported it as an important health problem.

(c) Lack of specialised female personnel as gender healthcare problem was reported by 52/400 (13.00 per cent) respondents from the general category and 4/200 (02.00 per cent) respondents from the professional category. A total of 56/600 (09.33 per cent) respondents reported it as an important health problem.

(d) Gender bias as a gender healthcare problem was reported by 34/400 (08.50 per cent) respondents from the general category and 14/200 (07.00 per cent) respondents from the professional category. A total of 48/600 (08.00 per cent) respondents reported it as an important health problem.

(e) Negligence of women in general as gender healthcare problem was reported by 17/400 (04.25 per cent) respondents from the general category and 14/200 (07.00 per cent) respondents from the professional category. A total of 31/600 (05.16 per cent) respondents reported it as an important healthcare problem.

(f) Late marriage as gender healthcare problem was reported by 15/400 (54.25 per cent) respondents from the general category and 08/200 (04.00 per cent) respondents from the professional category. A total of 23/600 (03.83 per cent) respondents reported it as an important health issue.

(g) Affordability to modern healthcare as gender healthcare problem was reported by 24/400 (06.00 per cent) respondents from the general category and 2/200 (01.00 per cent) respondents from professionals reported it. A total of 26/600 (04.33 per cent) respondents reported it as an important health problem.

(h) Transportation as gender health problem was reported by 34/400 (08.50 per cent) respondents from the general category and 22/200 (11.00 per cent) respondents from professionals reported it. A total of 56/600 (09.333 per cent) respondents reported it as an important health need.

(i) Hectic work schedule, negligence by women as gender healthcare problem was reported by 17/400 (04.25 per cent) respondents from the general category and 14/200 (07.00 per cent) respondents from the professional category. A total of 31/600 (05.16 per cent) respondents reported it as an important health problem.

(iii) Gender Healthcare and Child Healthcare

(a) Relation between child health and gender healthcare as interdependent was reported by 230/400 (57.50 per cent) respondents from the general category and 95/200 (47.50 per cent) respondents from professional category. A total of 325/600 (54.16 per cent) respondents reported the relationship.

(b) Relation between child health and gender healthcare as totally dependent was reported by 69/400 (17.25 per cent) respondents from the general category and 50/200 (25.00 per cent) respondents from professional category. A total of 119/600(19.83 per cent) respondents reported the relationship.

5. Perception of Gender Healthcare Issues

Major Gender Healthcare issues

The study found five major GHC issues identified and analysed by the respondents. These issues and their perceptions are as follows:

(i) Family Planning

Small family size has become a norm of society and is being accepted as one of the modern practices to attain **a** standard living. This response has been revealed by 158/600 (26.33 per cent) respondents. 45/600 (07.50 per cent) respondents believe that people don't have awareness related to family planning and many people who know about it don't accept it because of varied reasons like religious obligations, social pressures and myths related to it etc. Tubectomy is preferred as a permanent method of family planning, this has been revealed by 39/600 (06.50 per cent) respondents. Education and awareness regarding family planning methods is very essential for reproductive and child health has been revealed by 36/600 (06.00 per cent) respondents.

(ii) Sex Ratio

(a) Proper legislative measures are very important for bringing social control in the society. Enforce strict laws to prevent illegal abortions, these ideas have been put forth by 26/600 (04.33 per cent) respondents who compose of 22/400 (05.50 per cent) general respondents and 04/200 (02.00 per cent) professional respondents.

(b) Awareness and counselling to people is needed to combat such issues, this response has been revealed by 157/600 (26.16 per cent) respondents, of whom 102/400 (25.50 per cent) were general respondents and 55/200 (27.50 per cent) were professional respondents.

(c) Extensive moral and religious education can help in bringing a balance in society has been revealed by 30/600 (05.00 per cent) respondents who comprise 22/400 (05.50 per cent) general respondents and 08/200 (04.00 per cent) of professionals.

(iii) Female Foeticide

(a) Female foeticide is being illegally done at many places. It has been revealed by 153/600 (25.50 per cent) respondents, who compose of 110/400 (27.50 per cent) general respondents and 43/200 (21.40 per cent) professional respondents.

(b) Even if the case of female foeticide occur people usually do not report about it, the response has been put forth by 15/600 (02.50 per cent) respondents. Out of whom 13/400 (03.25 per cent) respondents belong to general category and 02/200 (01.00 per cent) are professional respondents.

(c) Private and unregistered clinics are mainly responsible for carrying out such operations has been revealed by 20/600 (03.33 per cent) respondents who compose of 11/400 (02.75 per cent) general respondents and 09/200 (04.50 per cent) professionals.

(d) Awareness regarding this issue needs to be improved has been revealed by 24/600 (04.00 per cent) respondents, composing of 11/400 (02.75 per cent) general respondents and 13/200 (06.50 per cent) professional respondents and social evils like dowry is mainly responsible for such issues has been revealed by 21/600 respondents who belong to general category.

(iv) Maternal Mortality

(a) Institutional deliveries has reduced MM has been revealed by 143/600 (23.83 per cent) respondents, of whom 90/400 (22.50 per cent) are general respondents and 53/200 (26.50 per cent) professionals.

(b) The main reasons of mm are Inadequate facilities and weak referral system was put forth by 55/600 (09.16 per cent) respondents, of whom 40/400 (10.00 per cent) are of general category and 15/200 (07.50 per cent) are professionals.

(c) Unavailability of maternity hospitals is one of the reasons for MM has been revealed by 41/600 (06.83 per cent) respondents, of whom 31/400 (07.75 per cent) are of general category and 10/200 (05.00 per cent) are professional respondents.

(v) Cultural Restrictions

(a) To overcome cultural restrictions, Gender specialised treatment is needed. The response has been given by 172/600 (28.66 per cent) respondents. The respondents compose of 105/400 (26.25 per cent) general respondents and 67/200 (33.50 per cent) professionals.

(b) Cultural restrictions had led to gender bias due to which women are being less cared. This response has been given by 59/600 (09.83 per cent) respondents, of whom 38/400 (09.50 per cent) are of general category and 21/200 (10.50 per cent) are professional respondents.

(c) Cultural restrictions are more prevalent in far flung areas, the response has been put forth by 22/600 (03.66 per cent) respondents. The respondents compose of 15/400 (03.75 per cent) general respondents and 07/200 (03.50 per cent) professionals.

6. Gender Healthcare System: Positive Views

(i) Limitations of the Healthcare System

(a) In all four districts, 395/600 (65.83 per cent) respondents who compose of 280/400 (70.00 per cent) general respondents and 115/200 (57.50 per cent) professionals have revealed that health centres lack the availability of female gynaecologists/specialised doctors in the entire valley.

(b) The health care system of the valley lacks proper facilities and adequate infrastructure required for gender health has been revealed by 370/600 (61.66 per cent) respondents, of whom 263/400 (65.75 per cent) are of general category and 107/200 (53.50 per cent) are professionals.

(c) There is no separate hospital for women has been put forth by 77/600 (12.83 per cent) respondents, who consist of 54/400 (13.50 per cent) general respondents and 23/200 (11.50 per cent) professionals.

(d) In-adequate supply of medicines in the hospitals has been revealed by 71/600 (11.83 per cent) respondents, from whom 45/400 (11.25 per cent) are from general category and 26/200 (13.00 per cent) are professionals.

(e) The ambulances in the hospitals are not well-equipped has been revealed by 45/600 (07.50 per cent) respondents, of whom 34/400 (08.50 per cent) are general respondents and 11/200 (05.50 per cent) professionals.

(f) In rural areas, there is very less accessibility to health care units has been put forth by 33/600 (05.50 per cent) respondents, of whom 30/400 (07.50 per cent) are from general category and 03/200 (01.50) are professionals.

(g) Majority of PHCs in the valley lack the facility of blood banks has been revealed by 28/600 (04.66 per cent) respondents, who compose of 17/400 (04.25 per cent) general respondents 11/200 (05.50 per cent) professionals.

(h) Lack of health educators and awareness programmes has been revealed by 26/600 (04.33 per cent) respondents, of whom 20/400 (05.00 per cent) are from general category and 06/200 (03.00 per cent) are professionals.

(ii) Role of the State

(a) The biggest role state can play in making the healthcare system of the valley more gender effective is by provision/availability of female doctors in all healthcare units. It has been revealed by 133/600 (21.16 per cent) respondents, of whom 83/400 (20.75 per cent) are general respondents and 50/200 (25.00 per cent) are professionals.

(b) Proper supervision and inspection by state authorities can help in improving this sector's functioning has been put forth by 105/600 (17.50 per cent) total respondents, of who 83/400 (20.75 per cent) are general respondents and 22/200 (11.00 per cent) are professionals.

(c) The state should improve hospital accessibility in far flung areas has been revealed by 72/600 (12.00 per cent) respondents, who composed of 41/400 (10.25 per cent) general respondents and 31/200 (15.50 per cent) professionals.

(d) Efforts need to be taken by state to maintain proper and needed doctor patient ratio in hospitals to prevent overcrowding and help in improving services has been revealed by 30/600 (05.00 per cent) respondents, who compose of 20/400 (05.00 per cent) general respondents and 10/200 (05.00 per cent) professionals.

(e) Proper implementation of programmes by state functionaries can help in providing better services has been put forth by 24/600 (04.00 per cent) respondents, who compose of 16/400 (04.00 per cent) general respondents and 08/200 (04.00 per cent) professionals.

(iii) Role of the Private Sector

(a) Private clinics, hospitals and Nursing Homes can play a big role in providing better gender healthcare facilities has been revealed by 134/600 (22.33 per cent) respondents, of whom 93/400 (23.25 per cent) are general respondents and 41/200 (20.50 per cent) are professionals.

(b) Non- governmental organisations and counsellors can informally play a better role in providing effective gender services has been revealed by 126/600 (21.00 per cent) respondents, who composed of 83/400 (20.75 per cent) general and 43/200 (21.50 per cent) professional respondents.

(c) To improve healthcare sector, public-private partnerships should be encouraged has been put forth by 15/600 respondents, who composed of 04/400 general respondents and 11/200 professionals.

(d) Poor women can't afford the costs of healthcare services in private sector has been revealed by 117/600 (19.50 per cent) respondents, of whom 84/400 (21.00 per cent) were general respondents and 33/200 (16.50 per cent) professionals.

(e) Government hospitals need to be strengthened for providing better services has been put forth by 52/600 (08.66 per cent) respondents, of whom 34/400 (08.50 per cent) were general respondents and 18/200 (09.00 per cent) professionals.

(iv) Need for Awareness Programmes

(a) Awareness and Counselling Programmes about GHC need to be started everywhere especially far-flung areas has been revealed by 152/600 (25.33 per cent) respondents, who compose of 99/400 (24.75 per cent) general respondents and 53/200 (26.50 per cent) professionals. Proper utilisation of funds meant for awareness programmes must be made.

(b) Cooperation of various agencies like schools, mohalla committees and PHC's can help in spreading awareness about GHC has been revealed by 58/600 (09.66 per cent) respondents, of whom 38/400 (09.50 per cent) are general and 20/200 (10.00 per cent) from professional category.

(c) Health camps can help in spreading awareness among people about Gender Health practices has been revealed by 36/600 (06.00 per cent) respondents, of whom 26/400 (06.50 per cent) are general respondents and 10/200 (05.00 per cent) are professionals.

(d) ICDS workers and ASHA can help in effective awareness programmes about GHC has been revealed by 12/600 (02.00 per cent) respondents, who composed of 11/400 (02.75 per cent) general respondents and 01/200 (00.50 per cent) professionals.

(v) Training Programmes for Medicos and Paramedics

(a) Conducting of short training courses during service for Gender Healthcare awareness was suggested by 213/600 (35.50 per cent) respondents, who composed of 150/400 (37.50 per cent) general respondents and 63/200 (31.50 per cent) professionals.

(b) Organising of Seminars and workshops to update the knowledge and technology of GHC to healthcare providers has been suggested by 128/600 (21.33 per cent) respondents, of whom 75/400 (18.75 per cent) are general respondents and 53/200 (26.50 per cent) professionals.

(c) Moral education should be given to Gender Healthcare providers so that they will develop the culture of GHC has been put forth by 92/600 (15.33 per cent) respondents, of whom 65/400 (16.25 per cent) are from general category and 27/200 (13.50 per cent) are professionals.

(d) Refresher courses for medicos and paramedics can help in improving their skills and knowledge as per current requirements has been put forth by 76/600 (12.66 per cent) respondents, who composed of 46/400 (11.50 per cent) general respondents and 30/200 (15.50 per cent) professionals.

(e) Proper supervision of doctors and paramedics can help in better GHC service delivery has been revealed by 21/600 (03.50 per cent) respondents, of whom 16/400 (04.00 per cent) are general respondents and 05/200 (02.50 per cent) are professionals.

7. Suggestions for Gender Healthcare System

(i) Suggestions for the Government of J and K

(a) Formulation and implementation of gender health policy must be carried out after taking into consideration the basic needs of women living in the state. The suggestions were presented by 25/600 [04.16 per cent] respondents who composed of 16/200 [08.00 per cent] professional and 09/400 [02.25 per cent] general respondents.

(b) Expansion and improvement in Gender Health Services. The suggestion was given by 75/600 [12.50 per cent] respondents who comprised of 36/200 [18.00 per cent] professional and 16/400 [04.00 per cent] general respondents.

(c) The number of female medical staff must be increased significantly in order to provide solace and satisfaction to a majority of gender patients. The suggestion was made by 24/600 [04.00 per cent] respondents who belonged to professional and general categories in the proportion of 18/200 [09.00 per cent] and 06/400 [01.50 per cent] respondents respectively.

(d) The existing health infrastructure in the state is neither according to the present needs nor according to the present standards. There seems an absolute need to increase the level of infrastructure in the health sector in J&K. The suggestion was put forth by 59/600[09.83 per cent] respondents who represented two sub-groups of professional [34/200, 17.00 per cent] and general 23/400, [05.75 per cent] respondents.

(e) In the context of acute shortage of gender healthcare services and facilities, the respondents suggested that maximum number of women's hospitals and other related healthcare centres must be established. This suggestion was presented by 17/600 [02.83 per cent] respondents who belonged to professional [14/200, 07.00 per cent] and general [03/400, 00.75 per cent] categories.

(f) The respondents, particularly from hilly areas, suggested that all necessary and basic gender healthcare facilities and services must be made available in far-flung areas in advance before the arrival of winter season. The suggestion was conveyed by 13/600 [02.16 per cent] respondents who included 07/200 [03.50 per cent] and 06/400 [01.50 per cent] professional and general categories of respondents respectively.

(g) It was suggested that modern ambulances well equipped with all gender healthcare emergency facilities and services must be made easily available at every tehsil/block level health centre. This suggestion was presented by 12/600 [02.00 per cent] who composed of 02/200 [01.00 per cent] professional and 10/400 [02.50 per cent] general respondents.

(h) It was strongly upheld by the respondents that a general mass movement about various aspects of health education must be started formally as well as informally. This suggestion was conveyed by 04/600 [00.66 per cent] respondents who were from professional [03/200,01.50 per cent] and general [01/400,00.25 per cent] categories.

(i) The busy schedule of doctors in health centres due to huge rush of female patients exhausts them and affects the quality of treatment. So, it is suggested that there must be realistic ratio between doctors and patients. This suggestion was made by 12/600 [02.00 per cent] respondents who belonged to professional [09/200, 04.50 per cent] and general [03/400, 00.75 per cent] categories.

(j) There should be proper inspection and supervision of doctors who evade their duties in the health centres and go for private practice in their clinics during the office hours. They must be dealt with strictly and even punished for their illegal acts. This was suggested by 25/600 [04.16 per cent] respondents who belonged to professional [15/200, 07.50 per cent] and general [10/40002.50 per cent] respondents categoris.

(k) Corruption, has become a common phenomenon in Kashmir, the heath sector has also fallen prey to this evil practice. The respondents suggested that government must uproot basis of corruption with people's support in the most sacred area of human life. This suggestion was made by 16/600 [02.66 per cent] respondents who were professional [09/200, 04.50 per cent] and general [07/400, 01.75 per cent] respondents.

(l) A significant number of respondents suggested that training in gender health issues is necessary and must be followed by developing a system of monitoring and accountability of medicos and others. These suggestions were conveyed by 13/600 [02.16 per cent] total respondents, out of which 07/200 [03.50 per cent] are professionals and 06/400 [01.50 per cent] are general respondents.

(ii) Suggestions for the NGOs

(a) The respondents suggested that NGOs can play effective role in developing and maintaining the gender health standard practices. This suggestion about active role of NGOs was conveyed by 290/600 [48.33 per cent] total number of respondents, of which 196/200 [98.00 per cent] were professional respondents and 95/400 [23.75 per cent] were general respondents.

(b) NGOs must highlight all major and minor aspects of gender health in Kashmir for the government and the gender health sufferers. This suggestion was put forth by 22/600 [03.66 per cent] total number of respondents, of which 12/200 [06.00 per cent] are professional respondents and 10/400 [02.59 per cent] are general respondents.

(c) The respondents suggested that number of gender health camps and '*melas*' must be organised by the NGOs with two specific objectives. First, to demonstrate gender health plans and programmes and second to present actual medical help to the sufferers. This suggestion was presented by 15/600 [02.50 per cent] respondents of which 13/200 [06.50 per cent] are professional respondents and 02/400 [00.50 per cent] are general respondents.

(d) The respondents suggested that sessions of family counseling must be held on regular basis for ensuring minimum standards of gender health to be maintained in the state. The suggestion was given by 17/600 [02.83 per cent] respondents out of which 15/200 [07.50 per cent] professionals and 02/400[00.50 per cent] are general respondents.

(e) The respondents suggested that regular and standard research-based surveys must be carried out by the experts. This will help to understand the problems and to put suggestions for their effective resolution. The suggestion was presented by 18/600 [03.00 per cent] total respondents, of which 17/200 [08.50 per cent] were professional respondents and 01/400 [00.25 per cent] were general respondents

(f) NGOs working in the field of gender healthcare must always show readiness for co-ordination which must be carried out at two levels, one, between these specialised NGOs and, two, between NGOs and government agencies and organisations. The suggestion was given by 26/600 [04.33 per cent] respondents out of which 14/200 [07.00 per cent] are professionals and12/400 [03.00 per cent] are general respondents.

(iii) Suggestions for Civil Society

(a) There should be organised mass campaign about gender health and its major problems in the Kashmir context. The civil society through its functional organs must play a central role in this campaign. The suggestion was given by 47/600 [07.83 per cent] respondents, out of which 37/200 [18.50 per cent] belong to professional category and 10/400[02.50 per cent] were general respondents.

(b) The facilities and services provided by the governmental institutions and organisations must be utilised properly and carefully, so that their effects are more extensive and deeply felt. The civil society can do a lot in this regard through its organs and agencies. This was expressed by 35/600 [05.83 per cent] respondents, of which 22/200 [11.00 per cent] were professionals and 13/400 [03.25 per cent] were general respondents.

(c) The civil society has a decisive role in the healthcare of individuals. It can emphasise upon them to adopt all concerned facilities and services and take full care of themselves, especially by women. This suggestion was given by the following number of respondents 36/600 [06.00 per cent], out of which 27/200 [13.50 per cent] were professionals and 09/400[02.25 per cent] were general respondents.

(d) Civil society can help gender health victims through organising counselling sessions for all women at the individual, family and community levels. This suggestion was put forth by the following respondents i.e. 15/600 [02.50 per cent], of which 13/200 [06.50 per cent] were professionals and 02/400 [00.50 per cent] were general respondents.

(e) The civil society must focus on all issues of gender healthcare before the government and people. This suggestion was put forth by the following respondents i.e. 91/600 [15.16 per cent], out of which 46/200 [23.00 per cent] were professionals and 45/400 [11.25 per cent] were general respondents.

8. Case Studies of Health Programmes, Healthcare Centres and Hospitals

In order to develop empirical perspective and realistic assessment of the Gender Healthcare situation in Kashmir, three types of case studies were conducted. The brief findings of these case studies are mentioned below:

(i) Case Studies of ICDS and NRHM

ICDS in Kashmir

(a) In the Sample of 200 ICDS centres, 56 (28.00 per cent) Anganwadi Centres (AWCs) were housed in *pucca* buildings, while 90 (45.00 per cent) of the AWCs were housed in semi-pucca houses. Other 54 (27.00 per cent) AWCs were in *katcha* houses which involved the danger to the life of the children. Most of the AWCs (87.00 per cent) are housed in the Anganwadi Helpers (AWHs) houses, while only nine per cent AWCs have their own building and 08 (four per cent) are rented.

(b) Those centres which are located in government buildings like 14 in district Anantnag and two in district Budgam have all necessary provisions of tap water, concrete latrine and adequate space.

(c) The 164 (82.00 per cent) AWCs covered under the study had no separate space for cooking purpose as cooking for AWCs was done in the AWHs personal kitchen.

(d) Only 76 (38.00 per cent) of the AWCs covered in the study had separate space for storage, 110 (55.00 per cent) had separate outdoor space for recreation and 106 (53.00 per cent) had some sort of space for indoor activity.

(e) The 160 (80.00 per cent) of the AWCs had no arrangement for heating. Consequently, the children got exposed to severe cold and viral infections like fever, cold, etc.

(f) On an average, the number of beneficiaries enrolled in all the ICDS centres range from 35 to 45.

(g) The 95 per cent of the beneficiary children were immunised but full immunisation rate is far from satisfactory. Only 78.00 per cent of the children had received all the doses of immunisation.

(h) The physically challenged and sick children only are allowed to take home the supplementary nutrition. But, in actual practice,

90 per cent of the beneficiaries take meals to home, where all the family members consume it.

(i) Almost all the respondents (98 per cent) were satisfied with the quality of supplementary nutrition received by their children from the AWCs.

(j) The 58 per cent AWCs receive the supply of supplementary nutrition yearly, while 27 per cent receive it half-yearly. The 07.00 per cent Anganwadi workers (AWWs) reported that they receive the supply when they need it. The 02.00 per cent AWCs have ready to eat food available at the AWC while all others give cooked food to the beneficiaries.

NRHM in Kashmir

(a) The number of Accredited Social Health Activists (ASHAs) is 9,764 in 6,654 villages in the state and most of them have been trained and had received drug kits in the year of 2008-09.

(b) AYUSH services are provided in majority of the PHCs (317/518) in the state.

(c) Number of Village Health and Sanitation Committees constituted are 6,788 in number with 5,215 operational joint bank accounts.

(d) Number of Village Health and Sanitation Days observed during 2008-2009 was reported to be 75,192 in the state.

(e) Number of registered Rogi Kalyan Samities (RKS) was reported 474 with 14 in district hospitals, 85 in Community Health Centres and 375 in Primary Health Centres.

(f) The 08.30 per cent respondents got the benefit of JSY/Institutional deliveries.

(g) The 83.30 per cent respondents got regular and complete immunisation.

(h) The 06.60 per cent respondents reported the proper attendance of health care workers in their professional duties.

(i) As much as 1.70 per cent respondents reported the significant improvement in the hospital infrastructure and cleanliness.

(ii) Case Studies of PHCs

The brief summary of the findings of case studies of PHCs is explained below:

(i) Primary Health Centre, Hazratbal, Srinagar

(a) According to the guidelines, minimum OPD attendance should be 40 patients per doctor per day, but, due to the shortage of doctors, a doctor at PHC Hazratbal, has to cater about 60 patients on an average per day.

(b) The 24 hours emergency services meant for appropriate management of injuries and accidents, first aid, stabilisation of the condition of the patient before referral, dog bite/snake bite/scorpion bite cases, and other emergency conditions are present at PHC.

(c) Referral services (two ambulances, one boat for Dal dwellers) are available in the concerned PHC.

(d) In-patient services (six beds) are available.

(e) The centre has achieved good results as far as immunisation of pregnant ladies and new born babies are concerned. The centre is active in providing antenatal, pre-natal, post-natal care to women. New-born care, care of the child, family planning, nutrition services, school health, adolescent healthcare services are also provided. Promotion of safe drinking water and basic sanitation, prevention and control of locally endemic diseases, collection and reporting of vital events is done actively by the staff of this PHC.

(f) Education about health/behaviour change communication (BCC), management of reproductive tract infections and sexually transmitted infections is given much importance.

(g) Besides, PHC plays a good role in referring the complicated delivery cases to specialised hospitals by providing free transport facilities. The center plays an active role in providing the benefits of NRHM programme to women and children like free medicines, free screening facilities, monetary allowances etc. The centre has performed well in promoting awareness related to various family planning methods and their benefits. The centre plays a good educative role for adolescent girls related to their health needs and is also spreading information regarding causes and consequences of various sexually transmitted diseases.

(ii) Primary Health Centre Harudpanzoo, Budgam

(a) The health centre was not totally normal in functioning, until it was covered under centrally sponsored programme, i.e., NRHM. With the advent of this programme, the condition of PHC somewhat improved because the centre received funds for every year for the improvement of infrastructure and other basic facilities like water supply, electricity etc. NRHM not only provided money for infrastructural development but also recruited additional staff in the PHC. With increase in manpower and other facilities, health centre started working on 24x7 basis from October 2007.

(b) The PHC Harudpanzoo caters to a population of 70,000 people and is heading one PHC, two sub-centres and a DMC (Designated Medical Centre) for diagnosis of TB.

(c) Various facilities available at the health centre are a labour room, laboratory for various hematological tests, dental section and a ward of six beds. The health centre has one ambulance also. All these facilities have been made available under NRHM programme.

(d) The health centre is having a Fair Price Shop though the drugs are sold on market prices, their quality is somewhat better than drugs available in open market.

(e) Health centre is having the facility of ECG but the technician to operate this machine is not available, thus the facility is not functional.

(f) Health centre lacks X- ray and USG facilities which are of immense importance for providing better gender healthcare services, and USG is very important for diagnosing pregnancy related issues.

(g) The biggest problem in the health centre is the non-availability of lady doctor. In addition, many posts are lying vacant in the health centre, which comprise of two posts of doctors, two nurses and multipurpose health workers (one male and one female). In this centre, there is no Health Educator or Community Health Officer. The night staff available in the hospital is just one doctor, one paramedic and a sweeper.

(h) The health centre faces a huge rush of patients every day. As per records, the PHC examines 1400-1600 patients every month in the out-patient department, 200-300 patients are admitted every month, two-three cases are referred everyday to other sub-district, district or super specialty hospitals for specialised treatment.

(i) The health centre performs three-five normal deliveries every week. The deliveries which need to be conducted by caesarian method are referred to other hospitals because it lacks various facilities which are important for such deliveries like USG, blood bank, and other emergency care.

(j) From last three years, two epidemics have affected the area, Cholera in the year 2010 and Enteric fever in the year 2011. To deal with the situation, all the medicines were bought from NRHM funds and were distributed among people free of cost

(k) The most prevalent diseases in the area are infectious diseases like upper and lower respiratory tract infections, Enteric fever, Tuberculosis, etc.

(1) Most of the gender related diseases remain unknown in the area because of non-availability of lady doctor as women folk don't feel comfortable in discussing their problems with male doctors and are forced tp visit to other hospitals, only when the condition becomes more severe.

(iii) Primary Health Centre, Achabal, Anantnag

(a) The OPD of health centre faces a huge rush of patients, almost 60 to 70 patients per day which compose mainly women and children.

(b) The diseases prevalent in the area are mostly seasonal like Hay fever, Flu, water-borne diseases, etc.

(c) The health centre provides facilities for in-patients with a bed facility of 24 of which 12 are for males and 12 for females. Generally, pregnant ladies that come to this centre for delivery purpose are admitted in the health centre. The staff on night duty available at the health centre is a doctor, senior nurse, FMPHW, pharmacist, nursing orderly, sweeper, and a driver.

(d) The health centre has a well-maintained immunisation section with good facilities like a deep freezer for storage of various kinds of vaccines. The health centre has well-maintained immunisation records of children and females who are registered there. But, the unavailability of electricity on 24×7 basis is responsible for inconvenience and untimely immunisation.

(e) The biggest problem that the health centre faces is the lack of a qualified Gynaecologist and thus the services are carried out by simple MBBS doctors due to which various gynaecological and obstetrics related diseases remain untreated.

(f) In the health centre, only normal deliveries are carried out because the hospital lacks the facilities for caesarian operations. The health centre lacks the facility of blood bank due to which most of the cases are referred to Maternity and child health hospital Anantnag.

All deliveries carried out in the health centre get all the benefits as per JSY scheme.

(g) As the health centre lacks the specialised services of permanent family planning methods like Tubal ligation and vasectomy, they carry out this function usually by education, motivation, counseling and by providing free of cost contraceptives such as condoms and oral pills.

(h) The X-ray section of the health centre is not working properly because of the irregular power supply due to which patients suffer a lot. For this service, the health centre is having one X-ray technician. However to cater to the huge rush of patients manpower is less. The health centre is also having USG facility for the patients.

(i) The health centre has two health educators, one extension educator, two local health workers and 105 recognised ASHAs who motivate women to avail the health facilities provided by the government. They also provide awareness and health education to the people and benefits of institutional deliveries and immunisation programmes.

(iv) Primary Health Centre, Delina, Baramulla

(a) Minimum laboratory investigations like haemoglobin, urine, albumin, sugar, etc., are available at minimum cost rates in the centre.

(b) PHC Delina has got a well-furnished building and has almost everything which a PHC should have. However, there are still certain shortcomings:

- It is not a 24x7 open PHC;
- Inadequate physical infrastructure and facilities, e.g., no blood banks;
- Drivers are posted but the ambulances are not there;
- Lack of set standards for monitoring quality care etc;
- Operation theater is available but is not functional;
- There is no labour room, so pregnant cases are always referred;
- There is huge deficiency of staff.

(c) The PHC Delina is promoting family planning through education, counselling and motivation techniques. Provision of contraceptives like condoms, Oral Pills, IUD etc is there. Permanent methods of family planning like tubal ligation and vasectomy is done free of cost. Monetary allowances are also given under NRHM.

(d) Free iron and folic acid tablets are being distributed among pregnant ladies.

(e) Health melas and free medical camps are organised in far flung areas to promote health culture and provide health services at their door steps.

(f) Health educators in this centre spread health education to adolescent girls.

(g) Referral system with proper transport facility is provided to the patients to improve their health.

(iii) Case Studies of Two Specialised Hospitals

(i) Lal Ded Maternity Hospital, Srinagar

(a) L.D. still stands as the sole hospital in the Kashmir region for maternity treatment.

(b) The bed strength of the hospital is 500, two patients per bed in every ward. Even the labour rooms are not exception.

(c) The labour section seems chaotic always. Each room contains four beds, eight patients and 16 attendants [two for each patient], two pregnant women, bearing the pain of their life, on a single bed. The post-operative ward is the only ward in the entire hospital where patients are provided a single bed, at least for a day.

(d) There are three operation tables in the hospital for the critical patients, one each for emergency, post-emergency and SOS, which is agonising for patients who need to be operated upon immediately. The situation is grim during night hours when only two operation tables remain functional due to insufficient theatre strength.

(e) The maternity hospital is attended by patients from nearby as well as from far flung areas. The records in the hospital confirm that on an average, the out-patient department [OPD] receives 600-700 obstetrics and gyneacological patients daily. Lal Ded hospital has an average number of 350-400 patients in the OPD daily with 250 obstetrics and 150 gynecological patients. About 115 patients are admitted everyday as IDPs with about 80 obstetrics and 35 gynaecological ailments.

(f) The hospital performs 45 major and 30 minor surgeries daily. About 20 deliveries and 40-45 lower segment caesarean operations are performed daily.

(g) The hospital has all necessary and modern equipments in the laboratory, radiology section, laundry, blood bank, and anesthesia.

(h) This hospital has the distinction of having the highest number of caesarean operations. As per official sources, about 80-100 children are born in the hospital. Officials confirm that nearly half of these births are caesarean.

(i) Every day around 120 patients are admitted in the hospital. Under such circumstances, it is not possible to provide a bed for each patient. Thus overcrowding in the hospital in general and OPD in particular tells upon the working of the staff as well as the health of patients, the efficiency of all medicos, non-medical staff and others involved.

(j) Lal Ded hospital is notorious for smuggling or stealing the new-born male babies at the time of their birth. The practice is that the para-medical staff member with the passive or silent support of her/his support smuggle/steal the babies inside or outside the hospital and hand over to the needed persons who pay them hefty amounts. Hundreds of such cases have been reported every month and every year in the local print media.

(ii) G.B. Pant Children Hospital, Srinagar

(a) In 1985, the children hospital was shifted to Sonawar from a city area in Srinagar by the government mainly because of lesser space and accommodation available at the earlier place. However, this decision with good intentions and objectives didn't prove purposeful because of three major reasons. *First*, the new area was a congested area in comparison to the earlier one, so was not more suitable for the hospital. *Second*, the new area fell within the cantonment area of the city, which is generally controlled by the army with no local administration's intervention. *Third*, this led to the problem of 'dual control' of the hospital, one the state authorities and second the army authorities. In this type of situation, the hospital at the new place could not prosper and developed the features of mis-management, mal-administration, and unaccountability and so on in the hospital.

(b) The cumulative effect of this situation was felt in the deterioration in the practices of treatment, facilities and services. This all reflected in the increasing number of infant deaths in the recent years, for which this hospital became notorious.

(c) Alarming number of infant deaths in hospital in recent years is a grave concern. The 480 infant deaths were registered in the year 2012 in the children's hospital; and a total number of 3,800 infant deaths were recorded since 2008 in the children's hospital.

(d) This hospital has one oxygen plant which is supposed to fulfill the concerned needs of the hospital. But, as was reported, it faces the threat of becoming non-functional mainly due to overloading. The information gained in this regard is that this plant at present is overloaded with 22,000 oxygen points and 314 ventilators are functional on it in different wards of the hospital. The fact is that the plant has the capacity of 446 liters per minute, but it is forced to supply 1,000 litres per minute to meet the emergency services and facilities.

The hospital is problem infected. The various problems pollute the environment of this hospital. These acute problems include the following:

- Absence of work culture.
- Corruption practices.
- Private practice of professional staff.
- Non-availability and non-issuance of medicines.
- No proper ambulance.
- Under performance of diagnostics lab.
- Non-availability and irresponsibility of the health administrators.

LIST OF TABLES

Abbreviations

AAY	Antyodaya Anna Yojana
AD	Allopathic Dispensaries
APL	Above Poverty Line
ASHA	Accredited Social Health Activist
ANM	Auxiliary Nursing Midwives
AWC	Anganwadi Centres
AWW	Anganwadi Workers
AYUSH	Ayurvedic Yoga Unani-Siddha Homeopathy
BCC	Behaviour Change Communication
BPL	Below Poverty Line
BMO	Block Medical Officer
CBR	Crude Birth Rate
CDR	Crude Death Rate
CHO	Community Health Officer
CHC	Community Health Centre
CMO	Chief Medical Officer
DLHS	District Level Health Survey
DMC	Designated Medical Centre
ECG	Electro-cardiography
FMPHW	Female Multipurpose Health Worker
HC	Health Centre
GDMOS	General Duties Medical Officers
GHC	Gender Healthcare
GMC	Government Medical College
GO	Governmental Organisations
ICDS	Integrated Child Development Service
IFA	Iron Folic Acid
IGMSY	Indira Gandhi Matritva Sahyog Yojana
IMNCI	Integrated Management of Neo-natal and Childhood Illness
IMR	Infant Mortality Rate

IPHS	Indian Public Health Standards
IUD	Intra Uterine Devices
IPD	Inpatients Department
ISM	Indian System of Medicine
JSY	Janani Suraksha Yojana
JSSK	Janani Shishu Suraksha Karyakram
LHV	Lady Health Visitor
MCH	Maternal and Child Health
MCTS	Mother Child Tracking System
MO	Medical Officer
MPHW	Multipurpose Health Worker
MS	Medical Superintendent
NGO	Non-governmental Organisation
NFHS	National Family Health Survey
NHP	National Health Policy
NHED	Nutrition and Health Education
NNR	Neonatal care
NRHM	National Rural Health Mission
OPD	Outpatients Department
PCOD	Poly Cyst Ovarian Syndrome
PHC	Primary Health Centre
PNC	Pre/post-Natal Care
PPP	Public Private Partnership
PSE	Pre-School Education
PTSD	Post Traumatic Stress Disorder
RCH	Reproductive and Child Health
RGSEAG	Rajiv Gandhi Scheme for Empowerment of Adolescent Girls
RKS	Rogi Kalyan Samiti
RTI	Reproductive Tract Infection
SDH	Sub-district Hospital
SC	Subcentre
SMHS	Shri Maharaja Hari Singh Hospital
STI	Sexually Transmitted Infections
SPM	Social and Preventive Medicine
TB	Tuberculosis
TFR	Total Fertility Rate
WHO	World Health Organisation

Section - A

Gender Healthcare Study

1

Introduction

1. Concept of Health

(i) Health generally refers to a state of complete physical, mental and social well-being and not merely absence of disease or infirmity. The major determinants of health are social, economic, cultural, physical environment and individual, behaviour. It has been observed that the real health status of any individual and community is determined by the mass factors which necessarily include income, social status, social support network, literacy-education, employment, social-physical environment, child development, personal health practices, coping skills, culture-social structure, gender status, values and traditions, and healthcare system.

(ii) It has been argued that health is maintained and improved constantly not only through an advancement and application of health science but also through the efforts and lifestyle choices of individuals and groups. Though biological factors are primary factors in this field, social, cultural, economic and other factors play equally important role in their respective spheres. Accordingly, health is interpreted in wider and broader terms of "a state of complete physical, mental and social well-being and not merely the absence of disease or infirmity." This is the definition maintained by the W. H. O., Geneva in its official documents.

***(c)** Gender Health:* Gender has globally been established as one of the primary, important, active and constant factor in determining the health conditions of individuals and groups. Consequently, it gave rise to the conception of 'gender health' which may be explained in terms of the status of physical, mental and social aspects of the health of womenfolk. In reality, it represents a set of positive features, conditions and factors in the broader societal and gender context. Various studies at regional and global levels concluded that women in general maintained or were compelled to maintain lesser standards of physical and mental health conditions in comparison to their men counterparts, especially in contemporary times. It was observed irrespective of women's multi-dimensional differences and had clearly identified the causative physical, mental and social-economic factors. Though the supreme importance of women's health in the survival and continuity of human race in a stable way could not be reduced, the gender health was neither attached the supreme importance nor the crucial priority in the health policies and programmes of the government and non-governmental organisations.

There exist some similar or synonymous concepts of health, which are directly or indirectly related to the gender healthcare and reveal its important features. Some of these positive concepts are mentioned below.

(ii) Healthcare: The concept of 'healthcare' refers to the practices of diagnosis, treatment and prevention of disease, illness, injury and other physical and mental impairments. It includes the facilities and services available in the primary, secondary and tertiary care in public health. It is generally considered as an important determinant in promoting the gender framework of healthcare system.

(iii) Reproductive Health: It implies that people at large have responsible, satisfying and safer sex life and that they have the capability to replace and freedom to decide if, when and how often to do so. Implicit in this is the right of men and women to be informed of and to have excess to safe, effective and acceptable methods of fertility regulation of their choice and the right of areas to appropriate healthcare services that will enable women to go safely through pregnancy and childbirth and provide couples with the best chance of having a healthy infant

(iv) Mental Health: According to the WHO, Geneva, mental health refers to a state of well-being in which the individual realises his or her own abilities, can cope with the normal stress of life and can work productively. In general, it reveals the level of psychological wellbeing or absence of mental disorder. It may include the individual's ability to enjoy life. It has been observed that cultural differences, assessments and competing professional theories have affected the precise explanation of conditions related to mental health.

(v) Women/Gender Health: It refers to the health conditions of female sex. Its major processes are caused by their specific hormones and its main issues involve menopauses, child birth, maternal health, menstruation, contraception, anemia and breast cancer. Women also face a medical situation which is not directly related to their biology, i.e., gender differentiated and gender discriminated access to medical treatment. This becomes the base for gender health problems in the society.

Since women's health is based on social determinants, it also affects the conditions of this health, which may be considered as input and output processes in the women's health. It was observed by experts that this help generally depends on:

- Social Status of women in broader society,
- Constitutional and legal rights to protect women's health in totality,
- Medical facilities and services on priority basis for reproductive health,
- Availability of health facilities with women medical experts,
- Adequate nutritional services,
- Independent economic status of women,
- Attitude towards gender discrimination and sexual inequality.

On the other hand, these input processes of gender healthcare affects the totality of health of women. The implication of this situation will be as follows. If the societal response is proper, positive and need based, the gender healthcare is normal to the minimum extent. But, if the societal response is not proper, nor need fulfilling and negative, the gender healthcare is not normal to the maximum extent. In the latter case, there is the incidence of maternal mortality that in turn gave rise to increasing number of female deaths and disabilities among women. This also led to the problems and complexities at the time of pregnancy and delivery. Consequently, a lot of unnatural births and deaths have been recorded in the recent past. Moreover, some disadvantages of gender healthcare in this context reflected in the cases of HIV and other diseases.

In addition to the above-mentioned problems, women in general face widespread practices of discrimination, domination, inequality and injustice in all traditional societies. These socially-culturally determined practices had completely negative impact on their health which can be characterised as exploitation and degeneration. This happened at the global level in all countries irrespective of their differences in many fields. Thus women in these countries, especially in Asia and Africa, suffered extremely in those times.

(vi) Comprehensive Healthcare: This term was introduced in India with the meaning of providing the provision of integrated preventive, curative and promotive healthcare services and facilities from 'womb to tomb' to every individual, which has to be applied in equal share and intensity in the cases of gender healthcare. This concept formed the basis of national health policy and planning in India and establishment of network of primary healthcare centres and sub-centres.

(vii) Changing Pattern: However, in the recent past, especially after the end of colonial rule collapsed in most of the countries, this situation about the gender and gender healthcare experienced some degree of change qualitatively as well as quantitatively. This happened in the twentieth century in many countries of the world and was experienced in India too.

2. Gender Healthcare in India

(i) The reality of gender healthcare in India revealed in its characterisation as the 'crucial problem' mainly because of its complexities and problems which could not be resolved for long. It was generally observed that the standard and status of gender healthcare was much lower and inferior in comparison to their men at the pan-Indian level. This could be explained in terms of biological/physiological, medical and social-economic-cultural factors. While the biological/physiological system of women stood and was prone to risks and complexities, the cultural limitations, social and economic standards made them discriminated in the negative sense. Both theses sets of factors led to deterioration and even degeneration of the gender healthcare. Moreover, non-response from the existing healthcare system and non-fulfillment of healthcare facilities created a situation of deprivation and desperation related to this system.

(ii) It has been found that the gender healthcare faced the negative social-cultural environment which had devastating effect throughout. This kind of situation imposed through social and cultural practices such as inequality, domination, discrimination values and other views, which all were integrated in the social-cultural ethos. In this socially structured and culturally integrated situation, women's health could not be improved in India.

(iii) However, after independence in 1947, this situation experienced significant degree of change, in women's healthcare. It was attempted by various regimes/governments to provide a comprehensive and integrated healthcare system which will fulfill the basic health needs of all people, particularly women and children. Several credible surveys and studies in the healthcare system in India have revealed that significant degree of success has been achieved in this regard. The following demographic and health data makes it clear:

[a] Demographic Data

S. No.	*Demographic indicator*	*1951*	*1981*	*2000*
1.	Life expectancy	36.7	54.0	64.6 [RG]
2.	Crude Birth Rate	40.8	33.9 [SRS]	26.1 [SRS]
3.	Crude Death Rate	25.0	12.5 [SRS]	8.7 [SRS]
4.	Infant Mortality Rate	146	110	70 [SRS]

[b] Infrastructure Available in India

S.No.	*Health indicator*	*1951*	*1981*	*2000*
1.	No. of SC/PHC/CHC	725	57,363	1,63,181
2.	No. of Dispensaries and A hospitals	9,209	23,555	43,322
3.	No. of Private and Public Health Centres	1,17,198	5,69,495	8.70,161
4.	No. of doctors [allopathic]	61,800	2,68,700	5,03,900
5.	No. of nursing personnel	18,054	1,43,887	7,37,000

Though the above-mentioned figures convey the heavy increase in numbers, but the data does not indicate as to how many people in total number got benefited by these facilities and services. There is a general opinion prevailing among experts and professionals in the health sector that the pace of development in this sector in India has proved impressive. The growth of healthcare sector has enabled majority of people in the country to avail medical facilities and services in the health sector. In fact, the national health policy [2000 - 2002] has guided this unprecedented growth of health sector. This policy was followed vigorously in the-post independence decades and recent past, whose objectives revolved around the following gender healthcare guidelines:

- Reduction of infant mortality rate to less than 30 infant deaths per 1,000 live births,
- Reduction of maternal mortality ratio to less than 100 mortality deaths per 1,00,000 live births,
- To achieve universal immunisation of children,
- Necessary delivery assistance by trained personnel for all births,
- 100 per cent registration of births, deaths, marriages and pregnancies,
- To achieve and maintain the balanced sex ratio in population,
- Complete stoppage of determination of female sex and subsequent abortions,
- To avoid the uneven progress in rural-urban areas in the healthcare sector for attainment of better health goals,
- Promotion of the principle of encouraging delayed marriages and discouraging early marriage,
- Universal access to family planning information and relevant services,
- Prevention of major infectious diseases, including reproductive tract infections and AIDS, and
- Decentralisation of health planning, implementation and programmes.

These declared objectives had direct and indirect impact on the health sector and gender healthcare in particular in India. This led to the broader transformation in the practices of healthcare related to women in India.

3. Gender Healthcare in Jammu and Kashmir State

[i] The Jammu and Kashmir State

Nature of the State: The J&K state occupies a strategic place on the country's map with its borders touching Pakistan, China, and Afghanistan. The three distinct regions, Jammu, Kashmir and Ladakh, have their specific resource base. Except for Jammu and Kathua districts, the entire state is mountainous. The Plateau of Ladakh, flanked the state on the east with lowest population density, is separated from rest of the state by high mountain ranges. In actuality, the state with its varied and diversified geographic, agri-climatic and topographic features and connectivity and other such features characterise development challenges. The land of the state is highly fertile and water resources are in abundance. Rice, maize and wheat are major cereals of J&K. The state stands as the largest producer of apples, walnuts, almonds and many other temperate dry and fresh fruits. It has also widespread occupational network of handicrafts. So, it stands as the major exporter of superior quality carpets, shawls, wooden articles, paper machie, embroidered clothes and many other valuable crafts. The state has a distinction in having maximum number of tourist spots and destinations and horticultural-floricultural activities.

[ii] Area and Population

The state of J&K has a geographical spread of 2,22,236 sq. kms. [including an area of 1,20,849 sq. kms. under occupation of Pakistan and China] accounting for 7.02 per cent of the total area of India, making it 6th largest state in the country. The forest area of the state is 20,230 sq. kms. which constitute 19. 95 per cent of its total geographic area.

The population of the state, according to census reports, was as shown in the table below:

Table 1.1:Population in J&K [district-wise and male-female], 2001-2011

			Total Population 2011			*Percentage of total*
S. No.	*District*	*2001*	*Total*	*Male*	*Female*	*State*
1.	Kupwara	650,393	875,564	475,126	400,438	06.98
2.	Budgam	607,181	735,773	390,705	345,048	05.86
3.	Baramulla	843,892	1,015,503	422,171	473,332	08.09
4.	Bandipore	304,886	385,099	201,531	183,568	03.07
5.	Srinagar	1,027,670	1,269,751	675,667	594,084	23.56
6.	Ganderbal	217,907	297,003	158,900	138,103	02.37
7.	Pulwama	441,275	570,060	297,988	272,072	04.54
8.	Shopian	211,332	265,960	136,303	129,658	02.12
9.	Anantnag	778,408	1,070,144	552,404	517,740	03.53
10.	Kulgam	394,026	422,786	216,672	206,114	03.37
11.	Leh	117,232	147,104	92,907	54,197	01.17
12.	Kargil	11,907	143,388	80,791	62,597	01.14
13.	Poonch	372,613	476,820	252,240	224,580	03.80
14.	Rajouri	483,284	619,266	332,424	286,842	04.93
15.	Kathua	511,455	615,711	327,953	287,758	04.91
16.	Doda	320,256	409,576	213,091	196,485	03.26
17.	Ramban	217,944	283,313	149,032	134,281	02.26
18.	Kishtwar	190,843	231,034	120,496	110,541	01.84
19.	Udhampur	459,684	555,357	298,094	257,263	04.43
20.	Reasi	247,694	314,714	166,392	148,322	02.51
21.	Jammu	13,570,777	1526,406	815,727	710,679	12.20
22.	Samba	272,539	318,611	168,948	149,663	02.54
	Total	**10,143,700**	**12,548,926**	**6,665,561**	**5,883,365**	**100.00**

There has been constant increase in population in all provinces of the state. That reflects in two tables below:

Table 1.2: Population Increase at the Province Level, 2001-2011

		Total Population				*Percentage*
			of the 2011			
S. No.	*Province*	*2001*	*Total*	*Male*	*Female*	*total*
1.	Kashmir province	5,476,970	6,907,623	3,647,466	3,260,157	55.03
2.	Ladakh province	236,539	290,492	173,698	116,794	02.31
3.	Jammu province	4,430,191	5,350,811	2,844,397	2,506,414	42.68

Table 1.3: Increasing Decadal Growth

S.No.	*District*	*Growth Rate*	*S.No.*	*District*	*Growth Rate*
1.	Kupwara	34.62	12.	Kargil	20.18
2.	Budgam	21.18	13.	Poonch	27.97
3.	Baramulla	20.34	14.	Rajouri	28.14
4.	Bandipora	26.31	15.	Kathua	31.81
5.	Srinagar	23.56	16.	Doda	27.89
6.	Ganderbal	36.30	17.	Ramban	31.81
7.	Pulwama	29.18	18.	Kishtwar	21.06
8.	Shopian	25.85	19.	Udhampur	20.86
9.	Anantnag	37.48	20.	Reasi	27.06
10.	Kulgam	27.03	21.	Jammu	12.48
11.	Leh	25.48	22.	Samba	16.90

According to census-2011 reports, the sex ratio of population in the state [district-wise and decade-wise] for all age groups has been as is noted in the following table:

Table 1.4: Sex Ratio in Population in J&K, 2001-2011

		Sex Ratio [number of females per 1,000 males]		
S.No.	*District*	*2001*	*2011*	*Decadal Rariation*
1.	Kupwara	906	843	63
2.	Budgam	911	883	48
3.	Baramulla	905	873	32
4.	Bandipore	894	911	17
5.	Srinagar	841	879	18
6.	Ganderbal	917	869	48
7.	Pulwama	942	913	29
8.	Shopian	950	951	01
9.	Anantnag	911	937	26
10.	Kulgam	945	951	06
11.	Leh	823	583	240
12.	Kargil	837	775	62
13.	Poonch	919	890	29

14.	Rajouri	878	863	15
15.	Kathua	898	877	21
16.	Doda	913	922	09
17.	Ramban	889	901	12
18.	Kishtwar	904	917	13
19.	Udhampur	846	863	17
20.	Reasi	880	891	11
21.	Jammu	865	871	06
22.	Samba	897	886	11
	State level	**872**	**883**	**09**

The sex ratio in the population in the age group of zero to six years was as noted in the following table:

Table 1.5: Sex Ratio of Population Zero to Six Years Age Group, 2001-2011

S.No.	*District*	*2001 Population*	*2011*	*Population of Total*
1.	Kupwara	1021	854	22.50
2.	Budgam	1004	832	20.69
3.	Baramulla	961	866	15.94
4.	Bandipoore	967	893	15.66
5.	Srinagar	928	869	12.28
6.	Ganderbal	1,014	863	17.02
7.	Pulwama	1,016	836	17.13
8.	Shopian	1,011	883	15.14
9.	Anantnag	977	832	19.28
10.	Kulgam	1,003	883	16.64
11.	Leh	955	944	08.03
12.	Kargil	980	978	14.21
13.	Poonch	959	895	17.64
14.	Rajouri	905	857	19.14
15.	Kathua	847	836	13.02
16.	Doda	959	932	17.34
17.	Ramban	968	931	19.32
18.	Kishtwar	977	922	16.83
19.	Udhampur	912	887	14.88
20.	Reasi	952	921	17.73
21.	Jammu	819	795	10.47
22.	Samba	798	788	11.93
	State	**941**	**859**	......

The literacy rate in the state was as mentioned in the following table:

Table 1.6: Literacy Rates in J&K, 2001-2011

S.No.	*District*	*2001–2011*	*Literacy Rate* *Male*	*Female*	*Total*	*Decadal.*
1.	Kupwara	43.24	77.10	54.79	66.92	23.67
2.	Budgam	42.20	68.19	46.60	57.98	15.78
3.	Baramulla	66.93	77.35	55.01	66.93	19.25
4.	Bandipora	39.01	68.41	46.24	57.82	18.81
5.	Srinagar	63.13	78.03	63.47	71.21	08.08
6.	Ganderbal	40.46	70.73	47.82	59.99	19.52
7.	Pulwama	51.87	75.41	53.81	65.00	13.13
8.	Shopian	44.67	71.87	52.77	62.49	17.82
9.	Anantnag	47.59	74.13	54.15	64.32	15.15
10.	Kulgam	44.40	70.60	49.74	60.35	15.15
11.	Leh	65.34	89.39	64.52	80.48	15.15
12.	Kargil	60.85	86.73	58.05	74.49	13.64
13.	Poonch	51.19	81.04	54.80	68.69	17.50
14.	Rajouri	57.99	78.19	57.20	68.54	10.54
15.	Kathua	64.81	8.1.40	64.56	73.50	08.69
16.	Doda	53.55	80.36	50.34	65.97	12.42
17.	Ramban	43.06	71.97	40.04	56.90	13.84
18.	Kishtwar	43.31	71.75	44.13	58.54	15.23
19.	Udhampur	5932	79.93	58.22	69.90	10.57
20.	Reasi	48.72	69.93	47.55	59.42	10.69
21.	Jammu	77.56	89.77	77.41	83.98	06.42
22.	Samba	73.98	89.77	74.39	....	....
State	**55.52**	**78.26**	**58.01**	**68.74**	**13.21**	

The following is the demographic profile in the statistical form [2011]:

- No. of Districts in J & K — 22
- No. of Towns — 86
- No. of Panchayats — 4, 130
- Density per sq. km. — 124
- Literacy [2011] — Total — 68.74 Per cent
- Males — 78.26 Per cent
- Females — 58.01 Per cent
- Growth Rate — 23.71 Percent
- No. of Tehsils — 82
- No. of Villages — 6,652
- No. of C. D. Blocks — 143
- Male-female Ratio — 1,000/83.

The following is the number of educational institutions in the state:

- No. of Primary Schools — 1,604
- No. of Middle Schools — 8,619
- No. of High/Higher Sec. Schools — 2,756

- No. of General Colleges 76
- No. of Universities 07
- No. of Engineering Colleges 12
- No. of B. Ed. Colleges 144

4. Gender Healthcare and Health Culture in Kashmir

[A] Inverse Relationship

The pattern and standard of gender health in Kashmir reflected in the following important features of the Kashmiri culture, especially related to health:

(a) ***Pattern of Differentiation:*** The difference between males and females was made systematically in the traditional situation. So, they were differentiated in all areas and at all levels in life. This was supported by actual cultural patterns, masculine ideology and religious idealism.

(b) ***Pattern of Gender Discrimination:*** The differentiation between males and females was followed necessarily in the practices of gender discrimination as reflected in inheritance laws, social practices, cultural patterns and extreme religious ideas. This discrimination spread to all fields of life and hurt every sector and segment of gender life in Kashmir.

(c) ***Attitudes and Behaviour:*** In the pre-determined environment of gender differentiation and discrimination, the relevant attitudes and related behaviour were adopted and followed seriously with ideational support in order to control and dominate the women in society at large.

(d) ***Domination and Suppression:*** Not only women in Kashmir were differentiated and discriminated, they were also dominated and suppressed in the social life. This kind of absolute male domination and female suppression were considered as common and unavoidable conditions of the then existing feudal social order. Women were not allowed any space outside family. In that situation, women did not think or work for their personal and social matters including their health problems. They had also no role in the planning and other efforts towards the requirements of gender health.

(e) ***Values and Norms:*** The values and norms of the traditional society of Kashmir were developed [like in other traditional societies] which attached women with a general lower social position with its cultural, social and ideological legitimacy. Thus women could not take an initiative at the ideation level or at the practice level in regard to their specific needs, especially of health needs. Even their health problems, including the delivery operations, were carried out by male doctors.

(f) ***Role and Status of Women:*** Since a gendered social order preferred an inferior and limited role for women in society, they were awarded the same kind of inferior status in the entirety of social life. It follows that women role [related to their personal and social matters] was exclusively limited to the family framework. In this way, they were not allowed to attain expanded or higher status in society.

(g) ***Division of Labour:*** The gender based social order in traditional Kashmir had made clear demarcation of areas/fields between the male and female areas of operation. While the female activities were mostly limited to the family framework, the male set of activities spread over the whole society. While in this social division of labour, female activities emerged as limited and dominated, the male activities were unlimited and had the dominant character. That was completely a male dominated social order. These propositions reflect in the following diagram :

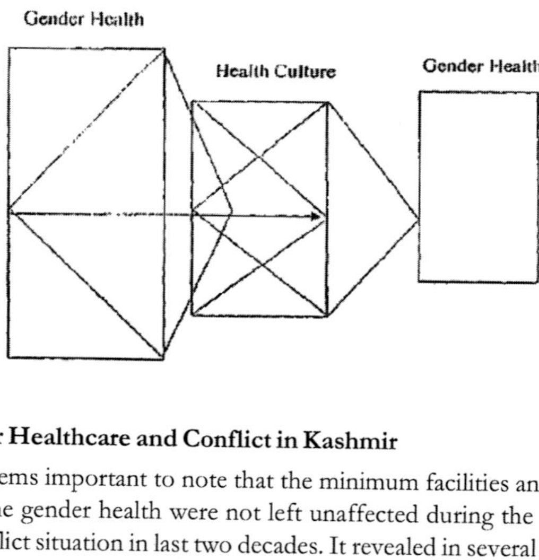

5. Gender Healthcare and Conflict in Kashmir

[i] It seems important to note that the minimum facilities and treatment to the gender health were not left unaffected during the hey days of conflict situation in last two decades. It revealed in several reports and studies that, like all other fields in Kashmir, the health sector was also affected and the effect on gender health proved more adverse. In actuality, the gender health was worst-affected due to militancy and the following details clarify it:

- Many public health centres were closed or were closed for most of the time, especially in the rural and hilly areas.

- Medical and para-medical staff of all health centres in rural and urban areas could or didn't attend their duties regularly and without any interference.
- No specialised expert could make the scheduled visit to the health centres weekly or monthly due to security reasons.
- At some places, militants and government. supported militants blasted the buildings of health centres due to various reasons, and at other places, security forces occupied these buildings.
- In many health centres, the infrastructure, particularly diagonastic machines and other sensitive items were misued or looted.
- Most of healthcare activities were carried out in the environment of threat, tension, stress and anxiety and most of gender healthcare facilities such as transport vehicles were either damaged, misused' or looted.
- The entire healthcare system collapsed for many years and women could not visit any specialised doctors or centres for proper treatment, particularly for pre-natal and post-natal regular healthcare.
- In the environment perpetual tension and depression, it was experienced that many problems related to normal sex life and diseases got initiated with no proper medical treatment available.
- Like many other social groups, women emerged as 'worst sufferer' in the field of mental health problems. It was reported that they suffered from various psychological diseases such as depression, perpetual tension, anxiety, trauma, stress, PTSD, suicide sensation and so on.
- Finally, as a result of the cumulative effect of all above conflict-related developments, the normal productive health of couples got disturbed that gave rise to many gynaecological and other problems in Kashmir.

6. Existing Healthcare Conditions

The existing conditions of gender health in JK, particularly in the Kashmir province, may not be characterised as better or superior to those conditions and standards prevailing at the national level. The former conditions are absolutely worst or inferior than the latter conditions. At the societal level, people in general in Kashmir, had neither proper-enough consciousness-awareness about the basic requirements of gender health, nor had the resources to get necessary medical advice and treatment. In addition, the following observations were made regarding gender health in JK, particularly in the Kashmir province:

- There was no proper awareness and commitment about minimum norms of gender health partly due to ignorance and illiteracy and partly clue to poverty and no access to the needs of health, especially gender health;
- The government and NGOs failed to provide all basic needs and least requirements of gender helth, especially in rural and hilly areas;
- It was revealed that there was extreme difference in the sex ratio [number of women per 1,000 population] in the state which was in 2001 and 2011. The lowest sex ratio was more extreme in the Kashmir province. In fact, six districts in the Kashmir were included in top 10 districts having least sex ratio in the whole of the country in the age group of zero to six. It was explained in terms of high rate of female foeticide/ abortions in the state. These statistical details reveal the deteriorating gender health standards in the state, especially the Kashmir region; and
- Since there was no proper knowledge and awareness about the gender health, the government was not able to facilitate important related facilities, it led to further deterioration and absolutely stopped improvement in the standards of health.

7. Data Support

The preceding explanation of gender health in Kashmir reveals its lowest standard which existed mainly before independence. However, in the period after 1947, some major or minor changes occurred due to official and unofficial efforts which reflected in the following statistics:

[i] Healthcare/Health Status Aspects

Health Status Indicators	*J&K*	*India*
Population (in 000), 2011	12,548,926	1,210,193,422
Decadal Growth Rate (Census 2001-2011)	23.71	17.64
Estimates of B.R. (Birth Rates) SRS, 2010	18.3	22.1
C.D.R (Crude Death Rate), 2011	5.7	8.1
Natural Growth Rate (SRS Bulletin - 2009)	12.8	15.2
Infant Mortality Rate, 2011	43	50
Sex ratio-overall (Females per 1,000 males) 2011	883	940
Sex ratio in Zero-6 age group	937	927
Child Zero-6 years population (Percentage of total)	16.01	13.12
Institutional delivery rate (HMIS 2010-11)	77.3	-
Total Fertility rate (NFHS-II) (SRS 2010)	2.2	2.6
Full Immunisation (DLHS-2007-08)	54per cent	62.5per cent
Antenatal Check-up (DLHS-2007-08)	75.2	84.5
Life expectancy at birth	65.8 m 68.1 f	65.0 m 67.0 f

[ii] Health Institutions in the State

Health Institutions in Kashmir Division

S.No.	Institution	Anantnag	Budgam	Bandipora	Baramulla	Kargil	Ganderbal	Kulgam	Kupwara	Leh	Pulwama	Shopian	Srinagar	Total Health Centres
1.	Provincial Hospital	0	0	0	0	0	0	0	0	0	0	0	0	0
2.	District Hospital	1	1	0	1	1	0	1	1	1	1	0	1	9
3.	General Hospital	0	0	0	0	0	0	0	0	0	0	0	0	0
4.	Sub District Hospital/CHC	6	9	3	6	4	4	2	7	0	3	2	1	47
5.	Emergency Hospital	0	0	0	0	0	0	0	0	0	0	0	0	0
6.	Primary Health Centre	27	36	6	28	2	29	19	31	14	21	6	9	228
7.	Allopathic Dispensary	14	9	6	21	14	4	9	8	3	17	4	16	125
8.	Urban Health Centre/Evening Clinic	0	0	0	0	0	0	0	0	0	0	0	0	0
9.	District TB Centre	1	0	0	1	1	0	0	1	1	1	0	1	7
10.	Medical Aid Centres	11	3	5	13	100	4	5	41	86	6	5	1	280
11.	Mobile Medical Aid Centre	0	0	0	0	0	0	0	0	0	0	0	0	0
12.	Sub Centres	123	121	39	126	33	84	70	154	24	80	44	41	939
13.	MCH	1	0	0	0	0	0	0	0	0	0	0	0	1
14.	Maternity Hospital	0	0	0	0	0	6	0	0	0	0	0	3	9
15.	Leprosy Hospital	0	0	0	0	0	0	0	0	0	0	0	1	1
		184	179	59	196	155	131	106	243	129	129	61	74	1,646

[iii] Health Infrastructure in J&K

Table 1.8: Available Infrastructures at Primary Health Centres by Districts Jammu and Kashmir

	Number of PHCs having					
	Residential Quarter Available for MO	*Functioning 24 hours basis*	*At least 4 beds*	*Regular power supply*	*Having functional Vehicle*	*Total number of PHCs*
Kupwara	9	7	13	0	12	19
Baramulla	3	7	13	2	12	20
Budgam	2	0	11	1	14	21
Srinagar	3	4	9	3	10	12
Pulwama	2	3	4	0	12	18
Anantanag	3	6	6	0	12	15
Leh (Ladakh)	3	8	2	2	8	8
Kargil	3	2	2	0	3	5
Doda	4	2	7	3	7	14
Udhampur	5	9	9	0	7	19
Poonch	3	5	11	2	6	18
Rajouri	4	5	6	0	6	15
Jammu	8	6	6	1	10	17
Kathua	6	8	6	0	8	21
Jammu and	58	72	105	14	127	222
Kashmir (per cent)	(26.10)	(32.40)	(47.50)	(06.30)	(57.20)	(100.0)

[iv] Available Human Resources at PHCs

Table 1.9: Available Human Resource at Primary Health Centres by Districts Jammu and Kashmir, 2007-08

	Human Resources Status of PHCs				
	Medical Officer	*Lady Medical Officer*	*AYUSH Doctor*	*Pharmacist*	*Total Number of PHCs*
Kupwara	10	5	1	17	19
Baramulla	14	11	7	19	20
Budgam	11	9	1	21	21
Srinagar	10	6	0	12	12
Pulwama	6	8	4	17	18
Anantnag	9	5	14	14	15
Leh (Ladakh)	2	4	0	7	8
Kargil	2	1	1	5	5
Doda	5	3	9	13	14
Udampur	9	4	9	18	19
Poonch	4	6	8	18	18
Rajouri	6	3	5	15	15
Jammu	13	14	10	15	17
Kathua	14	8	7	20	21
Jammu and	105	87	76	211	222
Kashmir (per cent)	(51.80)	(39.20)	(34.20)	(95.10)	(100.0)

[vi] Major Sociological Observations

[v] Total No. of Healthcare Centres

S No.	Institution	Name of Anantnag	Budgam	Bandipora	Baramulla	Kargil	Ganderbal	Kulgam	Kupwara	Leh	Pulwama	Shopian	Srinagar	Total Health Centres
1.	Provincial Hospital	0	0	0	0	0	0	0	0	0	0	0	0	0
2.	District Hospital	1	1	0	1	1	0	1	1	1	1	0	1	9
3.	General Hospital	0	0	0	0	0	0	0	0	0	0	0	0	0
4.	Sub District Hospital/CHC	6	9	3	6	4	4	2	7	0	3	2	1	47
5.	Emergency Hospital	0	0	0	0	0	0	0	0	0	0	0	0	0
6.	Primary Health Centre	27	36	6	28	2	29	19	31	14	21	6	9	228
7.	Allopathic Dispensary	14	9	6	21	14	4	9	8	3	17	4	16	125
8.	Urban Health Centre/Evening Clinic	0	0	0	0	0	0	0	0	0	0	0	0	0
9.	District TB Centre	1	0	0	1	1	0	0	1	1	1	0	1	7
10.	Medical Aid Centres	11	3	5	13	100	4	5	41	86	6	5	1	280
11.	Mobile Medical Aid Centre	0	0	0	0	0	0	0	0	0	0	0	0	0
12.	Sub Centres	123	121	39	126	33	84	70	154	24	80	44	41	939
13.	MCH	1	0	0	0	0	0	0	0	0	0	0	0	I
14.	Maternity Hospital	0	0	0	0	0	6	0	0	0	0	0	3	9
15.	Leprosy Hospital	0	0	0	0	0	0	0	0	0	0	0	1	1
	.	184	179	59	196	155	131	106	243	129	129	61	74	1,646

Keeping in view the preceding descriptive and statistical aspect of GHC in Kashmir, we can make the following major sociological observations:

[a] Women's health may be considered as an 'area of suffering' in the field of public health standards. In fact, the gender health situation can be characterised as of 'extremely lower standard' with negative features and conditions which are miserable and in some peripheral areas of 'sub-human standard'.

[b] On the one hand, there prevailed no requisite knowledge and proper awareness and relevant-complete treatment about gender health on the part of majority of women who belong to rural and hilly areas, were illiterate and mostly belonged to the lowest income group.

[c] On the other hand, there were neither specialised experts nor technological facilities available to the vulnerable cases of the gender health in Kashmir. The government was not able to provide these facilities in all towns and villages.

[d] Most of the gender health patients were not in a position to purchase the necessary required drugs at affordable prices in the market or at fair price shops. They could not even pay for diagonastic tests and surgeries because of their belonging to lowest economic groups.

[e] Near majority of women residing in areas outside cities and towns were not in a position to avail, partly or fully, the pre-natal and post-natal health care facilities. So, these women and their new-born babies suffered absolutely mainly because of non-availability of expert doctors and the related/relevant facilities.

[f] The most crucial problem for women was the absence of the transport facility at health centres in the backward areas at the time of delivery/ birth of child by the concerned women. It was reported in the local press repeatedly that, as a result of this situation, many women had to pay in terms of their own lives while delivering the babies. Some of them died in the process.

[g] From the cultural point of view, many women in Kashmir usually felt embarrassed at the presence of or treatment by the male doctors and complete absence of female doctors while dealing with the birth of child in different health centres. They felt perturbed physically as well as mentally on handling their deliveries by the male doctors.

[vii] Emerging Needs of Gender Healthcare

In the preceding background, we can identify the following emerging needs of GHC in Kashmir:

[a] establishment of public health centres in villages in rural and hilly areas in all gender specialties, expertise, technology and facilities;

[b] providing the relevant set of drugs available in the large scale distributive network on minimum affordable prices;

[c] ensuring the availability of minimum necessary transport facility at all health centres to help women before and after the delivery;

[d] providing systematically and in continuity the pre-natal and post-natal healthcare expertise and facilities;

[e] engaging necessarily the trained and specialist doctors in health centres at the time of delivery of the child and satisfying the female psyche; and

[f] keeping in touch with new developments in the treatment of problems and issues involved in gender health and identifying and implementing its implications in our healthcare system.

8. Statement of the Problem

[i] It has been established and confirmed by several sociological studies that women were generally dominated and discriminated in unequal and unjust social situations. This applies to all groups, classes and communities irrespective of their differences in income, status, culture, language, ethnicity and so on. As a result of this widespread and deep-rooted social-cultural environment, women at large suffered in all fields of life, which included their health status and its care. Since the healthcare facilities and services were not available in the state, their conditions deteriorated day. by day. These worst conditions of gender health are related to two major factors. *First,* unstable and uncertain political conditions in the state from 1947 onwards did not allow the government to concentrate and improve the health conditions of women. In this situation, women in Kashmir living in rural, hilly and far flung areas suffered more than men and women in urban areas. *Second,* the conflict which started in 1989 had completely negative impact which led to its debacle in most of the areas in the state. In reality, the existing healthcare system, particularly related to women, collapsed which hurt the women extremely. Thus, both these factors had deteriorating effect on the gender healthcare leading to absence of proper planning, schemes and programmes and their implementation, Thus, the government's efforts to these worst healthcare conditions could not be responded responsibly, realistically and properly. The private sector too did not play its voluntary role. In this situation of least care of the healthcare needs of women in the state, some centrally sponsored schemes and programmes, particularly the N. R. H. M. in recent decades, helped the women patients.

[ii] It is in the preceding situation of gender healthcare that the existing healthcare system was one which can be characterised as 'negative'. It

means that the system did not fulfill the basic health needs of women and did not serve their health interests, especially at the time of pregnancy and delivery. These negative features of the gender healthcare system dropped to its worst during conflict days. One may recall that in those days there was no road connection to any health centre or hospital due to blasting of the bridge in between, there was no ambulance available to take women from different villages to the hospital, there was no doctor available in the hospital/health centre, and there was no proper post-natal care available in the areas of residence or hospitals.

[iii] In the preceding situational background, there emerges the need for establishment and maintenance of the healthcare system, which has all gender-positive features in its functioning. It follows that this new healthcare system must provide all necessary facilities and services needed in the gender health sector on long-term basis. These healthcare practices must be formalised and institutionalised and made necessary part of the entire healthcare system in the state.

[iv] The ideas of this study have been developed in the background of views related to deterioration and degeneration of gender health care practices and dismal response of the health authorities towards this grave health situation. It intends to carry out this study within scientific and sociological framework and will thematically be bi dimensional:

[a] to develop an objective assessment and explanation of the past situation related to gender healthcare and its reflection in the negative healthcare system; and

[b] to present and analyse the basic health needs of women in the state and to highlight all positive features of the new positive healthcare system in the state.

9. Relevance and Scope of Study

[i] Taking in to consideration the poor condition of women's health in Kashmir at present, this kind of sociological study seems highly relevant and highly needed. It is because it will provide the causes and consequences of this grave situation, and will analyse the resolution of the problems cropped up during last many decades. In this context, this study must be considered seriously by the concerned governmental-non-governmental agencies and organisations. This will help in the totalistic and realistic understanding of gender healthcare and its crucial problems in the J&K state.

[ii] In fact, situation related to the health of women in the state was really distressing partly because of natural-cultural-local factors and partly because of political instability-conflict conditions. The existing health conditions of women and children are really pathetic. There have been reported many horrible cases of death of women and children, even in their respective hospitals, in recent years. All these and related health conditions and available healthcare demand a serious academic study which we had envisioned.

[iii] This study has focused on some relevant and important areas related to gender healthcare in J&K. In other words, the following set of questions, based on major topics/themes, was posed to the respondents and their responses were recorded/noted and, later on, explained and interpreted. The questions investigated scientifically and sociologically included the following questions:

- How the traditional culture in Kashmir contributed to the existing poor conditions of gender healthcare?
- How the chronic political instability-uncertainty from 1947 onwards in the state led to the pathetic conditions of gender healthcare?
- How all cultural, social and economic factors led to negative gender healthcare system in the state?
- How even this ailing healthcare system collapsed partly due to armed conflict in the state during last two decades?
- How this negative gender healthcare system can be changed with a positive gender healthcare system in the near future?
- How the professional and general respondents perceive the concerned issues and problems and their resolution?
- What is the role of various agencies/organisations, of the government and civil society in the establishment and maintenance of new and positive gender healthcare system in the state? And
- How the new healthcare system will serve the health interests of women in the state?

10. Broader Objectives of the Study

In the context of situational and thematic aspects, explained.in detail in two preceding sections, this study was oriented to follow the following major academic objectives:

[a] to develop a scientific, realistic and comprehensive perspective about existing gender health and healthcare conditions in the state after evaluating various practices, services and facilities in hospitals and other health centres throughout the state;

[b] to make a scientific and sociological understanding of the problems and issues of the existing healthcare system and as per the views and perceptions held by the professional and general respondents engaged in health sector;

[c] to make an integrated, comprehensive and multi-disciplinary approach to the study of negative as well as positive gender healthcare systems in the state;

[d] to make a scientific analysis of the causes and consequences of the collapse of existing system of healthcare facilities and services and the establishment of new positive gender healthcare system;

[e] to collect and present a set of suggestions for governmental and non-governmental agencies/organisations and for negation of existing gender healthcare system and establishment of positive gender healthcare system; and

[f] to make an objective critique of the health and related practices in the traditional Kashmiri society in the past and make observations about the health culture changes experienced in the recent decades.

2

Methodology

1. Theoretical Context

This study stands for a scientific, sociological and empirical study of women's health in Kashmir. No particular or theoretical perspective or framework was applied to explain and interpret the social phenomena related to women's health. In an attempt to carry out an objective analysis of the social phenomena, varying theoretical perspectives were applied to arrive at scientifically verifiable propositions and conclusions.

2. Focus of the Study

The main theme of this study was to observe and assess, scientifically and sociologically, all past and present aspects of women's health and to suggest ways of improvement and perfection in future. The focus of this was to investigate empirically the social, cultural, economic and other dimensions of women's health. In other words, the study was oriented to analyse the input-output processes and causes-consequences of the most crucial component of the society. The study has qualitative as well as quantitative dimensions and generally pursued inter-disciplinary approach.

3. Universe of the Study

The general and broader universe of this study is the Kashmir province in J&K state having ten administrative districts. But, four particular districts in this region have been made particular universe and unit of study. The names and some population details about these districts are given below:

District / code		*Population*		*Growth Rate*
		2001	2011	[Percentage]
D-1	Srinagar	1027670	1269751	23.56
D-2	Budgam	607181	736773	21.18
D-3	Baramulla	843892	1015503	20.34
D-4	Anantnag	778408	1070144	37.48

As revealed from the above, these districts represent urban or urbanising areas in the region and can provide a realistic picture about existing and changing gender health conditions.

4. Methods and Techniques Adopted

Since the study is empirically oriented, it depends mainly on empirical methods/techniques, especially questionnaire, interview and observation. All major propositions in the study are based on the gained information and data, and conclusions are drawn accordingly. The main steps taken in this investigation are as follows:

[i] ***Questionnaire:*** A detailed and theme-based questionnaire was formulated and it was reviewed taking into consideration relevance and suitability of the questions. It was tested in the field during pilot study in which about 15 per cent of the total number of respondents were questioned or were given questionnaires to fill. This led to further revision in the text of questionnaire, in other words, standardisation of the questions. Then the research investigators [RIs] were given training in the art of recording the responses in this questionnaire.

[ii] ***Pilot Study:*** The pilot study was carried out during which the relevance of questions and suitability of themes in the questionnaire were tested. This and other aims of this pilot study confirmed its authenticity and totality of sociological contents of this empirical study.

[iii] ***Interviews:*** This exercise was adopted in the process of getting proper responses from selected respondents. Moreover, it was the only source and instrument to get responses from those respondents who were not able to fill the questionnaire or did not like to fill it up.

[iv] ***Non-participant Observation:*** It was adopted simultaneously when the situation demanded. Several aspects of the concerned situation which could not be gathered through questionnaire or interview, were covered through non-participant observation method in which the RI could get the hidden, original, actual and sometimes document-based information.

Sometimes, the observation helped in the objective assessment of the situation where questionnaire and interview had failed. This is relevant to many themes such as health and work culture.

[v] ***Official and non-official Sources:*** In order to get the authentic information regarding gender health, all official and unofficial sources were tapped for the required purpose. In some cases, the official documents were the only source of health statistics of the state. In other cases, the non-official agencies, organisations and institutions provided the information related to health sector, which was not provided by other official and unofficial sources.

[vi] ***Written Primary and Secondary Sources:*** The study of written primary and secondary source documents was the next unlimited source of authentic information on health statistics of the state. This included periodical reports of surveys and studies [carried out regularly by international and national agencies, organisations and institutions], other research documents, books, research papers and newspaper-magazine articles. The objective study of all these important sources provided the most-needed information and other statistical details about the prevailing health situation in contemporary times.

[vii] ***Oral Methods:*** One more method adopted for seeking information about the reality of health problems and issues in the past and present times was the oral methods. In these methods, real and correct information was gathered in the informal oral sessions with several experts, professionals, scholars, researchers and others concerned held in different areas and different situations.

[viii] ***Case Studies/Surveys:*** In order to get exclusively specific, authentic and most primary source information about gender health in our units of analysis, i.e. four districts of D-1, D-2, D-3 and D-4, the following particular studies cum surveys were carried in Kashmir. The details follow:

[i] Four case studies of four PHCs:

[a] D-1 Hazratbal [Srinagar] PHC.

[b] D-2 Hardpanzu [Budgam] PHC.

[c] D-3 Achabal [Anantnag] PHC.

[d] D-4 Delina [Baramulla] PHC.

[ii] Two assessment studies of National Health Schemes:

[a] ICDS in Kashmir.

[b] NHRM in Kashmir.

[iii] Two assessment surveys of most important gender hospitals in Kashmir:

[a] Lal Ded Maternity Hospital, Srinagar.

[b] G. B. Pant Children Hospital, Srinagar.

These eight case studies/surveys provided the most crucial, original and comprehensive information and data which was fully utilised in the explanation of gender health conditions in Kashmir.

[ix] ***Field Investigation:*** Four trained RIs with the help of supervisor and PI, carried out detailed field investigation as objectively as possible. They adopted the above-mentioned methods-techniques, primary-secondary sources and recorded the findings in an objective manner and made the observation too. This important process went on for a period of four months and it concluded the work of data collection.

[x] ***Aggregation Tabulation:*** After all preceding stages, the information-data was aggregated, tabulated/classified, explained/analysed and interpreted according to the major themes and needs of this study. This enabled us to pursue the writing of the final report of this study.

5. Sample of Respondents

The total number of respondents in this study was 600 who were broadly divided among two categories of general and professional. The latter was further divided into three categories, i.e., medicos, para-medicos and health administrators. In totality, this was a highly representative and stratified sample.

The details of this sample follow:

Table 2.1: Details of the Sample of Study

S. No.	*Code*	*District*	*Respondents General*	*Medicos*	*Professional Para-medicos*	*Health admns.*	*Total*
1.	D-1	Srinagar	100	20	20	10	150
2.	D-2	Budgam	100	20	20	10	150
3.	D-3	Anantnag	100	20	20	10	150
4.	D-4	Baramulla	100	20	20	10	150
	Total		**400**	**80**	**80**	**40**	**600**

The other sociological compositions of the sample were age, sex, marital status, income, working status, language, family occupation and family structure. The details follow:

Table No. 2.2: Different Categories of the Sample of this Study

		D-1		*D-2*		*D-3*		*D-4*				
S.No.	*Category*	*G*	*P*	*G*	*P*	*G*	*P*	*G*	*P*	*Total*	*G*	*P*
i.	**AGE CATEGORIES**											
	14-30	39	19	44	26	30	08	31	11	207	143	64
	31-45	33	22	44	22	52	36	56	34	299	185	114
	46 AND ABOVE	29	09	12	02	18	06	13	05	94	72	22
	Total	**100**	**50**	**100**	**50**	**100**	**50**	**100**	**50**	**600**	**400**	**200**
ii.	**SEX CATEGORIES**											
	MALE	20	24	26	30	48	29	65	28	270	159	111
	FEMALE	80	26	74	20	52	21	35	22	330	241	89
	Total	**100**	**50**	**100**	**50**	**100**	**50**	**100**	**50**	**600**	**400**	**200**
iii.	**RESIDENCE**											
	RURAL	17	12	86	42	50	27	65	23	322	218	104
	URBAN	83	38	14	08	50	23	35	27	278	182	96
	Total	**100**	**50**	**100**	**50**	**100**	**50**	**100**	**50**	**600**	**400**	**200**
iv.	**MARITAL STATUS**											
	MARRIED	56	30	71	26	46	29	64	37	359	237	122
	UNMARRIED	42	20	21	24	51	19	34	11	222	148	74
	WIDOWED	02	00	08	00	02	01	00	00	13	12	01
	DIVORCED	00	00	00	00	01	01	02	02	06	03	03
	Total	**100**	**50**	**100**	**50**	**100**	**50**	**100**	**50**	**600**	**400**	**200**
v.	**INCOME GROUPS** (PER MONTH)											
	BELOW 100,000	98	44	89	35	65	10	86	29	456	338	118
	100000-300,000	02	06	**08**	15	30	35	13	21	130	53	77
	300000-500,000	00	00	03	00	05	05	01	00	14	09	05
	ABOVE 5,000,000	00	00	00	00	00	00	00	00	00	00	00
	Total									**600**	**400**	**200**
vi.	**WORKING STATUS**											
	DOMESTIC	43	00	66	00	50	00	07	00	166	166	00
	WORKING	57	50	34	50	50	50	93	50	434	234	200
	Total	**100**	**50**	**100**	**50**	**100**	**50**	**100**	**50**	**600**	**400**	**200**
vii.	**FAMILY TYPE**											
	NUCLEAR	86	43	34	20	58	44	52	27	364	230	134
	JOINT	14	07	66	30	42	06	48	23	236	170	66
	Total	**100**	**50**	**100**	**50**	**100**	**50**	**100**	**50**	**600**	**400**	**200**
viii.	**FAMILY OCCUPATION**											
	AGRICULTURE	06	04	34	04	47	00	28	9	132	115	17
	SERVICES	66	28	38	46	48	50	42	32	350	194	156
	TRADE AND COMMERCE	15	11	00	00	03	00	10	00	39	28	11
	BUSINESS	13	07	28	00	02	00	20	09	79	63	16
	Total	**100**	**50**	**100**	**50**	**100**	**50**	**100**	**50**	**600**	**400**	**200**
ix.	**LITERACY STATUS**											
	LITERATE	79	50	53	50	83	50	100	50	515	315	200
	ILLITERATE	21	00	47	00	17	00	00	00	85	85	00
	Total	**100**	**50**	**100**	**50**	**100**	**50**	**100**	**50**	**600**	**400**	**200**

6. Report of the Study

At the end of all these exercises, the way was cleared for writing the detailed report of this study. This was done in terms of writing the first draft of the report. It was submitted to the ICMR, New Delhi for changes/corrections/revisions, if any. After incorporating all suggestions and directions of the ICMR, the final draft of the report was prepared and submitted.

7. Difficulties Encountered

During the period of research project which lasted for 16 months, the team of researchers faced certain problems which affected the quality of this study. These problems encountered were as follows:

[i] The most serious problem of academic nature faced by our team of researchers was non-availability of particular information and related statistics on the topic of gender health in Kashmir. We faced a tough time in tracing the sources of this information and collect the statistics related to the topic of research.

[ii] Since the society is generally not research conscious and investigation friendly, it was very difficult, if not impossible, to collect descriptive as well as oral information and related statistics. More problems were faced in getting information and data about the impact of conflict situation for 22 years long period on the gender healthcare system, facilities and practices.

[iii] Severe cold weather conditions in Kashmir during the winter months from November to February hindered the normal progress of academic work. We had to carry out the field work during the months of December 2012 - February 2013. But, we did our work with determination. It is because of this hard work that we are able to complete and submit this report in time.

3

Gender Healthcare and Culture in Kashmir

1. Gender, Health and Culture

Generally, there exist certain set medical standards of the physical health of women which every society or culture has to ensure. It is because of the fundamental importance of the role of women in procreation and continuity of human race and society. It is not something extra which the women deserve in society. In reality, as man's health conditions are determined by social, economic, cultural, educational and other factors, women's health too is shaped by these crucial factors in addition to biological and hereditary factors. However, women's health is characterised with particular features because of female body organism and particular requirements which must be fulfilled necessarily. Though the biological factor has a dominant and basic role in the women health, the importance of culture also emerges as one of the determining factors, especially with the advancement in age after birth. At that stage, culture turns to be the single most important factor. So, the sociologists have emphasised the crucial and critical role of cultural context of gender health, especially in the under developed society like that of the Kashmiri society.

2. Ignorance and Gender Health

Despite the fundamental importance of gender health in the society, this field faced either the situation of ignorance or situation of negative differentiation and discrimination. It has been observed by the concerned experts that normally gender health has often been ignored consciously and this practice had a common character. In this particular conservative background, women's health in general was ignored in terms of leaving aside their health needs, avoiding and delaying their normal treatment, and keeping their health problems unattended leading to their multiplicity and deterioration. It has also been established during their observation by experts that women health problems were not treated properly, timely and completely. This may be explained partly in terms of illiteracy, poverty, ignorance, non-availability of doctors, facilities and medicines and partly by cultural lag, cultural ethos and cultural practices. In that ideal situation, if a male fell ill, he was normally treated medically, necessarily and immediately. On the other hand, if a female fell ill, she was not rushed to the experts immediately and necessarily. The cases were often delayed or ignored which deteriorated their condition. They were used to send to the then available health expert of institution at the last. These extremely negative gender health conditions prevailed in all areas and classes and communities. But, a considerable degree of change has been experienced in the present situation.

3. Gender Health and Kashmiri Culture

Like other traditional cultures in the Indian sub-continent, the Kashmiri culture in the distant past did not treat women equal, as a result of which they developed different, often unequal, status and role. They were generally differentiated, discriminated and maltreated. Their activities were restricted to the domestic jobs. The consequent attitudes and behavior patterns reflected at the broader societal level. The common practice in those pre-independent days was that while gender health was not responded properly and completely and most of its problems were not attended but kept pending, deferred or forgotten. This was the lack of interest among men about the health suffering of women.

It was found by the observers that this kind of attitude and behaviour was prevailing in rural as well as urban areas, among all classes, groups and communities, and in rich and poor families. The rationale provided to this kind of gender health treatment was explained in terms of heavy economic dependence of women on eldest male member of the family, absolute and dominant male authority, unequal role and status between male and female, cultural limitations and so on. Thus, a social environment was created whose last preference was the gender health. In that situation, while women were not treated medically in time and properly, there was no goal fixed related to women's health improvement. It was particularly bad for women's health as there existed no common health facility and there was no doctor available.

So, women had to opt for folk or faith-healing practices in which majority of them suffered damages in their health.

Moreover, a general situation in which women were teased, harassed and tortured continuously and systematically and with some ideological and cultural support, women developed several mental and physical health problems. These could neither be diagnosed in time and properly nor treated completely by their male family members. Even they were not allowed to go independently to avail the available medical treatment and facilities. In brief, the traditional cultural ethos in Kashmir in the distant past provided not a just and needed health care to women and they were not also allowed to avail the medical facilities. In addition, that situation was not condemned and was not considered undesirable.

4. Gender Health and Cultural Symbol Practices

It is now clear that gender health was totally affected by the cultural phenomena such as cultural notions, concepts, orientation, values, norms and practices. Even superstitions played a role and were practically detrimental to the ideals of gender health. It was observed that conscious and organised negation of gender health facilities were justified and legitimised on the basis of cultural notions and views which were practiced through the application of related values and norms. Even value oriented words like *'maa', 'behau', 'betee', 'biwi'* and *' bahu'* revealed differential treatment of heath care to them. Three particular examples of this differential treatment with women follow:

[i] The women in the past believed that their respective husbands were *'dekka'* [forehead], meaning like a crown and king without whose association her existence meant nothing. They reserved all honours and regards for that 'taj'. They also believed that their husbands must be always at top of hierarchy and must always be preferred irrespective of their social positions even at their cost.

[ii] Women used to occupy back seat after their husbands inside as well as outside their family. They never claimed first, superior or equal status to men. This crudely reflected in their habit of not consuming the fresh food with other male members of family and not at the same time at which male members consumed it. In many cases and on all special occasions like *Eid* and local festivals, when there used to be a variety of special foods prepared for the occasion/s, they used to consume either after the males consumed or consume the male's left-over food.

[iii] In the cultural context of Kashmir, even some gender health care has been deteriorated to such a level that it did not benefit the women nor could they avail it in ideal conditions. This revealed through the practical aspects of Kashmiri culture which again can be explained in three particular ways:

[a] When women fell ill, they usually go to their parent's home and get the treatment there on their expenses.

[b] Women usually go to parents home voluntarily before the time of delivery and stay there till she gets perfectly well.

[c] When the women feel tired or overburdened in in-laws home, they usually go to their parent's home for relaxing and entertaining. In cases of divorce and separation also, the women sufferers are provided shelter, security, support and help by the parents and their paternal relatives.

5. Culture and Religion in Kashmir

Like in other societies in the Indian sub-continent, religion was used in Kashmir directly or indirectly for gender healthcare in a particular way and through different methods and techniques. In this connection, we may mention about conventional and non-conventional methods of this gender health treatment in Kashmir. On the one hand, the conventional methods include religious, psychological and folk healing methods. On the other hand, the non-conventional methods include all traditional and modern forms of medical treatment. In the cultural background of Kashmir, women have utilised more conventional than non-conventional methods in treating different diseases and other health problems. The result is that their health has suffered and these conventional methods were not fully effective and realistic. Consequently, they had to opt for non-conventional methods for speedy recovery of diseases and from other health problems.

[i] The most common conventional method of gender health treatment was *'Peer-Faqir Illaj'* which has strong cultural and religious connotation. It has been observed that treatment is strongly imbedded in the cases, its effects have also shown positive impact and significant improvement in many cases. Thus, both conventional and non-conventional ways of treatment are in vogue in Kashmir, still a considerable number of women patients go for conventional ways of treatment, especially when modern medical facilities are not available fully. But, the emerging trend in this regard convey that increasing number of women in rural and urban areas are moving towards modern methods of healthcare.

The conventional, particular religious type health care revolves around some practices ordered by *peers* and *faqirs* and followed by women health sufferers. These practices include the following distinctive practices:

[a] Making a *'taveez'* and put/hang it on any particular or directed part of the body;

[b] Reciting some Quranic recitations and give the patient an air wave of it;

[c] Giving a cup on which some religious statements are written by the Peer with a bead of blue or black colour. The patient is directed to wash the cup with water and consume that water.

[d] Some dry fruits, especially *badaam, kishmish,* and other items like *shreen,* sugar pieces, and so on are given to the women patients to consume as per the orders of the *peer* and *faqir.*

[e] Some Quranic text on a small piece of paper [say around from 3 x 4 to 4 x 6 inches] is folded and given to women for burning it in *kangdi* [local firepot] and take its smoke on her body;

[f] Some *peers,* especially senior and experienced ones, go for *'jadoo'* [magic] technique. As per the healththe concerned woman has to take some serious oral or physical act in order to restore normalcy or negate the undesirable physical or psychological condition. The *peers'* belonging to the Shia Muslim community are considered more experienced and expert in this field.

[g] There is one *'jinn-pari* syndrome' in which a woman is caught mentally and physically and she performs abnormal acts. The particular type of *'peers'* have to work very hard in order to liberate these women from those non-human entities. While this disease is limited to the women, its treatment is available with the religious oriented *'peers'* only. Modern treatment is still irrelevant for this kind of female disease.

[ii] The other conventional type of gender health treatment is carried out by the folk practices and folk healers. Folk healers have power like lowest degree of *charisma* through which they treat women. Sometimes, they adopt religious oriented and religious ordained treatment to women health seekers. They ask for doing certain practices repeatedly. This action on the part of folk healers has a limited effect in practice. Normally, this treatment does not continue for longer period and women usually return to the medical treatment for speedy recovery and stable health.

[iii] It seems important to note here that these conventional and folk practices of gender healthcare have been distorted and exploited by some shrewd individuals. These folk *peers* and *faqirs* use these healing techniques for personal and financial gains. As a result, these practices got debunked, deteriorated and degenerated. Some fake-identity individuals use it for sexual purpose also. In reality, all these individuals involved in these practices stand for fraud, evil and criminal elements. Though the job of these fake *peers* and *faqirs* has been delegitimised, they still continue with these practices.

6. Gender Health, Heavy Workload and Inter-sex Cultural Practices

[i] It has been reported that, in the cultural background of Kashmir, there is heavy burden of domestic work on women in all areas, cities, towns and villages. In the rural areas, they have the further responsibility of activities related to agriculture. This is in addition to child-bearing and child-rearing practices performed by them. Even if there is separation between the couple, the 'duties' are performed by women only. This seems interesting to note that, in the traditional cultural context, women are not involved in heavy work load by men only but by women also. Thus, even in the intra-sex relationship and work allocation, the women emerge as the main burden taker and sufferer. That explains the complex relationship between daughter-in-law and mother-in-law, in which the latter, in league with elder male-female members of the family, impose heavy load of domestic work on the former. The sister-in-law too help her brother to impose heavy burden on his wife. In this way, women always suffer at the hands of their own and opposite sex.

[ii] It follows that in totality women have been assigned heavy workload which has affected their health adversely. In this kind of cultural environment, women felt compelled to undertake all sorts of work at the cost of her health, especially in the in-laws context because women want to please them always. It was in this type of cultural environment that married women generally took refuge in the parental home in order to take complete rest or relaxation or to avoid odd jobs.

7. Gender Health and Age at Marriage

[i] It was also found that one of the important culturally determined factor, i.e., age at marriage, affects the gender health condition in general. It follows that age of marriage in society, early or late, affect the entire

process of health maintenance and reproductive behaviour in the negative way. If the average age is due and proper, it will also affect but in positive way and will ensure proper reproductive cycle. It was observed in the Kashmiri society that while in majority of female cases, marriage was performed at earlier age or later age, these practices had negative physical and mental health implications. Moreover, they had to face several complications in the reproductive health. On the other hand, only minority, though significant, of women had married at the normal and proper age. This kind of marriage practice had comparatively better physical and mental health implications for the entire life.

[ii] It was also observed that women succumb to the motivation or the pressures of their male partners to undergo sex detection tests in the sonography centres. Subsequently, if the child is a girl, they are forced or motivate to undergo illegal abortion even at the cost of grave implications for their health. Even in the cases of family planning, the women motivated to undergo all types of operations in comparison to their respective men. The cumulative impact of all these practice on the health of women has not been found desirable or appreciable.

8. Common Diseases among Women

As is clear from the previous section, the culturall factors necessarily determined the nature, occurrence and frequency of main diseases among women in all areas of Kashmir. Though all women individuals didn't experience every single disease, but majority of them had this disease/s at one or the other time in life. These main and chronic diseases were identified as follows:

- Anaemia
- Mental health problems
- Depression
- Hyper tension
- PTSD
- Anxiety
- Suicidal tendency
- Thyroid
- Stomach Cancer

These diseases were found among all groups of women in Kashmir. Their causation can be explained in terms of culture-specific and women-specific factors and their long-term implication. The higher mortality rate in the Kashmir region in the state can also be explained in the context of this dreaded situation.

9. Gender Health and Cultural-religious Attitudes

Culture, with the support of mass religion, created an environment in the Kashmiri society which had clear negative implication for gender health. This reflects in the common cultural-religious attitude to avoid and to resist/oppose the exposure of their bodies in front of unknown and unrelated doctors. Consequently, they are not able to get proper and timely treatment of their diseases and other health problems in the absence of female doctors and other concerned professionals. This type of attitude in its extreme form hurt women at large at the time of their delivery. This complex problem aggravated and deteriorated the health condition of women in the situation characterised by shortage of female doctors and para-medical staff [especially nurses] in the speciality of gynecology and obstretics at all health centres and for all women. In totality, the culture-imposed restrictions on male-female interaction have created several structural and functional limitations and difficulties for women for their medical treatment. In that situation, there was neither any possibility of forced/imposed interaction between female patients and male doctors-professionals nor their former could expose before the latter.

10. Gender Health and Food Habits

It has been argued that socially the traditional food habits in Kashmir do not go in the best interests of the health of the people, especially of the female health. It follows that the pattern of food habits in Kashmir had not contributed to the betterment of gender health.

First, the argument in this regard is that present food habits in Kashmir are neither scientific nor balanced. The people, including women, consume heavy quantity of rice in the lunch and dinner which has had negative health implications on the consumers, especially women. Most of the local people, especially women in their marriage days and during pregnancy days, consume huge doze of spices which, after some limit, turn anti-body components and sources for dreaded diseases for them. Thus, they develop complex problems which never allow their bodies to reach desirable standards of health.

Second, there is hardly any fruit-consumption tradition in Kashmir. People generally eat less or very less fruits or didn't eat at all. It is occasionally said here that people used to eat fruits at the time they fell ill and on the advice of doctor or *hakim*. Now, this attitude has changed considerably. People in large numbers are consuming local and non-local varieties of fruits now.

Third, women in large numbers consume salt tea [which is boiled with the soda to the highest, even dangerous level] in large quantity, say two to four cups at a time in the morning and in the afternoon [at 4.00 pm.] This tea consumption has spoiled the stomach system of more women than men.

Fourth, Kashmiri people take very little breakfast in the morning, i.e., one piece of bread and several cups of salt tea, while as they, especially the working or labour class which most Kashmiris belong to, need heavy breakfast such as eggs, bread, milk, and other such varieties.

11. Gender Health and Cultural Change

The most important aspect of this entire situation is that a radical but partial type of change has been experienced in the Kashmiri society and its health sector, too. In reality, the educational, economic, and social changes in post-independence period provided the basis for change in attitudes and be-haviour towards health and nutrition. In other words, people in general and women in particular started giving due attention to their physical and mental health needs in the recent past. This gave rise to a gender-based response towards health and family welfare. This was also because the state after 1947 started taking concrete steps and introducing-implementing schemes and programmes for total gender health betterment. As a result of all these conscious and organised efforts by the government, we have a situation now where minimum gender health facilities are available in urban and rural areas and certain sections and groups of women utilise these fully according to their needs and problems. These groups are from middle-upper classes from rural and urban background. However, a large number of women from lower classes and communities and particularly from rural areas still wait for gender health facilities, expert doctors and professionals, medicines in order to fulfill their basic health needs.

4

Gender Healthcare and Conflict in Kashmir

Armed Conflict and its Impact

[i] The armed conflict between two combatant groups or countries has disastrous short-term and long-term implications for all sections of society and all sectors of human life. Various features of this situation have been, identified by global experts, international organisations and human rights groups. It has been established through a number of studies that the armed conflict between countries and between state and militant groups devastates and destroys the whole life, especially of women. It has been specifically observed that gender health has become the target and victim of armed conflict in many countries of the world. Now, it has been established that with convincing empirical evidence that in a conflict zone, the gender health suffered absolutely, particularly in the areas mentioned below:

- Existing health services and facilities got lost in the violent attacks;
- Functioning of infrastructure in terms of buildings, material apparatus and technological tools is disturbed and destroyed deliberately;
- Health personnel working in conflict areas are killed or injured or forced to flee;
- National and international medical aid reached not in time and not according to needs of the population in the conflict affected areas, especially women trapped in these areas;

- Access to gender healthcare facilities and services became difficult;
- Minimum reproductive healthcare needed in particular conflict situation was lacking, resulting even in pathetic condition of women;
- Even if the facilities and services were available in conflict areas, men engaged in armed activities may be given precedence over women;
- There was maximum possibility of disturbance in reproductive health of women from menstruation to life threatening pregnancy related health conditions during the conflict;
- Direct implication on the actual sex life of concerned family members within the conflict zone;
- Heavy increase in the deterioration of mental health conditions of women in the conflict environment;
- Comparatively, faster growth of home and physical distance, and
- Taking women away from family/domestic role.

2. Conflict in Kashmir and its Implications

[i] Though the conflict situation prevailed in Kashmir for last two decades, it was not a war between two sovereign countries. In actuality, it represented the armed militant movement organised on the part of local youth armed insurgents against the state for achieving their political objective of *'Azaadi'*. In effect, it also represented the limited-war situation during last 20 years. Thus it follows that these concepts of 'war' and 'militancy' are different qualitatively as well as quantitatively. While the war is fought between two countries, the militancy is fought between organised armed groups of youth and some little portion of state armed/security forces. In the former case, all military and armed forces get involved; the latter engages groups of armed youth and some portion of armedsecurity forces. Finally, while the war involves all people of the country, the militancy engages a particular group of militants and their supporters belonging to the same country, but, supported by other country. In this context, the conflict situation may be characterised as 'mass armed violence' between armed militants and state's security forces rather a full war between two sovereign countries.

[ii] So, the implications of militancy or violence are different. All global level short term and long term implications of war, mentioned above, cannot be generalised in the militancy hit state of J&K. The implications in the case of militancy are limited and have lesser long term implications. These implications have been observed more in the infrastructure,

facilities and services in the gender healthcare system than in the fields of mortality rates, reproductive health and general gender health practices in the healthcare centres at all levels in the state.

[iii] After observing the immediate consequences of the militancy on the gender healthcare system in last two decades among all respondents, the following gender health areas were identified as most crucial as follows:

- Loss of health infrastructure,
- Collapse of gender healthcare facilities and services,
- Major areas of gender health suffering, and
- Main gender health problems in Kashmir.

[iv] A detailed enquiry was carried out about these aspects of gender healthcare devastation and collapse of this system in Kashmir in last two decades among all respondents of this study. In this way, we got the respondents' views about the macro and micro-level impact of militancy conditions on important fields related to gender health. In the following, we present the relevant observations made during this investigation.

3. Loss of Healthcare Infrastructure

The loss of infrastructure in Kashmir due to conflict situation in last two decades reflected first in the total loss of health infrastructure in terms of the total collapse of system of healthcare facilities and services. This crudely reflects in the following table and its explanatory details:

Table 4. 1: Total Loss of Healthcare Infrastructure in Kashmir

		Response										
		D-1		*D-2*		*D-3*		*D-4*		*Total*		
S. No	*Theme/Question posed*	*P.*	*G.*	*P.*	*G.*	*P.*	*G.*	*P.*	*G.*	*T.*	*P.*	*G.*
1	2	3	4	5	6	7	8	9	10	11	12	13
		No	No	No	No	No	No	No	No	No	No	No
1.	Negligence to G. Health Sector	00	07	07	05	27	33	43	07	292	177	115
2.	Infrastructure destroyed completely	79	37	35	09	09	00	08	01	168	121	47
3.	Rural areas more effected	00	00	06	04	00	01	67	28	106	73	33
4.	No new hospital was constructed	00	00	00	00	08	03	45	20	76	53	23
5.	Loss of medical manpower	00	00	07	07	00	00	40	17	71	47	24

The preceding table reveals that

[i] The 292/600 [48.66 per cent] respondents felt that, due to conflict situation in Kashmir, the local government does not pay proper attention to the gender health. It could not even stop its extreme deterioration, in other words, the government ignored completely the gender health and its basic needs. This response was shared by 115/200 [57.50 per cent] professional and 177/400 [44.25 per cent] general respondents.

[ii] Conveying the same line of response, 168/600 [28.00 per cent] respondents said that there was complete collapse of the gender health infrastructure available in the healthcare centres after 1989. It was revealed by 47/200 [23.50 per cent] professional and 121/400 [30.25 per cent] general respondents.

[iii] The 106/600 [17.66 per cent] respondents opined that the gender healthcare facilities and services collapsed more in rural than urban areas after 1990. This response was conveyed by 33/200 [16.50 per cent] professional and 73/400 [18.25 per cent] general respondents.

[iv] The 76/600 [12.66 per cent] respondents upheld the view that since government was extremely busy in countering militancy, it had no time to plan and subsequently construct new hospitals. So, there could be no new construction of hospital here. This view was shared by 23/200 [11.50 per cent] professional and 53/400 [13.25 per cent] general respondents.

[v] The 71/600 [11.83 per cent] respondents said that Kashmir lost the professional and trained manpower from different healthcare centres after 1990. They could not withstand the threats and humiliation. This reply was shared by 24/200 [12.00 per cent] professional and 47/400 [11.75 per cent] general respondents.

[vi] The following responses were also recorded regarding the loss of healthcare infrastructure in Kashmir during two decades of conflict:

Table 4.1: Total Loss of Healthcare Infrastructure

S. No.	*Response*	*Total response*	*Professional response*	*General response*
1.	Many ambulances were burnt	39/600 [06.50]	12/200 [0.6.00]	27/400 [06.75]
2.	Facilities disrupted partly	222/600 [37.00]	122/200 [61.00]	100/400 [25.00]
3.	Medical and paramedic. Staff left the area	46/600 [07.66]	30/200 [15.00]	16/400 [04.00]
4.	Insufficient supply of medicines	92/600 [15.33]	81/200 [40.50]	11/400 [02.75]

5.	Fast rise in the number of patients	25/600 [04.16]	14/200 [07.00]	11/400 [02.75]
6.	Less utilisation of funds and facilities	11/600 [01.83]	08/200 [04.00]	03/400 [00.75]
7.	Buildings occupied by security forces	07/600 [01.16]	03/200 [01.50]	04/400 [01.00]

4. The Areas of Women Suffering

The second major aspect of the impact of conflict situation was related to the specific health areas in which women suffered extremely. When probed about this aspect of gender healthcare, our respondents identified some particular areas/fields which we recorded in the following table:

Table 4.2: Areas of Women's Suffering Due to Conflict

1	*2*	*3*	*4*	*5*	*6*	*7*	*8*	*9*	*10*	*11*	*12*	*13*
1.	Collapse of system of facilities/services	92	49	69	41	100	50	10	50	551	361	190
2.	Heavy rise of mental health cases	14	07	58	39	39	17	36	21	230	146	84
3.	Specific gender negative effects	00	00	12	13	75	32	00	00	132	87	45
4.	MCH and RCH	49	23	00	00	14	07	13	08	114	76	38
5.	Acute psychological diseases	24	20	34	15	01	02	00	00	96	59	37
6.	Limited physical movement	00	02	00	00	00	00	00	00	02	00	02
7.	Physical/domestic violence	00	03	00	00	00	00	00	00	03	03	00
8.	Increase in IMR-MMR	00	00	17	05	00	01	00	00	23	17	06

The preceding table reveals that:

[i] The 551/600 [91.83 per cent] respondents said that the conflict situation in Kashmir had collapsed the entire system of facilities-services which led to many serious hardships for women during emergency times, especially in rural and hilly areas. This response was shared by 146/200 [73.00 per cent] professional and 84/400 [21.00 per cent] general respondents.

[ii] There was heavy increase in the mental health cases among women due to conflict. In fact, this was completely unprecedented in the. past history in completely peaceful society in Kashmir. This was conveyed by 230/600 [38.33 per cent] respondents who belonged to professional 146/200 [73.00 per cent] and general 84/400 [21.00 per cent] respondents.

[iii] The conflict period in Kashmir experienced special impact on women in terms of rise of women specific diseases/problems among them. This was revealed by 132/600 [22.00 per cent] respondents who included 87/200 [43.50 per cent] and 45/400 [11.25 per cent] professional and general respondents respectively.

[iv] The MCH and RCH rise was noticed in the conflict situation and was conveyed by 114/600 [19.00 per cent] respondents who were from professional, 76/200 [38.00 per cent] and general 38/400 [09.50 per cent] categories.

[v] The conflict gave rise to acute psychological diseases/problems. In reality, it had develcped dangerous proportions and implications. This was suggested by 96/600 [16.00 per cent] respondents who belonged to professional 59/200 [29.50 per cent] and general 37/400[09.25 per cent] categories.

[vi] The conflict had general effect of restricting the normal mobility of women which directly affected their health condition in the negative direction. This was upheld by 02/600 [00.33 per cent] respondents who all [02/400, 00.50 per cent] belonged to the general category.

[vii] It was generally observed that violence against women started in an organised way after the conflict started in Kashmir. While criminal violence took place outside family, domestic violence took place inside family. This was conveyed by 03/600 [00.50 per cent] respondents who were all 03/200[01.50 per cent] from professional category.

[viii] It was observed by the experts and general people that constant situation of conflict over two long decades gave rise to the trends of MMR and IMR in Kashmir. This was confirmed by the decadal census reports.

5. Other Gender Healthcare Related Problems

The other area of investigation was the impact of conflict on gender healthcare services, facilities and other aspects. The responses to these questions are noted in Table 4.3:

Table 4.3: Other Gender Healthcare-related Problems

1	*2*	*3*	*4*	*5*	*6*	*7*	*8*	*9*	*10*	*11*	*12*	*13*
1.	Over burdening/ crowding of hospitals	00	00	00	00	05	06	40	21	72	45	27
2.	Funds diverted to other sector/region	00	00.	05	02	12	03	38	06	66	55	11
3.	Loss of medical transport	00	00	00	00	07	00	00	00	07	07	00
4.	Emergence of late marriage	00	02	00	00	00	00	00	00	02	02	00

5.	Hurdles to gender healthcare facilities	00	03	01	00	00	00	00	00	04	03	01

Table 4.3 conveys that

[i] The 72/600 [12.00 per cent] respondents said that the continuous armed conflict between the militants and security forces led to over-crowding and over-burdening in all hospitals because a large number of people were injured during these encounteres This had negative effect on the gender healthcare facilities. These respondents belonged to professional 45/200, [22.50 per cent] and general 27/400,[06.75 per cent] categories.

[ii] The 66/600 [11.00 per cent] respondents reported that the funds meant for local gender healthcare facilities and services could not be utilised in the abnormal conditions of conflict. In many cases, these funds were diverted to other healthcare sectors or to other regions and provinces. This information was revealed by 55/200 [27.50 per cent] professional and 11/400 [02.75 per cent] general respondents.

[iii] The general impact of conflict was felt seriously in the absence of transport provided by health institutions and centres. This condition had completely negative implications on women, especially in the cases of delivery. This response was conveyed by 07/600 [01.16 per cent] respondents of whom all 07/200, [03.50 per cent] belonged to the professional category.

[iv] One of the indirect implications of conflict was felt in the rise of late marriage as a common practice, which had certain implications for gender health in the long term. This was conveyed by 02/600 [00.33 per cent] respondents of whom [02/200, 01.00 per cent] of professional category.

[v] It was reported that various hurdles were created in the implementati of gender healthcare facilities mainly due to prevailing conflict conditions in Kashmir. This hurt the interests of gender health a lot. This was reported by 04/600 [00.66 per cent] respondents who belonged to professional 03/200, [01.50 per cent] and general 01/400, [00.25 per cent] categories.

6. Fulfillment of Medical Loss

After covering all important aspects of gender healthcare which suffered due to conflict, the investigation shifted to a question of crucial importance, i.e., how to recover these medical losses during last two decades ? The responses we received have been recorded in Table 4.4.:

Table 4. 4: How Can Medical Losses be Recovered

1	2	3	4	5	6	7	8	9	10	11	12	13
1.	Establish medical facilities fast	00	00	03	02	26	07	77	44	106	73	33
2.	Recruit female staff urgently	24	05	05	05	01	14	100	10	74	55	19
3.	Increase no. of Women Hospitals	05	05	03	02	12	11	15	10	63	35	28
4.	Formulate pro-gender policy	00	00	11	03	03	06	10	10	43	24	19
5.	Full Use of existing facilities	00	00	06	03	15	05	00	00	26	18	08
6.	Cooperation bet. G+P Sectors	00	00	14	08	03	00	00	00	25	17	08
7.	Introduce Gender-related schemes	05	04	02	03	00	01	23	06	44	34	10
8.	Separate hospitals for women	02	02	01	03	14	10	04	04	40	21	19
9.	Female administrators need	02	01	01	01	00	00	03	02	10	05	05
10.	proper training to medicos	01	00	02	01	02	03	05	06	20	10	10
11.	Focus on mental health	05	02	08	04	06	06	10	10	51	39	12
12.	Resolve the Kashmir Issue	03	02	07	07	09	11	10	15	64	39	25

Table 4.4 reveals 12 points of response which we explain here:

[i] The 106/600 [17.66 per cent] respondents maintained that in order to overcome the medical losses during the conflict, the government has to initiate and present all gender health facilities and services as early as possible. If people get medical facilities fast again, they may forget the medical losses. This response was shared by 73/200 [36.50 per cent] professional and 33/400 [08.25 per cent] general respondents.

[ii] As there is acute shortage of female staff, especially doctors, which was further increased due to conflict, the government immediately recruits female medicos and para-medicos in all hospitals and health centres. This was conveyed by 74/600 [12.33 per cent] respondents who belonged to professional—55/200, [27.50 per cent] and general 19/400, [04.75 per cent] categories.

[iii] The number of hospitals has remained static in Kashmir for past many years. The feeling of this least number of hospitals got intensified during the conflict. This was revealed by 63/600 [10.50 per cent] respondents who composed of 35/200 [17.50 per cent] professional and 28/400 [07.00 per cent] general respondents.

[iv] It was opinion of 43/600 [07.16 per cent] respondents that the government must formulate many pro-gender health schemes and implement these seriously. It was because this opinion got developed in the context of conflict in which there was no gender help or particular scheme to help them. This opinion was shared by 24/200 [12.00 per cent] professional and 19/400[04.75 per cent] general respondents.

[v] The 24/600 [04.00 per cent] respondents presented the view that since conflict has reduced the availability of gender healthcare facilities, the concerned existing facilities and services must be utilised to the

maximum extent. The upholders of this opinion were from professional and general respondents in the proportion of 18/200 [09.00 per cent] and 08/400 [02.00 per cent] respectively.

[vi] In the post-conflict period, there must be complete cooperation between government and private sectors in the field of gender healthcare facilities and services. This will prove highly purposeful and will fulfill all requirements. These views were expressed by 25/600 [04.16 per cent] respondents who composed of 17/200 [08.50 per cent] professional and 08/400 [02.00 per cent] general categories.

[vii] The 44/600 [07.33 per cent] respondents repeated the views [mentioned at No. IV] that the state must start the specific healthcare schemes in the state. They were from professional [34/200, 17.00 per cent] and 10/400 general [02.50 per cent] categories.

[viii] There must be separate hospitals and health centres established at all levels in order to help the women in totality. That was suggested by 40/600 [06.66 per cent] respondents who composed of 21/200 [10.50 per cent] professional and 19/400 [04.75 per cent] general categories.

[ix] There is a serious and urgent need of appointing female administrators in the health sector for making gender healthcare a successful and effective exercise. This was conveyed by 10/600 [01.66 per cent] respondents who belonged to professional [05/200, 02.50 per cent] and general, 05/400 [01.25 per cent] categories.

[x] The 20/600 [03.33 per cent] respondents put forward the view that there should be necessary training imparted to all medical and para-medical staff in gender healthcare. They belonged to the professional 10/200, [05.00 per cent] and general 10/400, [02.50 per cent] categories.

[xi] Since the prominent diseases related to gender health were mental health diseases which increased and intensified during the conflict situation of stress, depression, anxiety, insecurity and PTSD. So, the 51/600 [08.50 per cent] respondents opined that women's mental health problems must be focused and treated on preference basis. These respondents were from professional 39/200, [19.50 per cent] and general 12/400, [03.00 per cent] categories.

[xii] Finally, the respondents felt that the root cause of all these health problems was the conflict and its implications for gender health. So, there is the need to resolve this issue peacefully. This was conveyed by 64/600 [10.66 per cent] respondents who composed of professional 39/200, [19.50 per cent] and general 25/400, [06.25 per cent] respondents.

Section - B

Findings of the Study

5

Gender Healthcare Areas and Needs

1. GHC Areas

In order to ascertain the specific nature and number of fields (specialities), we carried out an investigation which gave the relevant information mentioned below:

Table 5.1: Gender Healthcare Fields

		D1		*D2*		*D3*		*D4*		*Responses*		
		Srinagar		*Budgam*		*Anantnag*		*Baramulla*		*(No. and per cent.)*		
S.No	*Fields*	*G*	*P*	*G*	*P*	*G*	*P*	*G*	*P*	*GT*	*G*	*P*
1.	Gynaecology	81.0	46.0	70.0	20.0	82.0	33.0	88.0	48.0	468 78.00	321 80.25	147 73.50
2.	Reproductive child health and maternal health	36.0	15.0	06.0	20.0	66.0	21.0	33.0	08.0	205 34.16	141 35.25	64.0 32.00
3.	Pre/post-delivery and natal care	18.0	03.0	00.0	00.0	09.0	10.0	03.0	04.0	47.0 07.83	30.0 07.50	17.0 08.50
4.	Cardiology	04.0	05.0	00.0	00.0	01.0	01.0	00.0	00.0	11.0 01.83	05.0 01.25	06.0 03.00
5.	Child health-care	04.0	03.0	00.0	00.0	00.0	00.0	00.0	00.0	07.0 01.16	04.0 01.00	03.0 01.50
6.	Adolescent health	23.0	20.0	00.0	00.0	02.0	00.0	00.0	00.0	45.0 07.50	25.0 06.25	20.0 10.00
7.	Mental health	18.0	13.0	00.0	04.0	00.0	00.0	01.0	01.0	37.0 06.16	19.0 04.75	18.0 09.00
8.	Nutritional care	09.0	11.0	00.0	00.0	00.0	00.0	00.0	00.0	20.0 03.33	09.0 02.25	11.0 05.50
9.	Social and	00.0	00.0	04.0	09.0	00.0	00.0	01.0	08.0	22.0	05.0	17.0

preventive medicine									03.66	01.25	08.50
10. Oncology	00.0	00.0	15.0	04.0	00.0	00.0	03.0	16.0	38.0	18.0	20.0
									06.33	04.50	10.00
11. Reproductive endocrinology	00.0	00.0	11.0	08.0	09.0	09.0	09.0	18.0	64.0	29.0	35.0
									10.66	07.25	17.50
12. Anaemic care	00.0	00.0	00.0	01.0	00.0	00.0	00.0	00.0	01.0	00.0	01.0
									00.16	00.00	00.50
13. Gastroenterology	00.0	00.0	00.0	02.0	00.0	00.0	00.0	00.0	02.0	00.0	02.0
									00.33	00.00	01.00
14. Immunology	00.0	00.0	02.0	02.0	00.0	00.0	00.0	00.0	04.0	02.0	02.0
									00.66	00.50	01.00
15. Nephrology	00.0	00.0	00.0	02.0	00.0	00.0	00.0	00.0	02.0	00.0	02.0
									00.33	00.00	01.00
16. Clinical bio-chemistry	00.0	00.0	00.0	02.0	00.0	00.0	00.0	00.0	02.0	00.0	02.0
									00.33	00.00	01.00
17. Caesarian	00.0	00.0	00.0	00.0	00.0	00.0	02.0	00.0	02.0	02.0	00.0
									00.33	00.50	00.00
18. Orthopaedics	00.0	00.0	00.0	00.0	01.0	03.0	00.0	00.0	04.0	01.0	03.0
									00.66	00.25	01.50
19. Paediatrics	00.0	00.0	00.0	00.0	05.0	00.0	00.0	00.0	05.0	05.0	00.0
									00.83	05.00	00.00

The following explanation can be made of the above table:

(i) Gynaecology as a major gender healthcare field was reported by 321/400(80.25 per cent) respondents from the general category and 147/200(73.50 per cent) respondents from the professional category. A total of 468/600(78.00 per cent) respondents reported it as the gender health field. This response composes of the following district-wise responses. In district Srinagar, 81.0 respondents from general category and 46.0 respondents from professional category reported it. In district Budgam, 70 respondents from general category and 20 respondents from professional category reported it. In district Anantnag, 82 respondents from general category and 33 respondents from professional category reported it. In district Baramulla, 88 respondents from general category and 48 respondents from professional category reported it. Respondents from all the four districts reported Gynaecology as the most needed gender healthcare field.

(ii) Reproductive child health and Maternal Child Health as a gender healthcare fields were reported by 141/400 (35.20 per cent) respondents from the general category and 64/200 (32.00 per cent) respondents from the professional category. A total of 205/600(34.16 per cent) respondents reported these as important gender health fields. This response composes of the following district-wise responses. In district Srinagar, 36 respondents from general category and 30 respondents from professional category reported it. In district Budgam, 30 respondents from general category and six respondents from professional category reported it. In district Anantnag, 40 respondents from general category and 66 respondents from professional category reported it. In district Baramulla, 42 respondents from general category and 33 respondents from professional category reported it. Respondents from all four districts reported reproductive and child health and maternal child health as important healthcare field.

(iii) Reproductive endocrinology as a gender healthcare field was reported by 29/400 (07.25 per cent) respondents from the general category and 35/200 (17.50 per cent) respondents from the professional category. A total of 64/600(10.66 per cent) respondents reported it as important health field gender. This response composes of the following district wise responses. In district Budgam, 11 respondents from general category and eight respondents from professional category reported it. In district Anantnag, nine respondents from general category and nine respondents from professional category reported it. In district Baramulla, nine respondents from general category and 18. respondents from professional category reported it. Respondents from above mentioned districts reported Reproductive as important healthcare field.

(iv) Issues pertaining to adolescent health as a gender healthcare field were reported by 25/400 (06.25 per cent) respondents from the general category and 20/200 (10.00 per cent) respondents from the professional category. A total of 45/600(07.50 per cent) respondents reported them as important health fields. This response composes of the following district-wise responses. In district Srinagar, 23 respondents from general category and 20 respondents from professional category reported it. In district Anantnag, two respondents from general category respondents from above mentioned districts reported issues pertaining to adolescent health as important gender healthcare field.

(v) Pre/post-delivery and natal care was reported by 30/400(07.50 per cent) respondents from the general category and 17/200(08.50 per cent) respondents reported it from the professional category. A total of 47/600(07.83 per cent) respondents reported these as important gender health care field. This response composes of the following district-wise response. In district Srinagar, 18 respondents from general category and six respondents from professional category reported it. In district

Anantnag, nine respondents from general category and 20 respondents from professional category reported it. In district Baramulla, three respondents from general category and eight respondents from professional category reported it. Respondents from all four districts reported pre/post-delivery and natal care as important gender healthcare fields.

(vi) Mental health as a gender healthcare field was reported by 19/400 (04.70 per cent) respondents from the general category and 18/200 (09.00 per cent) respondents from the professional category. A total of 37/600 (06.16 per cent) respondents reported these as important gender health care field. This response composes of the following district-wise responses. In district Srinagar, 18 respondents from general category and 13 respondents from professional category reported it. In district Budgam, four respondents from professional category reported it. In district Baramulla, one respondent from general category and one respondent from professional category reported it. Respondents from above mentioned districts reported mental health as important gender healthcare field.

(vii) Social and Preventive Medicine (SPM) as a gender healthcare field was reported by 5/400 (01.25 per cent) respondents from the general category and 17/200 (08.50 per cent) respondents from the professional category. A total of 22/600 (03.66 per cent) respondents reported this as important gender health care field. This response composes of the following district-wise responses. In district Budgam, four respondents from general category and nine respondents from professional category reported it. In district Baramulla, three respondents from general category and 16 respondents from professional category reported it. Respondents from above mentioned districts reported SPM as important gender healthcare field.

(viii) Cardiology was reported by 5/400 (01.25 per cent) respondents from general respondents and 6/200 (03.00 per cent) respondents reported it from professionals. A total of 11/600 (01.38 per cent) respondents reported it as a gender healthcare disease. Though this disease is not gender specific but creates problems in the body which give rise to other gender specific problems. This response composes of the following district-wise response. In district Srinagar, four respondents from general category and five respondents from professional category reported it. In district Anantnag, one respondent from general category and one respondent from professional category reported it. Respondents from all four districts reported cardiology as an important gender healthcare field.

(ix) Child healthcare as a gender health care field was reported by 4/400 (01.00 per cent) respondents from the general category and 3/200 (01.50 per cent) respondents from the professional category. A total of 7/600 (01.16 per cent) respondents reported it as an important gender healthcare field. This response composes of the following district-wise responses. In district Srinagar, four respondents from general category and three respondents from professional category reported it. Respondents from district Srinagar reported reproductive and child healthcare as important gender healthcare field.

(x) Nutritional care as a gender healthcare field was reported by 9/400 (02.25 per cent) respondents from the general category and 11/200 (05.50 per cent) respondents from the professional category. A total of 20/600 (03.33 per cent) respondents reported this as important healthcare field. This response composes of the following district-wise responses. In district Srinagar, nine respondents from general category and 11 respondents from professional category reported it. Respondents from Srinagar district reported nutritional care as important gender healthcare field.

(xi) Oncology as a gender healthcare field was reported by 18/400 (04.50 per cent) respondents from the general category and 20/200 (10.00 per cent) respondents from the professional category. A total of 38/ 600(06.33 per cent) respondents reported it as important gender healthcare field. This response composes of the following district-wise responses. In district Budgam, 15 respondents from general category and four respondents from professional category reported it. In district Baramulla, three respondents from general category and 16 respondents from professional category reported it. Respondents from above mentioned districts reported oncology as important gender healthcare field.

(xii) Anemia as a gender healthcare field was reported by 1/200 (01.00 per cent) respondent from the professional category. one respondent from professional category reported it in district Budgam.

(xiii) Gastroenterology was reported by 2/200 (01.00 per cent) respondents from the professional category. A total of 2/600 (00.33 per cent) respondents reported it as important gender field. In the professional category of district Budgam two respondents reported it.

(xiv) Immunology as a gender health care field was reported by 2/400 (00.50 per cent) respondents from general category and 2/200 (01.00 per cent) respondents from professional category. A total of 4/600 (00.60 per cent) respondents reported it. In district Budgam two from general category and two from professional category reported it as an important gender healthcare field.

(xv) Nephrology as an important gender healthcare field was reported by 2/200 (01.00 per cent) respondents from the professional category. A total of 2/600 (00.33 per cent) respondents reported it. In district Budgam 02.0 respondents from the professional category reported it as an important gender healthcare field.

(xvi) Clinical biochemistry was reported by 2/200 (01.00 per cent) respondents from professional category. A total of 2/600 (00.33 per cent) respondents reported it. In the professional category of district Budgam two respondents reported it as an important gender healthcare field.

(xvii) Caesarian as an important healthcare field was reported by 2/400 (00.50 per cent) respondents from general category. A total of 2/600 (00.33 per cent) respondents reported it. In district Baramulla two respondents from general category reported it.

(xviii) Orthopaedics as an important healthcare field was reported by 1/400 (00.25 per cent) respondents from general category and 3/200 (01.50 per cent) respondents from professional category reported it. A total of 4/600 (00.66 per cent) respondents reported it. In district Anantnag one respondent from general category and three respondents from professional category reported it as an important healthcare field.

(xix) Paediatrics as an important gender healthcare field was reported by 5/400 (05.00 per cent) respondents from general category. A total of 5/600 (00.83 per cent) respondents reported it. In district Anantnag five respondents from general category reported it as an important healthcare field.

2. Common Gender Healthcare Needs

There are numerous needs of gender health care in Kashmir, in which some are more important while others are less important. The differentiation in the health needs of women can be explained in social, cultural and economic factors. It is essentially in this background that women responed differently to the treatment of diseases (common and dreaded) and other health problems in Kashmir. So, there are different patterns of responses to disease and other health problems existing in the Kashmiri society.

We made an investigation in this regard, and the broader response we got from respondents has been noted in Table 5.2.

Table 5.2: Gender Healthcare Needs

S. No.	*Needs*	*D1 Srinagar*		*D2 Budgam*		*D3 Anantnag*		*D4 Baramulla*		*Responses (No. and Per cent.)*		
		G	*P*	*G*	*P*	*G*	*P*	*G*	*P*	*GT*	*G*	*P*
1.	Separate hospitals for women	00.0	00.0	00.0	00.0	02.0	02.0	37.0	31.0	72.0	39.0	33.0
										12.00	09.75	16.50
2.	Specialised female staff	00.0	02.0	00.0	01.0	10.0	05.0	60.0	14.0	91.0	70.0	21.0
										15.16	17.50	10.50
3.	Health Education	26.0	38.0	09.0	01.0	13.0	03.0	57.0	34.0	162	105	57.0
										27.00	26.25	28.50
4.	Equipped with referral transport	00.0	00.0	00.0	02.0	05.0	05.0	26.0	12.0	50.0	31.0	19.0
										08.33	07.75	03.80
5.	Awareness programmes	03.0	16.0	26.0	30.0	44.0	26.0	06.0	15.0	158	79.0	79.0
										26.33	19.75	39.50
6.	Improved facilities and infrastructure	02.0	00.0	10.0	01.0	02.0	00.0	34.0	13.0	62.0	43.0	14.0
										10.33	12.00	07.00
7.	Regular health checkups	29.0	02.0	00.0	00.0	00.0	00.0	00.0	00.0	32.0	29.0	03.0
										05.33	07.25	01.50
8.	Immunisation	03.0	02.0	17.0	06.0	27.0	00.0	00.0	00.0	59.0	47.0	12.0
										09.83	11.75	03.50
9.	Stress free Healthy environment	42.0	18.0	01.0	00.0	00.0	00.0	00.0	00.0	52.0	43.0	09.0
										08.66	10.75	04.50
10.	Pre and post marital counselling	09.0	00.0	04.0	03.0	00.0	01.0	00.0	00.0	17.0	13.0	04.0
										02.83	03.25	02.00
11.	Family care	06.0	08.0	00.0	00.0	00.0	00.0	00.0	00.0	10.0	06.0	04.0
										01.66	01.50	02.00
12.	Nutrition	69.0	00.0	68.0	24.0	45.0	13.0	00.0	00.0	207	182	25.0
										34.50	45.50	12.50
13.	Maternity care	00.0	00.0	01.0	06.0	00.0	00.0	00.0	00.0	04.0	01.0	03.0
										00.66	00.25	01.50
14.	Adequate supply of medicines	00.0	00.0	00.0	00.0	17.0	13.0	00.0	00.0	30.0	17.0	13.0
										05.00	04.25	06.50
15.	Blood banks of PHCs	00.0	00.0	00.0	04.0	03.0	05.0	00.0	00.0	10.0	03.0	07.0
										01.66	00.75	03.50
16.	Women Empowerment	00.0	06.0	01.0	04.0	02.0	01.0	00.0	00.0	57.0	03.0	06.0
										01.50	00.75	03.00
17.	Pre and post-delivery care	00.0	00.0	18.0	22.0	03.0	02.0	00.0	00.0	09.0	21.0	11.0
										05.33	05.25	05.50
18.	Familial support to women	00.0	00.0	00.0	00.0	01.0	00.0	00.0	00.0	32.0	01.0	00.0
										00.16	00.25	00.00
19.	Early diagnosis of disease	00.0	00.0	00.0	02.0	00.0	00.0	00.0	00.0	01.0	00.0	01.0
										00.16	00.00	00.16

Table 5.2 reveals that:

(i) Nutrition as gender healthcare need was reported by 182/400 (45.50 per cent) respondents from the general category and 25/200 (12.50 per cent) respondents from the professional category. A total of 207/600 (34.50 per cent) respondents reported it as an important gender healthcare need. This response composes of the following district-wise responses. In district Srinagar, 69 respondents reported it from general category. In district Budgam, 68 respondents reported it from general category and 24 respondents from professional category. In district Anantnag, 45 respondents from general category and 13 respondents from professional category reported it. Respondents from above mentioned districts reported it as the most required health need.

(ii) Health education as required gender healthcare need was reported by 105/400 (26.25 per cent) respondents from the general category and 57/200 (28.25 per cent) respondents from the professional category. A total of 162/600 (27.00 per cent)) respondents reported it as an important gender health need. This response composes of the following district-wise responses. In district Srinagar, 26 respondents reported it from general category and 38 respondentst from professional category. In district Budgam, nine respondents reported it from general category and one respondent from professional category. In district Anantnag, 13 respondents from general category and three respondents from professional category reported it. In district Baramulla, 57 respondents from general category and 34 respondents from professional category reported it. Respondents from above mentioned districts reported it as the most required gender health care need.

(iii) Familial support as required gender healthcare need was reported by 1/400 (26.25 per cent) respondent from the general category. A total of 1/600 (27.00 per cent) respondent reported it as an important health care need. This response composes of the following district-wise responses. In district Anantnag, one respondent from general category. Respondents from Anantnag district reported it as the most required gender health need.

(iv) Awareness programmes as gender healthcare need was reported by 79/400 (19.75 per cent) respondents from the general category and 79/200 (39.50 per cent) respondents from the professional category. A total of 158/600 (26.33 per cent) respondents reported it as an important gender healthcare need. This response composes of the following district-wise responses. In district Srinagar, 26 respondents reported it from general category and 38 respondents from professional category. In district Budgam, nine respondents reported it from general category and one respondent from professional category. In district Anantnag, 13 respondents from general category and three respondents from professional category reported it. In district Baramulla, 57 respondents from general category and 34 respondents from professional category reported it. Respondents from above mentioned districts reported it as the most required gender health need.

(v) Specialised female staff for women as most required gender healthcare need was reported by 70/400 (17.75 per cent) respondents from the general category and 21/200 (10.50 per cent) respondents from the professional category. A total of 91/600 (15.16 per cent) respondents reported it as an important gender healthcare need. This response composes of the following district-wise responses. In district Srinagar, two respondents reported it from professional category. In district Budgam, one respondent reported it from professional category. In district Anantnag, 10 respondents from general category and five respondents from professional category reported it. In district Baramulla, 60 respondents from general category and 14 respondents from professional category reported it. Respondents from above mentioned districts reported specialised female staff for women as the most required gender health need.

(vi) Improved facilities and infrastructure as gender healthcare need was reported by 48/400 (12.00 per cent) respondents from the general category and 14/200 (07.00 per cent) respondents from the professional category. A total of 62/600 (10.33 per cent) respondents reported it as an important gender health care need. This response composes of the following district-wise responses. In district Srinagar, two respondents reported it from general category. In district Budgam, 10 respondents reported it from general category and one respondent from professional category. In district Anantnag, two respondents from general category. In district Baramulla, 34 respondents from general category and 13 respondents from professional category reported it. Respondents from above mentioned districts reported it as the most required gender health need.

(vii) Immunisation as required gender healthcare need was reported by 47/400 (11.75 per cent) respondents from the general category and 12/200 (03.50 per cent) respondents from the professional category. A total of 159/600 (09.83 per cent) respondents reported it as an important gender health need. This response composes of the following district-wise responses In district Srinagar, three respondents reported it from general category and two respondents from professional category. In district Budgam, 17 respondents reported it from general category and six respondents from professional category. In district Anantnag, 27 respondents from general category reported it. Respondents from above mentioned districts reported it as the required gender health need.

(viii) Healthy/stress-free environment as required gender healthcare need was reported by 43/400 (10.70 per cent) respondents from the general category and 9/200 (04.50 per cent) respondents from the professional category. A total of 52/600 (08.60 per cent) respondents reported it as an important gender health need. This response composes of the following district-wise responses. In district Srinagar, 42 respondents reported it from general category and 18 respondents from professional category. In district Budgam, one respondent reported it from general category. Respondents from above mentioned districts reported it as the most required gender healthcare need.

(ix) Separate hospitals for women as a gender healthcare need was reported by 39/400 (09.75 per cent) respondents from the general category and 33/200 (16.50 per cent) respondents from the professional category. A total of 72/600 (12.00 per cent) respondents reported it as an important gender healthcare need. This response composes of the following district-wise responses. In district Anantnag, two respondents from general category and two respondents from professional category reported it. In district Baramulla, 37 respondents from general category and 31 respondents from professional category reported it. Respondents from above mentioned districts reported separate hospitals for women as an important gender healthcare need.

(x) Equipped referral transport for women as most required gender healthcare need was reported by 31/400 (07.75 per cent) respondents from the general category and 19/200 (03.80 per cent) respondents from the professional category. A total of 50/600 (08.33 per cent) respondents reported it as an important gender health need. This response composes of the following district wise responses. In district Budgam, two respondents reported it from professional category. In district Anantnag, five respondents from general category and five respondents from professional category reported it. In district Baramulla, 26 respondents from general category and 12 respondents from professional category reported it. Respondents from above mentioned districts reported well equipped referral transport as the most required gender health need.

(xi) Regular health checkups as required gender healthcare need was reported by 29/400 (07.25 per cent) respondents from the general category and 3/200 (01.50 per cent) respondents from the professional category. A total of 32/600 (05.33 per cent) respondents reported it as an important gender healthcare need. This response composes of the following district-wise responses. In district Srinagar, 29 respondents reported it from general category and two respondents from professional category. Respondents from above mentioned district reported it as the required gender health need.

(xii) Pre and post-delivery care as required gender healthcare need was reported by 21/400 (05.25 per cent) respondents from the general category and 11/200 (05.50 per cent) respondents from the professional category. A total of 32/600 (05.33 per cent) respondents reported it as an important gender health-care need. This response composes of the following district-wise responses. In district Budgam, 18 respondents reported it from general category and 22 respondent from professional category. In district Anantnag, three respondents from general category and two respondents from professional category reported it.In district Baramulla, one respondent from general category Respondents from above mentioned districts reported it as the most required and basic gender health need.

(xiii) Adequate supply of medicines as required gender healthcare need was reported by 17/400 (04.25 per cent) respondents from the general category and 13/200 (06.50 per cent) respondents from the professional category. A total of 30/600 (05.00 per cent) respondents reported it as an important gender health need. This response composes of the following district-wise responses. In district Anantnag, 17 respondents from general category and 13 respondents from professional category reported it. Respondents from above mentioned district reported it as the prominent gender healthcare need.

(xiv) Pre/post-marital counselling as required gender healthcare need was reported by 13/400 (03.25 per cent) respondents from the general category and 4/200 (02.00 per cent) respondents from the professional category. A total of 17/600 (02.83 per cent) respondents reported it as an important gender health-care need. This response composes of the following district-wise responses. In district Srinagar, nine respondents reported it from general category. In district Budgam, four respondents reported it from general category and three respondents from professional category. In district Anantnag, one respondent from professional category reported it. Respondents from above mentioned districts reported it as the most required gender healthcare need.

(xv) Family care as required gender healthcare need was reported by 6/400 (01.50 per cent) respondents from the general category and 4/200 (02.00 per cent) respondents from the professional category. A total of 10/600 (01.66 per cent) respondents reported it as an important gender healthcare need. This response composes of the following district-wise responses. In district Srinagar, six respondents reported it from general category and eight respondents from professional category. Respondents from above mentioned district reported it as the most required gender healthcare need.

(xvi) Blood banks in PHCs as required gender healthcare need was reported by 3/400 (00.75 per cent) respondents from the general category and 7/200 (03.50 per cent) respondents from the professional category. A total of 10/600 (01.66 per cent) respondents reported it as an important gender healthcare need. This response composes of the following district-wise responses. In district Budgam, four respondents reported it from professional category. In district Anantnag, three respondents from general category and five respondents from professional category reported it. Respondents from above mentioned districts reported it as important gender healthcare need.

(xvii) Women empowerment as required gender healthcare need was reported by 3/400 (00.75 per cent) respondents from the general category and 6/200 (03.50 per cent) respondents from the professional category. A total of 9/600 (01.66 per cent) respondents reported it as an important gender health-care need. This response composes of the following district- wise responses. In district Srinagar, six respondents reported it from professional category. In district Budgam, one respondent reported it from general category and four respondents from professional category. In district Anantnag, two respondents from general category and one respondents from professional category reported it. Respondents from above mentioned districts reported it as prominent gender healthcare need.

(xviii) Maternity care as required gender healthcare need was reported by 01/400 (00.25 per cent) respondent from the general category and 3/200 (01.50 per cent) respondents from the professional category. A total of 4/600 (00.66 per cent) respondents reported it as an important gender healthcare need. This response composes of the following district-wise responses. In district Budgam, one respondent reported it from general category and six respondents from professional category.

Respondents from above mentioned district reported it as the gender healthcare need.

(xix) Early diagnosis of disease as required gender healthcare need was reported by 1/200 (00.50 per cent) respondent from the professional category. A total of 1/600 (27.00 per cent) respondent reported it as an important gender health care need. This response composes of the following district-wise responses. two respondents reported it from professional category. Respondents from above mentioned district reported it as the most required gender healthcare need.

(xx) Preventive education as required gender healthcare need was reported by 2/400 (00.50 per cent) respondents from the general category and 6/200 (03.00 per cent) respondents from the professional category. A total of 8/600 (01.33 per cent) respondents reported it as an important gender healthcare need. This response composes of the following district-wise responses. In district Budgam, two respondents reported it from general category and 12 respondents from professional category. Respondents from district Budgam reported it as the most required gender healthcare need.

(xxi) Night services as required gender healthcare need was reported by 1/400 (00.25 per cent) respondent from the general category and 1/200 (00.50 per cent) respondent from the professional category. A total of 2/600 (00.33 per cent) respondents reported it as an important gender health care need. This response composes of the following district-wise responses. In district Budgam, one respondent reported it from general category and two respondents from professional category. Respondents from district Budgam reported it as the most required gender healthcare need.

(xxii) Mobile medical units as required gender healthcare need was reported by 1/400 (00.25 per cent) respondent from the general category A total of 1/600 (00.16 per cent) respondent reported it as an important healthcare need. This response composes of the following district-wise responses. In district Budgam, two respondents reported it from professional category. Respondents from above mentioned district reported it as the most required gender healthcare need.

6

Case Studies of Primary Health Centres

1. Introduction

The concept of Primary Health Centre (PHC) is not new to India. The Bhore Committee in 1946 gave the concept of a PHC as a basic health unit to provide as close to the people as possible, an integrated curative and preventive health care to the rural population with emphasis on preventive and promotive aspects of health care.

The health planners in India have visualised the PHCs and its Sub-Centres (SCs) as the proper infrastructure to provide health services to the rural population. The Central Council of Health at its first meeting held in January 1953 had recommended the establishment of PHCs in community development blocks to provide comprehensive healthcare to the rural population. These centres were functioning as peripheral health service institutions with little or no community involvement. Increasingly, these centres came under criticism, as they were not able to provide adequate health coverage, partly because these were poorly staffed and inadequately equipped and lacked basic amenities.

PHCs are the cornerstone of rural health services–a first port of call to a qualified doctor of the public sector in rural areas for the sick and those who directly report or referred from sub-centres for curative, preventive and promotive health care. As per IPHC Guidelines 2006, it acts as a referral unit for six sub-centres and refer out cases to Community Health Centres (CHCs-30 bedded hospital) and higher order public hospitals at sub-district and district hospitals. It has four to six indoor beds for patients (IPHC Guidelines, March 2006).

In order to provide optimal level of quality healthcare, a set of standards are being recommended for Primary Health Centre to be called Indian Public Health Standards (IPHS) for PHCs. These standards check the parameters covering all the essential elements of preventive, promotive, curative and rehabilitative primary health care which are necessary for the proper working of the PHCs.

The PHC evaluated by the team under ICMR project are:

1. District Srinagar — PHC Hazratbal.
2. District Budgam— PHC Hardepanzu.
3. District Baramulla— PHC Delina.
4. District Anantnag— PHC Achabal.

2. Primary Health Centre Hazratbal District Srinagar

(i) Population

Hazratbal lies in Srinagar city at a distance of 12 kms from main city centre. Hazratbal is situated on the western bank of world famous Dal Lake. Famous Hazratbal Dargah shrine is situated there. This area is famous for pilgrimage as well as scenic tourism.

Health Centre Hazratbal has been a block headquarter falling within the administration of Medical College Srinagar. However, it is also the office of the Block Medical Officer under whose jurisdiction there are more or less 14 SC/AD health care centres. The main villages/*mohallas* having population of 59,189, with SC/AD are as follows:

S. No.	*Health-institution*	*Population*
1.	AD Tailbal	3,778
2.	SC Hazratbal	8,857
3.	SC Khushipora	840
4.	SC Durbagh	2,272
5.	AD Nishat	10,371
6.	SC Takinwari	2,650
7.	SC Aadibal	6,664
8.	SC Nandpora	3,138
9.	SC Ishbar	5,030
10.	SC Dara	2,269
11.	SC Fakirgujri	1,640
12.	SC Theed	5,729
13.	SC Saidepora	1,805
14.	SC Shanpora	4,146
	Total	**59,189**

The following table gives the description of staff in the PHC:

(ii) Staff Strength at PHC

S. No.	*Position*	*Existing*
1.	BMO	01
2.	LMO	02
3.	Doctor (family welfare)	01
4.	Doctor–support staff from NRHM (Gynaecologist)	04
5.	Dental surgeon	01
6.	CHO	01
7.	Food inspector	01
8.	Senior pharmacist	01
9.	Supervisory pharmacist	01
10.	Sanitary inspector	01
11.	Senior assistant	02
12.	Junior assistant	01
13.	Health educator	01
14.	X-ray assistant	02
15.	Driver	02
16.	ANM	05
17.	Junior gardener	01
18.	Junior pharmacist	01
19.	Basic Health Workers	08
20.	FMPHW	01
21.	PMA	01
22.	Nursing Orderly	04
23.	Dental boy	01
24.	*Chowkidar*	01
25.	*Aaya*	01
26.	*Jamadar*	01
27.	Boatman	01
28.	*Mashki Shia*	06
29.	*Safayee Wala*	25

The strength of the staff is more than satisfactory according to the existing guidelines of Indian Public Health Standards. During the discussion with the concerned officials, it was revealed that the sub-centres functioning under the supervision of PHC Hazratbal are more than the existing norms which clearly shows that in the near future PHC will be upgraded as Community Health Centre.

(iii) Medical care

The different facilities available in the PHC arc discussed as follows:

(i) ***OPD Services:*** According to the guidelines, minimum OPD attendance should be 40 patients per doctor per day, but due to the shortage of doctors, a doctor at PHC Hazratbal, has to cater about 60 patients on an average day.

(ii) The 24 hours emergency services meant for appropriate management of injuries and accident, first aid, stabilisation of the condition of the patient before referral, dog bite/snake bite/scorpion bite cases, and other emergency conditions are present at PHC.
(iii) Referral services (two ambulances, one boat for Dal dwellers) are available in the concerned PHC.
(iv) In-patient services (six beds) are available.
(iv) Maternal and child health care, family planning.

The maternal and child healthcare services which are provided at PHC Hazratbal are grouped in thirteen categories under the following headings:

(i) Ante-natal care

(a) Registration of all pregnancies is done at PHC in the first trimester (before 12th week of pregnancy). However, even if a woman comes late in her pregnancy for registration she is registered and care is given to her according to gestational age.
(b) Minimum three antenatal checkups and provision of complete package of services are provided according to norms. First visit as soon as pregnancy is suspected/between 4th and 6th month (before 26 weeks), second visit at 8th month (around 32 weeks) and third visit at 9th month (around 36 weeks). Associated services like providing iron and folic acid tablets, injection Tetanus Toxoid etc (as per the guidelines for ante-natal care and skilled attendance at birth by ANMs and LHVs) are provided.
(c) Minimum laboratory investigations like haemoglobin, urine albumin, sugar, etc., are available at minimum cost rates.
(d) Nutrition and health counselling by proper health educators.
(e) High-risk pregnancies are referred to the nearest community health centres.

(ii) Intra-natal care

(a) Promotion of institutional deliveries with the help of ASHAs, JSY, JSSK, etc.
(b) Conducting of normal deliveries.
(c) Assisted vaginal deliveries including forceps/vacuum delivery whenever required.
(d) Manual removal of placenta.
(e) Appropriate and prompt referral for cases needing specialist care.
(f) Management of pregnancy induced hypertension including referral.

(g) Pre-referral management (Obstetric first-aid) in Obstetric emergencies that need expert assistance (Training of staff for emergency management is ensured).

(iii) Post-natal Care

(a) A minimum of two postpartum home visits, first within 48 hours of delivery, second within seven days through Sub-centre staff.
(b) Initiation of early breast-feeding within half-hour of birth and the counseling for the same with help of ASHAs and Health Educators.
(c) Education on nutrition, hygiene, contraception, essential new born care, etc., with the help of concerned staff and at times through the Health *Melas.*
(d) Others: Provision of facilities under Janani Suraksha Yojana (JSY) and Janani Shishu Suraksha Karyakaram (JSSK).

(iv) New Born Care

(a) Facilities and care for neonatal resuscitation.
(b) Management of neo-natal hypothermia/jaundice.

(v) Care of the Child

(a) Emergency care of sick children including Integrated Management of Neonatal and Childhood Illness (IMNCI).
(b) Care of routine childhood illness.
(c) Essential Newborn Care.
(d) Promotion of exclusive breast-feeding for 6 months.
(e) Full Immunization of all infants and children against vaccine preventable diseases as per guidelines of NRHM.

(vi) Family Planning

(a) Education, motivation and counselling to adopt appropriate family planning methods.
(b) Provision of contraceptives such as condoms, oral pills, emergency contraceptives, IUD insertions.
(c) Permanent methods like Tubal ligation and vasectomy/NSV.
(d) Follow up services to the eligible couples adopting permanent methods (Tubectomy/Vasectomy).
(e) Counselling and appropriate referral for safe abortion services for those in need.
(f) Counselling and appropriate referral for couples having infertility.

(vii) Nutrition Services (Co-ordinated with ICDS)

(a) Diagnosis of and nutrition advice to malnourished children, pregnant women and others.

(b) Diagnosis and management of anemia, and vitamin. A deficiency.

(c) Co-rdination with ICDS-in conducting VHNDs and health awareness programmes.

(d) Training in healthcare services and first aid to the concerned ICDS workers.

(viii) School Health

(a) Regular check ups, appropriate treatment including deworming, referral and follow-ups are the concerns of the PHC. This is done with the help of health educators and other counsellors through the visits to the concerned schools.

(ix) Adolescent Health Care

(a) Lifestyle education, counselling, appropriate treatment and other programmes meant for the adolescent care is provided by health counsellors and Educators.

(x) Promotion of Safe Drinking Water and Basic Sanitation

(a) With the help of Rogi Kalyan Samitis, Disinfection of water sources, Testing of water quality and promotion of sanitation including use of toilets and appropriate garbage disposal.

(xi) Prevention and Control of Locally Endemic Diseases

(a) Like Malaria, Kalaazar, TB, Hepatitis, etc., with the help of Health *Melas* and awareness programmes.

(xii) Collection and Reporting of Vital Events

(a) Like various diseases and other health issues with the help of ASHAs, health educators and other field staff.

(xiii) Education about Health/Behaviour Change Communication (BCC)

a) With the help of counselling to the masses by ASHAs and other staff.

(xiv) Management of Reproductive Tract Infections/Sexually Transmitted Infections

(a) With the help of health education for prevention of RTI/STIs by concerned staff and other Treatments.

(xv) Shortcomings

PHC Hazratbal is not spared from issues such as the inability to perform up to the expectation due to:

(i) Non-availability of specialised doctors;
(ii) Even if posted, doctors do not stay at the PHC;
(iii) Inadequate physical infrastructure and facilities like Blood Banks;
(iv) Insufficient quantities of drugs;
(v) Lack of accountability to the public and lack of community participation;
(vi) Lack of set standards for monitoring quality care, etc.

(xvi) Contribution of Health Centres Towards Gender Health

Primary Health Centre of Hazratbal has a step forward in providing awareness to the women regarding their health needs. They are provided with awareness regarding nutrition and health counseling by proper health educators. This PHC caters to a large population particularly the down trodden lot of Dal community, Fakir Gujri and Dhara. The centre has achieved good results as far immunisation of pregnant ladies and new born babies are concerned. The Centre is active in providing Antenatal, pre-natal, postnatal care to women. New born care, Care of the child, family planning, nutrition services, school health, Adolescent healthcare services are also provided. Promotion of safe drinking water and basic sanitation, prevention and control of locally endemic diseases, collection and reporting of vital events is done actively by the staff of this PHC. Education about health/behaviour change communication (BCC), Management of reproductive tract infections and sexually transmitted infections is given much importance. Besides, it plays a good role in referring the complicated delivery cases to specialised hospitals by providing them free transport facilities. The center plays an active role in providing the benefits of NRHM programme to women and children like free medicines, free screening facilities, monetary allowances etc. The center has performed well in promoting awareness related to various family planning methods and their benefits. The center plays a good educative role for adolescent girls related to their health needs and is also spreading information regarding causes and consequences of various sexually transmitted diseases.

3. Primary Health Centre Hardipanzoo District Budgam

I. Area and Facilities

Hardipanzoo is a hilly area inhabited by some tribes (Gujars) Khans and backward class communities which comes under district Budgam. It is about 30 kms away from the main district headquarter. The PHC Hardipanzoo was established in the year 1985. It comprised two-rooms building without electricity and water supply and with staff of only one Lab Assistant and one Pharmacist. The health centre was totally in shambles till 2007, when it was covered under centrally sponsored programme, i.e., National Rural Health Mission (NRHM), implemented in Jammu and Kashmir in the year 2005. With the advent of NRHM, the condition of PHC somewhat improved as under this programme the health centre received the fund every year for the improvement of infrastructure and other basic facilities like water supply, electricity, etc. NRHM not only provided money for infrastructural development but also recruited additional staff in the PHC. With increase in manpower and other facilities, health centre started working on 24x7 basis from 18 October 2007. The PHC Harudpanzoo caters to a population of 70,000 people and is heading one PHC, two sub centers and a DMC (Designated Medical Centre) for diagnosis of TB.

The following health institutions are operating under the supervision of PHC Harudpanzoo.

S. No.	*Health-institution*
1.	PHC Zaanigam
2.	SC Chill
3.	SC Rawalpora
4.	1 DMC

The various facilities available at the health centre are a labour room, laboratory for various hematological tests, dental section and a ward of six beds. The health centre has one ambulance also. All these facilities have been made available under NRHM programme. The health centre is having a Fair Price Shop, which as per doctors is by name only. The drugs are sold on market prices but the quality of drugs is somewhat better than drugs available in open market. Health centre is having the facility of ECG but the technician to operate this machine is not available thus the facility is useless. Health centre lacks X- ray and USG facilities which is of immense importance for providing better services, and USG is very important for diagnosing pregnancy related issues.

II. Manpower and Functioning

The total manpower available in the health centre is 14 employees–four Doctors, three Nurses, two Lab Assistants, one Allopathic Pharmacist, one Ayurvedic Pharmacist, one Block Health Worker, one Driver, and one Sweeper. In addition to it, 9 ASHA's are associated with the health centre who work in different areas of Harudipanzoo. The elaborat description of staff strength in the PHC is as follows:

Specialisation	*Number*	*Recruited By*
Doctors		
M.B.B.S	02	NRHM
B.U.M.S	01	NRHM
B.D.S	01	J K Health Deptt. (On contractual basis)
PARAMEDICS		
Nurses	03	NRHM
Lab assistant	02	1 by NRHM 1 by JK Health Deptt.
Block Health Worker	01	JK Health Deptt.
Allopathic Pharmacist	01	NRHM
Ayurvedic Pharmacist	01	NRHM
SUPPORT STAFF		
ASHA	09	NRHM
Driver	01	NRHM
Sweeper	01	NRHM

As the population to which this health centre is serving is very huge but manpower available in the centre is not sufficient, due to which people suffer to a greater extent. The biggest problem in the health centre is the unavailability of lady doctor which has become a major hurdle for both healthcare providers as well as patients because of prevalence of cultural and religion sensitivity. In addition to it, many posts are lying vacant in the health centre, which comprises two post of doctors, two nurses and multipurpose health workers (one male and one female). In this centre, there is no Health Educator or Community Health Officer. The night staff available in the hospital is just one Doctor, one Paramedic and a Sweeper.

The health centre faces a huge rush of patients every day. As per records, the PHC examines almost 1400-1,600 patients every month in the out-patient department, 200-300 patients are admitted every month, two to three cases are referred everyday to other sub-district, district or super specialty hospitals for specialised treatment. The health centre performs three to five normal deliveries every week. The deliveries which need to be conducted by caesarian method are referred to other hospitals because health centre lacks various facilities which are important for such deliveries like USG, blood bank, other emergency care.

As per doctors, due to NRHM programme IMR & MMR has decreased to a greater extent. The awareness about benefits of institutional deliveries has also increased due to the effective role played by ASHA workers. All the pregnant ladies who get registered in the health centre come for ante and post-natal check- ups and also avail the benefits of JSY scheme.

From last three years, two epidemics have affected the area Cholera in the year 2010 and Enteric Fever in the year 2011. To deal with the situation, all the medicines were bought from NRHM funds and were distributed among people free of cost. The most prevalent diseases in the area are infectious disease like upper and lower respiratory tract infections, Enteric fever, Tuberculosis,etc. The diseases in the area are mainly due to impoverished hygienic conditions in the area and ignorance among people. Most of the gender related diseases remain unknown in the area because of non-availability of lady doctor as women folk don't feel comfortable in discussing their gender related issues with male doctors and are forced to visit other hospitals, only when the condition becomes more severe. As reported many a time, lady doctors who were posted in the PHC didn't felt comfortable there owing to long and troublesome travelling from the city/town and got themselves immediately transferred using corrupt means.

III. Contribution of PHC Hardipanzoo Towards Gender Health

The PHC Hardipanzoo has been serving the people of this area since1985 and till date it is more so concerned about providing better facilities to women and children. Till 2005, the centres was not able to provide good facilities, due to lack of infrastructure and manpower. But with the advent of NRHM programme the centres were provided with necessary facilities to provide better services. The health centre is playing very good role as far gender health is concerned, although much needs to be done as the biggest problem in this centre is the lack of female doctors. The centre cater mainly to the needs of tribal women who now prefer institutional deliveries, which is a positive change as far as gender health is concerned. As far as the immunisation of pregnant ladies and new born is concerned, the centre is playing good role in spreading awareness related to its benefits and has achieved good results. Family planning and child spacing methods are not much used in the area, although health educators and ASHAs are trying their best to make people understand about its benefits and remove the various misconceptions related to it. The centre is actively carrying out various functions of NRHM programme and thereby providing free services to pregnant ladies and new born children. The centre is active in conducting health *melas* and medical camps in far flung areas to provide services to people at their door steps and spread awareness among people related health needs. The health centres have achieved good results in controlling MMR and IMR rates. Doctors in the health centres give extensive counselling to women related hygienic needs and about sexually transmitted diseases, their prevention and cure. In health centres three to five normal deliveries are carried out every week and monetary allowance is provided to them under NRHM programme, to motivate women for institutional deliveries. Door to door immunisation campaigns are also carried out by this health centre. The health centre lack many facilities both in terms of infrastructure and manpower, but still the role played by it especially in case of maternal and child health is appreciable and cannot be ignored.

4. Primary Health Centre Achabal District Anantnag

1. Area and Population

Achabal is one of the well known tourist destinations of Kashmir valley which is known for its stunning beauty and fresh water. It comes under district Anantnag and is almost 10 kms away from the district head quarter. The primary health centre Achabal is just a few miles away from the beautiful Achabal garden. Apparently, the infrastructural facility available in this health centre is having two buildings. In one building there is an OPD department and a ward for inpa-tients and in other building there is separate chamber of gynaecology and obstetrics with an attached labour room and also an immunisation section.

The HC caters to the needs of 42,302 persons. The area is divided into three zones Achabal, Brakpora and Anchidora. The description of the various healthcare centres falling in zone Achabal, for which it serves as first referral centre are mentioned in table below with villages and population:

S. No.	*Name of the Institution*	*Name of Villages*	*Population of Village*	*Total Population*
1.	PHC Achabal	Achabal	3,019	
		Check Achaba	686	
		Jogigund	676	4,381
2.	Sub-centre Khundroo	Khundroo	1,886	
		Darpora	385	
		Check Khundroo	335	
		Pingwan	549	3,155
3.	Sub-centre Sunsum	Sunsum	1,252	
		Traphoo	1,441	
		Thajwan	1,743	
		Kulgud	310	4,746
4.	Sub-centre Kanganhall	Kangan hall	1,940	
		Magraypora	1,240	
		Kadpora	667	
		Rumini	1,260	
		Kralpora	387	5,494
5.	Sub-centre Issuses	Issus	1,376	
		Odsoo	576	
		Patnoo	58	2,010
6.	Sub-centre Dass	C.iDass	1,350	

S. No.	Centre	Village	Population	Total
		Qawngan	1,246	
		Buntroo	1,412	
		Hertruroo	1.180	5,188
7.	Sub-centre C.S. Pora	C.s pora	1,920	
		Darpora	1,050	
		S.T Mavda	665	3.635
8.	Sub-centre Hard Pora	Hardpora	2,050	
		Budroo	610	2.660
9.	Allopathic Dispensary Telwan	Telwani	3,421	
		Tumbripora	385	3 806
10.	Allopathic Dispensary Gopalpora	Gopalpora	4,468	4.468
11.	Medical Aid Centre Damhall	Damhall	2110	
		Palpora	649	2,759

II. Various Services

The elaborate description of various services provided by this health centre is as follows:

a. Outpatient Department

The OPD of health centre cater to a huge rush of patients almost 60 to 70 patients per day which comprise (mainly) women and children. The diseases prevalent in the area are mostly seasonal like Hay fever, Flu, water borne diseases etc. The total doctors present in the OPD are six of which two are female doctors, one ayurvedic doctor, two male doctors and a dental surgeon. Both the female doctors and Ayurvedic doctor have been recruited under NRHM programme. In addition to the routine patients, the OPD also deals with the first aid of emergency patients and do the appropriate referrals.

b. Inpatient Department

The health centre provides facilities for inpatients with a bed facility of 24 of which 12 are for males and 12 for females. Generally, pregnant ladies are admitted in the health centre who come to this centre for delivery purpose. The staff on night duty available at the health centre are a doctor, senior nurse, pharmacist, nursing orderly, sweeper, and a driver.

c. Immunisation Section

The health centre has a well maintained immunisation section with good facilities like a deep freezer for storage of various kinds of vaccines. The health centre has well maintained immunisation records of children and females who are registered there.

d. Gynaecology

The biggest problem that the health centre faces is the lack of a qualified Gynaecologist and thus the services are carried out by simple MBBS doctors due to which various gynaecological and obstetrics related diseases remain untreated. In the health centre only normal deliveries are carried out because the hospital lacks the facilities for caesarian operations. The health centre lacks the facility of blood bank due to which most of the cases are referred to Maternity and child health hospital Anantnag. All the deliveries carried out in the health centre get all the benefits as per JSY scheme.

e. Referrel Services

As the health centre is not fully equipped, so a number of cases are referred to other sub-district, district and other specialised hospitals. To ferry the patients to other hospitals, health centre has four ambulances. In case of pregnant ladies who are referred to other hospitals, the cost of transportation is provided under JSY scheme and in case of other patients paid ambulance service is only for emergency patients.

f. Dental Section

The health centre has dental section with some basic facilities like consultation, tooth extraction, cavity fillings, etc. To provide these services the health centre has one dental surgeon and a dental assistant.

g. Hemaotology

The health centre has a well maintained laboratory for testing facility, almost all the routine tests are carried out in the centre. Free of cost testing facility is available to pregnant ladies and for other patients there is paid facility as per government rules.

h. Family Planning Services

As the health centre lacks the specialised services of permanent family planning methods like Tubal ligation and vasectomy, they carry out this function usually by education, motivation, counselling and by providing free of cost contraceptives such as condoms and oral pills.

i. X-Ray Section

The X-ray section of the health centre is not working properly because of the irregular power supply due to which patients suffer a lot. For this service the health centre is having one X-ray technician. However, to cater to the huge rush of patients manpower is less. The health centre is also having USG facility for the patients.

j. Drug Store

Almost all the PHCs complain about the scarce supply of drugs from the JK health department and same is the case with this centre. Due to which the drugs provided by the department does not meet the requirement of the centre. Thus, usually the people have to buy the medicines from the market. There is no fair price medical shop at the health centre. The health centre has two pharmacists, one of Ayurvedic and other allopathic medicine.

k. Accounts Section

The account section of the health centre mainly comprises the NRHM staff who deals with the salaries of the staff, honorarium to the field staff and monetary benefits to the pregnant ladies.

In addition to these facilities, the health centre has a good number of field staff who work in the field and educate masses about the health needs. The health centre has two health educators, one extension educator, two local health workers and 105 recognised ASHAs who motivate women to avail the health facilities provided by the government. They also provide awareness and health education to the people and benefits of institutional deliveries and immunisation programmes. As per doctors there, "with the advent of NRHM programme and the benefits provided under JSY scheme a large number of women are being registered in the health centre at the time of conception of pregnancy with the help of ASHAs and after that they remain in complete supervision of doctors throughout the pregnancy period and even after delivering the baby, both the baby and the mother receive full medical care till the immunisation schedule of the child comes to an end. With the advent of NRHM a lot of improvement has been made in decreasing the maternal and infant mortality rates".

In comparison to the other PHCs of the rural areas, the staff here is comparatively better. Most of the staff in the PHC is recruited under NRHM programme both the female doctors in the health centre are working under NRHM. The health centre is headed by a Block Medical Officer. The elaborate description of the staff in the PHCs is as under:

SUPERVISORY STAFF	
Block Medical Officer	
SPECIALISATION	*NUMBER*
DOCTORS	
M.B.B.S	02 Male & 02 Female
B.U.M.S	01 Male
B.D.S	01 Male
PARAMEDIC STAFF	
Staff Nurses	02 by NRHM, 01 by Health Dept.
Nursing Orderly	06
Laboratory Assistant	01
Dental Assistant	01
X-ray Assistant	01
Allopathic Pharmacist	01
Ayurvedic Pharmacist	01
ANM	19 by NRHM, 21 by Health Dept.
Multi-purpose Health Worker	04 by NRHM,03 by Health Dept.
FIELD STAFF	
Extension Health Educator	01
Community Health Officer	02
Health Educators	02
Block Health Worker	01
Local Health Workers	02
ASHA	105
SUPPORT STAFF	
Accounts Manager NRHM	01
Senior Assistant	02
Junior Assistant	02
Drivers	04
Sweepers	06

1. Contribution of PHC Achabal Towards Gender Health

The PHC Achabal is serving a large chunk of population and is providing better facilities for maternal and child health. The center is playing very good role in providing better facilities to pregnant ladies and new born children. The center is providing awareness regarding health, nutrition, prevention of various diseases. Referral system with proper transport facilities is provided to the patients to specialised hospitals who have complicated pregnancies and can't be treated in the primary health centre. Besides imparting antenatal, pre-natal and post- natal care

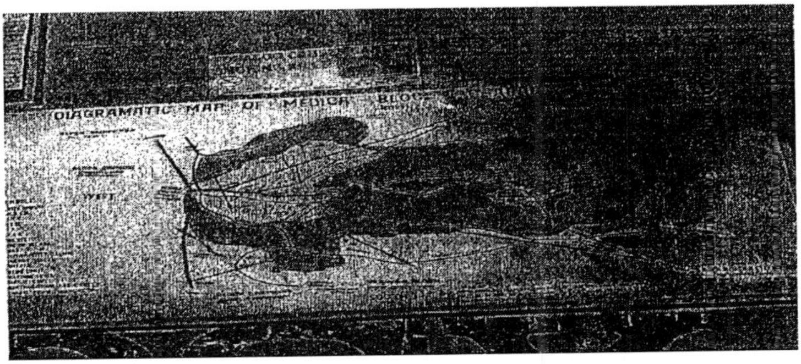

awareness regarding healthcare of the new mother and child is given. The staff here engaged is quite co-operative and helpful. With the advent of NRHM in the state, even the poor families prefer institutional deliveries due the cash benefit they receive in the Centre under the programme. Health *melas* are done by the centre to make aware the common masses regarding various health issues.Introduction of ASHA in NRHM ensures tracking system of the pregnant lady, i.e., Mother Child Tracking System (MCTS) so that all the necessary immunisation is done on time to prevent any complications in the future.

5. Primary Health Centre Delina District Baramulla

I. Area and Population

Delina is a village situated at a distance of five kms from Baramulla district headquarter. It lies on Srinagar Baramulla highway. The PHC Delina caters to the needs of 12,273 population of the villages all around it. The sub-centers falling within its jurisdiction are as follows:

S. No.	*Health-institution*
1.	SC Kanispora
2.	SC Johama
3.	SC Khawajabag

PHC Delina is a two storey building. It is a newly constructed PHC. It is functional since December 2012 however its foundation stone was laid way back in August 2006 and due to some unknown reasons the completion took so much of time. It is headed by a Medical Officer.

The building has been divided into several sections so that the patients can easily identify the appropriate place of treatment and other purposes. These sections are identified through different names as follows:

- Male OPD
- Female OPD/GYNEA
- X-Ray Section
- ECG/USG
- Dental OPD
- OPD AYUSH
- Dental section
- Sanitation room
- Dispensary
- Registration section
- Immunisation section
- Labour room
- Operation theatre
- Male ward
- Female ward
- Office
- Store
- Laboratory
- Male bathroom
- Female bathroom.

II. Staff Strength at PHC Delina

S. No.	*Position*	*Sanctioned*	*Occupied*	*Vacant*
1.	Assistant Surgeon	01	01	–
2.	Dental Surgeon	01	01	–
3.	ISM Doctor	01	01	–
3.	Pharmacist	01	01+01 =02	–
4.	Junior Grade Nurse	01	01	–
5.	FMPHW	01	01	–
6.	Lab tech/Asstt.	01	01	–
7.	X-Ray Tech.	01	01	–
8.	Dental Tech./Asstt.	01	–	01
9.	Nursing Orderly	01	01	–
10.	Sweeper	01	01	–
11.	Driver	02	2	–
12.	Chowkidar	01	01	–
13.	Junior Assistant	–	–	–

*Under NRHM Scheme

Besides the above staff, three ASHAs and 13 ICDS AWs are affiliated with the PHC who from time to time get training and other information from the

PHC, Delina, for improving the health conditions of the people, particularly gender health.

III. The Following Facilities are Available at the PHC Delina

(a) Medical care

1. ***OPD services:*** Regular OPD services are provided at the PHC. The doctors provide the required treatment and there was no complaint against the attitude of doctors from the patients
2. ***The eight hours emergency services:*** meant for appropriate management of injuries and accident, first aid, stabilisation of the condition of the patient before referral, Dog bite/snake bite/scorpion bite cases, and other emergency conditions are treated in the PHC
3. ***Referral services are available in the concerned PHC:*** There is problem with referral transport service. No ambulances are available at the PHC but the drivers are working there. Therefore, patients have to bear the cost of transportation for referral cases.
4. *In-patient services:* There are 16 beds available for in patients

(b) Ante-natal care

(i) Registration of all pregnancies is done at PHC in the first trimester (before 12th week of pregnancy). However, even if a woman comes late in her pregnancy for registration she is registered and care is given to her according to gestational age.

(ii) Minimum three antenatal checkups and provision of complete package of services are provided according to norms. First visit as soon as pregnancy is suspected/between four and six months (before 26 weeks), second visit at eight months (around 32 weeks) and third visit at ninth month (around 36 weeks). Associated services like providing iron and folic acid tablets, injection Tetanus Toxoid, etc., (as per the guidelines for ante-natal care and skilled attendance at birth by ANMs and LHVs) are provided.

(iii) Minimum laboratory investigations like haemoglobin, urine albumin, sugar, etc., are available at minimum cost rates.

(iv) Nutrition and health counselling is done by proper health educators.

(v) Pregnancies are referred to the block headquarters and the nearest health centres as the Operation Theater is still not functional in this PHC.

(c) Post-natal Care

(a) A minimum of two postpartum home visits, first within 48 hours of delivery, second within seven days through sub-centre staff.
(b) Initiation of early breast-feeding within half-hour of birth and the counselling for the same with help of ASHAs.
(c) Education on nutrition, hygiene, contraception, essential new born care, etc., with the help of concerned staff and at times through the Health *Melas.*
(d) Others: Provision of facilities under Janani Suraksha Yojana (JSY) and Janani Shishu Suraksha Karyakaram (JSSK).

(d) New Born Care

(a) Facilities and care for neonatal resuscitation.
(b) Management of neonatal hypothermia/jaundice.

(e) Care of the Child

(a) Emergency care of sick children including Integrated Management of Neo-natal and Childhood Illness (IMNCI).
(b) Care of routine childhood illness.
(c) Essential Newborn Care.
(d) Promotion of exclusive breast-feeding for six months.
(e) Full Immunisation of all infants and children against vaccine preventable diseases as per guidelines of NRHM.

(f) Family Planning

(a) Education, motivation and counselling to adopt appropriate family planning methods.
(b) Provision of contraceptives such as condoms, oral pills, emergency contraceptives, IUD insertions.
(c) Permanent methods like Tubal ligation and vasectomy/NSV.
(d) Follow up services to the eligible couples adopting permanent methods (Tubectomy/Vasectomy).
(e) Counselling and appropriate referral for safe abortion services for those in need.
(f) Counselling and appropriate referral for couples having infertility.

(g) Nutrition Services (Co-ordinated with ICDS)

(a) Diagnosis of and nutrition advice to malnourished children, pregnant women and others.
(b) Diagnosis and management of anemia, and vitamin. A deficiency.

(c) Co-ordination with ICDS in conducting VHNDs and health awareness programmes.

(d) Training in healthcare services and first aid to the concerned ICDS workers.

(h) School Health

Regular check ups, appropriate treatment including deworming, referral and follow-ups are the concerns of the PHC. This is done with the help of doctors particularly Medical Officer and other staff members through visits to the concerned schools (It must be noted that there is no post for the health educator.)

(i) Adolescent Health Care

Lifestyle education, counselling, appropriate treatment and other programmes meant for the adolescent care is provided.

(j) Promotion of Safe Drinking Water and Basic Sanitation

With the help of Rogi Kalyan Samitis, disinfection of water sources, testing of water quality and promotion of sanitation including use of toilets and appropriate garbage disposal.

(k) Prevention and Control of Locally Endemic Diseases

Like Malaria, *Kalaazar,* TB, Hepatitis, etc. treated with the help of Health Melas and awareness programmes.

(l) Collection and Reporting of Vital Events

Like various diseases and other health issues with the help of ASHAs and other Field Staff.

(m) Education about Health/Behaviour Change Communication (BCC)

With the help of counselling to the masses by ASHAs and other staff.

(n) Management of Reproductive Tract Infections/Sexually Transmitted Infections

With the help of health education for prevention of RTI/STIs by concerned staff.

(o) Training

(a) Health workers and traditional birth attendants.

(b) Initial and periodic training of paramedics in treatment of various diseases.

(c) Training of ASHAs.
(d) Periodic training of doctors through continuing Medical courses, conferences, skill development training, etc., on emergency obstetric care.
(e) Training of ANM.

(p) Drawbacks

There is no doubt that PHC Delina has got a well furnished building and has almost everything which a PHC should have. However, there are still certain shortcomings which came into our observation during the case study. These are:

(a) It is not a 24x7 PHC.
(b) Inadequate physical infrastructure and facilities, e.g., no Blood Banks.
(c) Drivers are posted but the ambulances are not there. This causes problems for the patients when they are referred.
(d) Lack of accountability to the public due to lack of community participation.
(e) Lack of set standards for monitoring quality care, etc.
(f) Operation Theater is available but is not functional.
(g) There is no labour room so pregnant cases are referred.
(h) There is deficiency of staff.

(IV). Contribution of PHC Delina towards Gender Health

The PHC Delina is promoting family planning through education, counselling and motivation techniques. Provision of contraceptives like condoms, Oral Pills, IUD, etc., is there. Permanent methods of family planning like tubal ligation and vasectomy is done free of cost. Monetary allowances are also given under NRHM. Free iron, and folic acid tablets are being distributed among pregnant ladies, health melas and free medical camps are organised in far flung areas to promote, health culture and provide health services at their door steps. Health educators in this centre spread health education to adolescent girls, referral system with proper transport facility is provided to the patients to improve their health. Registration of all pregnant women is done at PHC in the first trimester, minimum three anti-natal check-ups and provision of services is done according to norms. Laboratory investigations are done at minimum cost rates in post-natal care, a minimum of two post-partum home visits first within 48 hours of delivery, second within seven days through PHC staff. The infrastructure of this PHC is well developed and can provide much more facilities in the near future under proper administration.

(V). Conclusion

Primary Health Centre is to provide healthcare that is quality oriented and sensitive to the needs of the community. The broader objectives of the PHC's are to provide appropriate advice, treatment, referral and support that would help to cure the ailment to the extent medically possible. However, in almost all rural areas PHCs are not spared from issues such as the inability to perform up to the expectation due to:

(a) Non-availability of doctors at PHCs.
(b) Even if posted, doctors do not stay at the PHC Headquarter.
(c) Inadequate physical infrastructure and facilities.
(d) Inadequate supply of drugs.
(e) Lack of accountability to the public and lack of community participation.
(f) Lack of set standards for monitoring quality care, etc.

The case of health centres discussed above is no exception to it like:

- Unavailability of specialised doctors especially Gynaecologists.
- Inadequate facilities for surgical procedures.
- Inadequate supplies of drugs from health department even IFA tablets for pregnant women are not available as per requirement.
- Irregular power supply to the health centre hampers its overall functioning.
- No blood bank facility.
- Sanitary conditions of the health centre is not upto the mark.
- Less supervision and administrative checks.
- Health *melas* and awareness programmes are not held according to norms.
- There is no Health Educator or Counsellor at PHC Harudpanzoo.
- Water supply and sanitation of the centre is not upto the mark.

In PHCs in urban settings like Hazratbal, there are comparatively less problems as compared to those in rural ones. This is due to the fact that administrative heads are in their close proximity to it. There are chances of close watch and supervision by the higher authorities. Any complaint in these cases will come immediately in to the eyes of media.

Despite all these shortcomings, the staff present in the health centres is trying their best to provide services to the people especially to pregnant ladies and new born children. The health centre has well maintained record for immunisation of children and pregnant ladies. JSY benefits are also provided to women as per government norms. The centre is also playing a good role in community health awareness programmes and thereby trying to educate people about health needs.

7

Gender Health Policy and Health Administration in Kashmir

1. Gender Health Policy

[i] Gender health stands as a necessary component part of the general health. The governments in modern times are supposed to take care of all these aspects of health. But the existing reality reveals that all governments have not responded in a similar manner to their crucial health problems. It has been observed by experts that while some states are ahead in responding to health needs of its citizens, others are extremely backward because of failing to offer minimum health services. Between these two extremes, the Indian society in general and Kashmiri society in particular have positive as well as negative aspects of gender health. On the one hand, minimum health services and medical facilities have been provided to many sections of society. On the other hand, all services and facilities to all needy sections of society have not been provided. It is in such a situation that vulnerable sections of society such as women and children face acute problems and gender health emerges as a problematic field.

[ii] It is essentially in the preceding context that governments developed a particular role in making available all health services and medical facilities through its formal planning process and subsequently the formation and implementation of relevant programmes. Since women's health is of

basic importance in the human survival, every government attempts to provide these basic facilities. However, different societal groups and communities got benefited differently mainly because of their belonging to different social, economic, cultural and educational background. In this situation, these people developed varying ideas, views and opinions about government's health policy and its aspects of implementation. In this situational context, we carried out a detailed enquiry about various aspects of gender health policy and its implementation among the group of sample respondents. Their response has been recorded in the following table:

Table 7.1: Various Aspects of Gender Health Policy and its Implementation

		D-1		*D-2*		*D-3*		*D-4*			*Total*	
S.No	*Nature of Response*	*G.*	*P.*	*G.*	*P.*	*G.*	*P.*	*G.*	*P.*	*T.*	*G.*	*P.*
1	2	3	4	5	6	7	8	9	10	11	12	13
1.	No proper-independent	29	23	06	08	18	05	00	00	89	53	36
	GH policy									13.25	18.00	14.83
2.	Purposes served	13	03	00	09	27	21	67	02	162	97	65
	by NRHM	00	00							25.50	24.25	37.50
3.	Delivery related	00	00	05	04	00	00	00	00	09	05	04
	services provided									01.50	01.25	01.20
4.	Organise health *melas*	00	00	00	01	00	00	00	00	01	00	01
										00.17	00.00	00.50

The above table reveals that:

[i] A significant number of respondents, i.e., 89/600 [14.83 per cent] conveyed that the state of J&K has not developed a proper and independent health policy for women separately. It was because of the prevailing situation in which they don't get proper attention and health care. So, they usually suffer in terms of surviving on least standards of health. Out of these respondents, while 53/400 [13.25 per cent] respondents were from general category, 36/200 [18.00 per cent] were from professional category. That shows equal or near to equal response regarding government's policy towards gender health and its chronic problems. These views were upheld by respondents in all districts, but urban dominated district of Srinagar conveyed the response of 51/150 [29+23] respondents. It follows that consciousness about government's policy of women's health is more in urban areas than in rural areas. Other districts, Budgam and Anantnag, also show lesser consciousness about gender health.

[ii] About one-fourth of the respondents, i.e., 162/600 [25.50 per cent], said that basic and necessary features of gender health were provided directly or indirectly by the centrally-sponsored programme of NRHM. It provided more funds, facilities, services, professional and semi-professional expertise and health infrastructure. Among these respondents, while 97/400 [24.25 per cent] respondents belonged to the general category, 65/200 [37.50 per cent] were from professional category. So, the latter category felt more about wider use of funds, facilities and services from NRHM. These things became necessary as the state health department faced shortage of funds. The maximum response came from Anantnag and Baramulla districts which was [27+21] 48/150 and [67+32] 69/150 respondents respectively. These districts are rural dominated. In direct comparison, the urban-dominated districts of Srinagar and Budgam showed [03+03] 06/150 and [00+09] 09/150 respondents' response respectively. It follows that more professional and less general respondents felt about effective role of NRHM in the urban context.

[iii] The third aspect of the gender health situation in Kashmir touched by respondents in this study was related to the availability of some needed medical facilities and services of women's health, especially at the time of pregnancy and delivery. At these crucial times, maximum facilities and services were provided at every level of health administration. This response was conveyed by 09/600 [01.50 per cent] respondents who belonged to general [05/400; 01.25 per cent] and professional [04/200; 01.24 per cent] categories. This smaller number of respondents, mainly from Budgam district, was of the opinion that all facilities and services were not made available by the government hospitals and other health centres, but minimum number of such facilities and services were provided. Though respondents from other districts did not mention anything in this regard, the situation may be similar there in all possibilities.

[iv] A meager number of respondents, i.e., 01/600 [00.50 per cent] mentioned a particular item or act which has helped in the area of gender health. This area was the organisation of health 'melas' at all block, tehsil, sub-district and district and province level. Though the number of respondents is very less, the item of '*melas*' seems important and relevant as several health demonstrations on this occasion benefited many women in their local cultural context.

2. Policy Reflection in Planning and Programmes

[i] Though a significant number of respondents [i.e. 89/600; 14.83 per cent] conveyed that there exists no clear, independent and proper gender health policy, they didn't mean that there was no health policy objective at all with government. That is why 577/600 [96.16 per cent] respondents revealed that gender health policy and its objectives reflect in the health planning and programmes of the government. This response came from general as well as professional respondents. While general category of 368//400 [92.08 per cent] respondents felt that gender health facilities in the functional form, the professional category of 189/200 [94.50 per cent] respondents also conveyed the same views. Moreover, these responses were conveyed in all rural and urban dominated districts. More or less similar responses were shown by general and professional categories as manifests in their 92.88 per cent and 94.50 per cent responses respectively. On the other hand, 23/600 [03.83 per cent] respondents replied in 'no' which means that they felt gender health did not figure in governmental planning and programmes. What they wanted to convey is actually the non-serious handling of the problems of gender health, while as the policy and objectives of gender health reflect clearly in the planning and programme. These opposite responses and their reasons have been recorded in the following table:

Table 7.2: Policy Reflection in Planning and Programmes

		D-1		*D-2*		*D-3*		*D-4*			*Total*	
S.No	*Nature of Response*	*G.*	*P.*	*G.*	*P.*	*G.*	*P.*	*G.*	*P.*	*Total*	*G.*	*P.*
1	2	3	4	5	6	7	8	9	10	11	12	13
1.	G.H. Policy in Plan.											
	and progs.	10	47	94	50	86	45	88	47	577	368	189
	[i] YES									96.16	92.00	94.50
	Reasons:											
	[a] Functioning of											
	JSY, JSSK, RCH	00	07	00	00	00	15	00	00	17	00	17
	[b] Decrease in											
	MMR, IMR etc.									02.83	00.00	08.50
	[c] NRHM Help	00	01	00	00	04	00	00	00	00.55	00.05	00.50
										00.55	00.05	00.50
	[d] Improvement in	00	00	00	00	05	00	00	00	05	05	00
	facilities									00.83	01.25	00.00
	[ii] NO	02	04	03	02	01	03	03	05	23	09	14
										03.83	02.25	17.00
	Reasons:											
	[i] No specific											
	programme	00	02	00	03	01	02	00	01	09	04	05

[ii] No gender health progs.	00	00	00	02	00	00	00	01	03	01	02
[iii] No success achieved	01	00	00	01	00	02	00	00	04	02	02
[iv] General apathy	00	00	00	00	00	03	00	02	05	02	03
[v] Conflict situation	00	01	02	00	00	00	00	00	03	01	02

The above table reveals that the reasons for the first positive response were conveyed by the respondents as explained below:

[a] The 17/600 [02.83 per cent] respondents felt that gender policy of the government reflects through functioning of various health schemes and programmes such as JSK, JSSK, MCTC, and ICDS. Though these arc central government sponsored schemes, these were adopted by the state government with equal importance. It seems important to note that the entire response came from, professional and not from general respondents. It was because the former had full knowledge about it than the latter.

[b] Following the preceding pattern, 05/600 [00.55 per cent] respondents felt that government's gender health policy which is implemented through various schemes reflect in the general trend of decrease in MMR, IMR and other such relevant schemes in the state. Like in the preceding case, this response came from professional than general respondents.

[c] The third response came from same number and percentage of respondents and proportion between professional and general respondents was also more or less same.

[d] The last reason quoted by 05/600 [00.80 per cent] respondents in favour of policy reflection in government planning and programmes was that there has been general improvement in the women's health condition due to these official activities. Unlike the earlier responses, this response came mainly from the general category of respondents. This represents general social attitude of people towards the health programmmes, services and facilities, particularly in rural areas.

The second response which was 'negative' was supported by five major reasons by the respondents. The details follow:

[a] The 09/600 [06.66 per cent] respondents opined that there was no particular health scheme implemented by government of India or the state meant specifically for the women's health, though they need it more. The professional and general response was as follows:

Response	*Total*	*Professional*	*General*
Negative	09	05	04
	06.66	02.50	01.20

[b] The second reason quoted was that there is no serious and effective implementation of gender health medical activities. This response was shown by the number of respondents as is noted below:

Response	*Total*	*Professional*	*General*
Negative	03	02	01
	00.50	01.00	00.25

[c] Another reason for negative response referred by respondents was that though there may be some health related programmes and schemes in the policy and planning, but their positive effect is least noted. This response was presented by following number of respondents:

Response	*Total*	*Professional*	*General*
Negative	04	02	02
	00.67	00.50	01.00

[d] The fourth reason quoted by respondents was that there prevails a general apathy towards women's health. It becomes a serious matter when the condition of women deteriorates. This response was given by the following:

Response	*Total*	*Professional*	*General*
Negative	05	03	02
	00.83	00.50	01.50

[e] The fifth reason revolved around the conflict situation factor which contributed to the abnormality in providing gender healthcare. In fact, women suffered more than others though legally and constitutionally they were supposed to get preference and priority. This response was shown by the following:

Response	*Total*	*Professional*	*General*
Negative	03	02	01
	00.50	01.00	00.25

3. Attitude of Health Administrators

[i] The health administrators generally compose of three following groups:

[a] Professionals - doctors, experts, specialists, technocrats, etc.

[b] Para-medical staff of nurses, lab tech. assistants and professional helpers, etc.

[c] Health bureaucrats, administrators and technocrats, etc.

It has been observed that all these groups, especially of C-category who are more influential in health planning and its implementation are not very serious about gender health and its problems in Kashmir. In the last few decades, they have neither pleaded for proper response for emerging needs of gender health nor have they bothered to take care of proper implementation of programmes and schemes related to this health. It has also been observed that sometimes these powerful bureaucrats have taken the issues and problems of gender health casually. Some of them were found without administrative-technical skills. So, their role turns negative *vis-a-vis* the prime objective of gender health. This also seems the general opinion of respondents of this study. This response was conveyed by 134/600 [22.33 per cent] respondents. These views came from general and professional categories of respondents in proportion of 97/400 [24.25 per cent] and 37/200 [18.50 per cent] respondents respectively.

[ii] Our investigation among the professional respondents revealed that they often follow gender health guidelines provided in relevant documents clearly emphasising gender related medical facilities and health programmes. Our study revealed that the number and percentage of these respondents was not large. As we recorded, there were 49/600 [08.16 per cent] respondents who thought of positive health attitudes and following policy guidelines regarding gender health. While 18/400 [04.50 per cent] were general respondents, 31/200 [15.50 per cent] belonged to professional category.

Another dimension of gender health was the introduction and implementation of centrally sponsored and state sponsored schemes and programmes related to gender health. About 04/600 [00.66 per cent] respondents clearly upheld that centrally sponsored items are more beneficial and serve the community better. As a result of this situation, the state institutions, organisations, hospitals and other health centres conduct minimum number of health activities, while as the same institution carry out a lot of such activities from the central governments funds. This clearly shows the effective, successful and expanding health activities in rural areas, particularly related to rural women in the centre sponsored programme of NRHM. It has been observed that this programme, in addition of providing finances for all important health services run by the state health departments, gave boost to three types of health activities which are:

[a] Providing financial support to most of the important and basic health facilities including those meant for women exclusively.

[b] Providing stability and continuity to various health activities aimed at to serve the women in rural context.

[c] All major problems of gender health were taken care of financially by this programme.

In this context, while 1/600 [00.16 per cent] respondent conveyed that there was no worthwhile health programme introduced by the state government, 2/600 [00.33 per cent] respondents reported that NRHM as the main source of finances for state government health programmes.

[iii] One of the most crucial issues involved in health in Kashmir is the deep rooted corruption in the health administration. Successive regimes in the state have failed to curb this dangerous trend. A significant number of respondents [30/600; 05.00 per cent] opined in this way. There are also reports published in the local printing press regularly about corruption practices in the health sector, especially hospitals. The net result of this situation has led to extreme deterioration in women's and children's health. This widespread corruption is around the acts of fraud, scams, fake drugs, private practice during office hours, bribery or commission paid to medicos by pharmaceutical companies and conscious negligence of patients and hospitals. Kashmir experiences all these acts of corruption and its effect reflects crudely in the functioning of the state's sole maternity hospital, i.e., Lal Ded Maternity hospital.

These failures in the health sector reveals clearly in the responses of majority of respondents. While 30/600 [05.00 per cent] respondents reported this extreme form of corruption in the gender health sub-sector, 08/200 [04.00 per cent] professional and 22/400 [05.50 per cent] general respondents conveyed this type of corruption.

(iv) Two Case Studies:

(i) ICDS in Kashmir

(a) Introduction

(i) ICDS in Kashmir,

(ii) NRHM in Kashmir.

Many sections of society are not in a position to provide due care and security needed for normal growth of their children. Therefore, they require additional support through outside interventions to enable the family to fulfil its obligations towards proper healthcare, nutrition, education and social well-being of their children. Government concern for the promotion of services for the growth and development of pre-school children is evident from the constitution of National Children's Board and also from the Resolution of National Policy for Children, 1974. In pursuance of the National Policy for Children, which laid emphasis on the integrated delivery of early childhood services and services for expectant and nursing women, the scheme of Integrated Child Development Services (ICDS) was evolved to make a coordinated effort for an integrated programme to deliver a package of such services. The blueprint for the scheme was drawn by the Ministry of Social Welfare, Government of India, in 1975. The scheme was launched throughout the country in the same year on experimental basis in almost all states including Jammu and Kashmir in 1975 with the establishment of a project at Kangan in Srinagar district (now Ganderbal). The scheme called for coordinated and collective effort by different ministries, departments and voluntary organisations.

The programme approaches the child health in terms of health, nutrition, and education components for pregnant women, lactating mothers, and children less than six years of age. The programme is implemented through a network of community-level Anganwadi Centres. The range of services are targeted at young children and their mothers for growth monitoring, immunisation, health check-ups and supplementary feeding, as well as nutrition and health education, to improve the childcare and feeding practices that mothers adopt.

In order to assess objectively the gender health aspect in the functioning of ICDS programmes in J&K, we carried out the following studies to fulfil this objective:

1. ICDS project Batwara (Srinagar).
2. ICDS project Khansahib (Budgam).
3. ICDS project Bijbehara (Anantnag).
4. ICDS project Singpora (Baramulla).

(b) The assessment about the functioning related directly or indirectly to gender health in four particular districts follows:

1. ICDS Project Batwara (Srinagar)

(i) Population: The block level project has carried out a survey about population of project and the different ICDS services available to them. The details of this official survey reflect in the following table:

Table 7.3: Population Totals for ICDS Programes

1.	Total Population of the Block		99,227
2.	Urban Population		95,777
3.	Schedule Tribe Population		3,450
4.	Child Population 0-6 years		16,869
5.	No. of Anganwadi Centres in the Block	Urban areas	227
		Tribal areas	15

(ii) *Enrolled and Eligible Beneficiaries:* The official records reveal that there are more number of eligible beneficiaries in comparison to enrolled beneficiaries, who get the services from the centre at present. This reflects in the following table:

Table No. 7.4: Enrolled and Eligible Beneficiaries

S.No.	*Category of Beneficiaries*	*No. of Eligible Beneficiaries*			*No. of Enrolled Beneficiaries*		
		SC	*General*	*Total*	*SC*	*General*	*Total*
1.	Pregnant Ladies	82	2,289	2,381	31	465	496
2.	Nursing Mothers	57	1,532	1,589	21	509	530
3.	Below six months Boys	30	800	830	11	269	280
4.	Below 6 months Girls	27	732	759	10	240	250
5.	Six months-three year Boys	138	3,862	4,000	99	1,425	1,524
6.	Six months-three year Girls	120	3,223	3,343	77	1,475	1,552
7.	Three-six year Boys	146	3,824	3,970	100	1,537	1,637
8.	Three-six year Girls	134	3,833	3,967	88	1,630	1,718
9.	Adolescent Girls	310	8,619	8,929	110	2,122	2,232

According to the government official record, there is a gap between actual number of deserving eligible beneficiaries for the scheme and persons to be enrolled in ICDS centres because (according to the guidelines and norms of the scheme), they have to enrol 45 beneficiaries in one Anganwadi centre. So, the population is increasing in the area, but the number of ICDS centres is not increasing accordingly.

As the above table indicates in block Batwara, as in June 2013, the pregnant ladies eligible for ICDS services were 2,381 who consisted of 82 from tribal population and 2,289 from urban population, but they have enrolled only 496, i.e., 31 from tribal population and 465 from urban population because of constraints of the scheme. The total number of nursing mothers eligible for the scheme was 1,589 composed of 57 from tribal population and 1532 from urban population, and they could enrol only 530, i.e., 21 from tribal population and 509 from urban population.

The total number of (below six months) boys' children eligible for the scheme was 830 composed of 30 from tribal population and 800 from urban population, and they could enrol only 280 composed of 11 from tribal population and 269 from urban population. The total number of (below six months) Girl children eligible for the scheme was 759 composed of 27 from tribal population and 732 from urban population, and they could enrol only 250 consisting of 10 from tribal population and 240 from urban population. The total number of (six months to three years) boy children eligible for the scheme was 4,000 composed of 138 from tribal population and 3,862 from urban population, and they could enrol only 1,524 consisting of 99 from tribal population and 1425 from urban population. The total number of (six months to three years) girl children eligible for the scheme was 3,343 composed of 120 from tribal population and 3,223 from urban population, and they could enrol only 1,552 consisting of 77 from tribal population and 1,475 from urban population.

The total number of three to six year boy children eligible for the scheme was 3970 composed of 146 from tribal population and 3,824 from urban population, and they could enrol only 1,637 consisting of 100 from tribal population and 1,537 from urban population. The total number of three to six years girl children eligible for the scheme was 3967 composed of 134 from tribal population and 3,833 from urban population, and they could enrol only 1,718 consisting of 88 from tribal population and 1,630 from urban population. The total number of adolescent girls eligible for the scheme was 8,929 composed of 310 from tribal population and 8,619 from urban population and because of supply constraints they could enrol only 2,232, i.e., 110 from tribal population and 2,122 from urban population.

(iii) Gap between Enrolled in ICDS Centres and Beneficiaries of Supplementary Nutrition.

Table 7.5: No. of Beneficiaries Enrolled for Supplementary Nutrition

S.No.	*Category*	*ST*	*General*	*Total*
1.	Children 6-36 months Boys	33	656	689
2.	Children 6-36 months Girls	26	962	718
3.	Children 36-72 months Boys	33	688	721
4.	Children 36-72 months Girls	30	723	753
5.	Pregnant and Lactating Mothers	18	449	467
6.	Adolescent Girls	37	964	1,001
7.	**Total**	**177**	**4,192**	**4,349**

Even if there are more number of beneficiaries enrolled to avail other services of the scheme, but because of insufficient supply of supplementary nutrition and inadequate community response supplementary nutrition is not provided to all those registered. The above table reveals the number of beneficiaries to whom supplementary nutrition is provided:

According to the official data in areas like posh colonies of Raj Bagh and Jawahar Nagar, there are insufficient children available for availing supplementary nutrition because of two reasons: *one,* there are other institutions like Crèches, etc., to cater to the needs of children, *second,* elite community as they perceive the scheme do not avail charity.

In addition to this, there is no sufficient supply to cater to the needy, especially in tribal areas of Fakirkajri, Dhara, etc. As there are more number of deserving people eligible for the scheme, the supply is very insufficient to cater to this massive growing population. As the above table indicates, out of total number of 1,524, six months to three years boy children enrolled in ICDS centres only 689 are provided supplementary nutrition, i.e., 33 from schedule tribe category and 656 from general urban population. Out of total number of 1,552, six months to three years girl children enrolled in ICDS centres only 718 are provided supplementary nutrition i.e. 26 from schedule tribe category and 692 from general urban population.

Out of total number of 1,637, three to six years boy children enrolled in ICDS centres only 721 are provided supplementary nutrition, i.e., 33 from schedule tribe category and 688 from general urban population. Out of total number of 1,718, three to six years girl children enrolled in ICDS centres only 753 are provided supplementary nutrition, i.e., 30 from schedule tribe category and 723 from general urban population. Out of total 1,026 pregnant and lactating mothers enrolled in ICDS centres 467 avail the facility of supplementary nutrition, i.e., 18 from tribal category and 964 from general urban population. Out of 2232 adolescent girls enrolled in ICDS centers only 1,001 avail supplementary nutrition, i.e., 37 from tribal category and 964 from general urban population.

From the overall table *7.4 (c)*, it is clear that only 46 per cent six months to three year children, 45 per cent pregnant and lactating mothers and 45 per cent adolescent girls from those who are registered avail the benefit of supplementary nutrition.

(iv) Immunisation: Immunisation in the centres during the year 2013 is satisfactory, as Anganwadi workers and helpers have motivated the beneficiaries for timely immunisation of children. According to ICDS workers, the schemes of NRHM like JSY and JSSK, which provide monetary and other benefits for timely immunisation, is another dominant motivational force for the purpose. As in the year 2013, in block Batwara, 96 pregnant ladies, 424 Zero to three years children, and 105 three to six years children have been fully immunised. As the official figures in this regard indicate as follows:

(a) Pregnant Ladies Immunised 96

(b) Children 0-3 fully Immunised 424

(c) Children 3-6 years fully Immunised 105

(v) Pre-schooling

Table 7.6 .Pre-school Education

S. No.	*Gender*	*ST*	*General*	*Total*
1.	Boys	100	1,537	1,637
2.	Girls	88	1,630	1,718
3.	**Total**	**188**	**3,167**	**3,355**

According to ICDS official, pre-school education is held according to the norms in all 242 Anganwadi centres. As per these records, 1,637 boys and 1,718 girl children are enrolled for the same. The official records also reveal these children attend minimum of 16 days in a month for preschool education. As the table 7.6 indicates that pre-school education is provided to 100 per cent enrolled children. But during the field study, it was observed that education is not provided for the prescribed time of about four hours per day according to norms of the scheme.

2. ICDS Project Khansahib (Budgam)

(i) ***Population:*** The block level project has carried out a survey about its population and different ICDS services available to them. The details in this regard reflect in the following table:

Table 7.7: Population Totals for ICDS Services

1.	Total Population of the Block	11,809
2.	Urban population	0
3.	Rural population	11,809
4.	Child population 0-6 years	7,939
5.	No. of Anganwadi Centres in the Block	243

(ii) ***Gap between Those Eligible for the Scheme and Enrolled in ICDS Centres:*** According to the government official records, there is a gap between actual number of deserving eligible beneficiaries for the scheme and the persons to be enrolled in ICDS centres. It is because, according to the official guidelines and prevailing norms, they have to enrol 45 beneficiaries in one Anganwadi centre. Though the population is increasing in the area, the number of ICDS centres is not increasing in the same speed. table 7.8 below indicates this:

Table 7.8: Enrolled and Eligible Beneficiaries

S. No.	Category	Deserving eligible for scheme	Enrolled because of Supply Constraints
1.	Pregnant Ladies	739	729
2.	Nursing Mothers	661	486
3.	Six months- three years	4,771	4,374
4.	Three years-six years	3,168	2,916
5.	Adolescent Girls	2,470	2,430

According to official records, in block Khansahib, as in June 2013, the pregnant ladies eligible for ICDS services were 739, but they have enrolled only 729 because of constraints of the scheme. The total number of nursing mothers eligible for the scheme was 661 and they could enrol only 486. The total number of six months to three years children eligible for the scheme was 4,771 and they could enrol only 4,374. The total number of three years to six years children eligible for the scheme was 3,168 and they could enrol only 2916. The total number of adolescent girls eligible for the scheme was 2,470 and because of supply constraints they could enrol only 2,430.

(iii) Immunisation: The Immunisation in year 2013 is satisfactory, as Anganwadi workers and helpers have motivated the beneficiaries for timely immunisation. According to ICDS workers, the schemes of NRHM like JSY and JSSK, which provide monetary and other benefits for timely immunisation, is another dominant motivational force for the same. As in year 2013, in block Khansahib, 729 pregnant ladies, 2,186 zero to one year children, 2,188 one to three years children, and 2,916 three to six years children have been fully immunised. The following official figures in this regard follow:

(a) Pregnant Ladies Immunised	729
(b) Children 0-1 fully Immunised	2,186
(c) Children 1-3 fully Immunised	2,188
(d) Children 3-6 years fully Immunised	2,916

(iv) Infrastructure: There are only two Anganwadi centres in block Khansahib, which are operating from government constructed buildings, rest all other 241 centres are located in the houses of Anganwadi helpers. Those centres which are located in helpers houses sans the facilities like separate water supply, concrete washroom, separate kitchen, separate store, etc.

(v) ***Pre-schooling:*** According to ICDS officials, pre-school education is held according to norms in all 243 Anganwadi centres, as per the official records 1,449 boy and 1,467 girl children are enrolled for the same. But the provision of this service of pre-school education for four hours a day, according to norms, is least observed in remote tribal areas of Ringzabal, Konzabal, Zagoo and Kharian etc of district Budgam especially in winters because of absence of Anganwadi workers. There are some unique issues with respect to ICDS centres in block Khansahib. The two ICDS centres are under stay order by the district court Budgam since last year because of the dispute about location of the centre and in turn beneficiaries are the sufferers. There are no malnourished children in the area.

(vi) ***Previous Year Progress:*** The table No. 7.9 below shows the progress of ICDS project Khansahib in year 2012. According to official records, 3,560 zero to six years boys, 3,400 zero to six years girls, 696 pregnant ladies, 464 nursing mothers, and 2,320 adolescent girls have been benefited from the scheme.

Table 7.9: Progress Report, 2012

S. No.	*Beneficiaries*	*Covered in year 2012*
1.	Boys 0-6 years	3,560
2.	Girls 0-6 years	3,400
3.	Pregnant Ladies	696
4.	Nursing Mothers	464
5.	Adolescent Girls	2,320

3. ICDS Project Bijbehara (Anantnag)

(i) ***Population:*** The block level project has carried out a survey about population of project area and different ICDS services available. The details of this official survey reflect in the following Table:

Table 7.10: Population Totals for ICDS Services

1.	Total Population of the Block	126,499
2.	Urban Population	21,851
3.	Rural Population	104,648
4.	Child Population 0-6 Years	18,794
5.	No. of Anganwadi Centres in the Block	318

(ii) ***Gap between Those Eligible for the Scheme and Enrolled in ICDS Centres:*** According to the official records, there is a gap between actual number of deserving eligible beneficiaries for the scheme and the persons to be enrolled in ICDS centres. It is because, according to the official

guidelines and prevailing norms, they have to enrol 45 beneficiaries in one Anganwadi centre. Though the population is increasing in the area, the number of ICDS centres is not increasing so fast. This is revealed in the table No. 7.11 below:

Table 7.11: Enrolled and Eligible Beneficiaries

S. No.	*Category*	*Deserving Eligible for Scheme*	*Enrolled Because of Supply Constraints*
1.	Pregnant Ladies	1,134	793
2.	Nursing Mothers	962	816
3.	Six months-one year Boys	1,060	933
4.	Six months -one year Girls	975	851
5.	1 -3 years Boys	2,207	1,939
6.	1-3 years Girls	2,191	1,934
7.	3-6 years Boys	2,897	2,722
8.	3-6 years Girls	2,818	2,663
9.	Adolescent Girls	4,308	3,170

According to official records, in block Bijbehara, in June 2013, the pregnant ladies eligible for ICDS services were 1,134, but they have enrolled only 793 because of constraints of the scheme. The total number of nursing mothers eligible for the scheme was 962 and they could enrol only 816. The total number of six months to one year boys eligible for the scheme was 1,060 and they could enrol only 933. The total number of six months to one year girls eligible for the scheme was 975 and they could enrol only 851. The total number of one to three years boys eligible for the scheme was 2,207 and they could enrol only 1,939. The total number of one to three years Girls eligible for the scheme was 2191 and they could enrol only 1,934. The total number of three to six years boys eligible for the scheme was 2,897 and they could enrol only 2,722. The total number of three to six years girls eligible for the scheme was 2,818 and they could enrol only 2663. The total number of adolescent girls eligible for the scheme was 4,308 and because of supply constraints they could enrol only 3,170.

(iii) Immunisation: The Immunisation in the year 2013 is satisfactory, as Anganwadi workers and helpers have motivated the beneficiaries for this timely act. The unique schemes in the district, which provide monetary and others benefits for timely immunization is another dominant motivational force for the same. As in year 2013, in block Bijbehara, 358 pregnant ladies, 1,815 zero to one year children, 252 one to three year children, and 181 three to six year children have been fully immunised. As the following official figures indicate:

(a) Pregnant Ladies Immunised 358

(b) Children 0-1 fully Immunised 1,815

(c) Children 1-3 fully Immunised 252

(d) Children 3-6 years fully Immunised 181

(iv) Infrastructure: There are only 14 Anganwadi centres in block Bijbehara, who are operating from government constructed buildings, rest all other 304 centres are located in the houses of Anganwadi helpers. Those centres which are located in helpers houses sans the facilities like separate water supply, concrete washroom, separate kitchen, separate store, etc.

(v) Pre-schooling: According to ICDS officials, pre-school education is held according to the prevalent norms in all 318 Anganwadi centres. Other official records reveal that 2,722 boy and 2,663 girl children are enrolled for the same. Even though the mere enrolment of the children does not guarantee their pre-schooling education, as it was observed that in remote rural settings this practice is least held as per standard norms.

(vi) Schemes: There are some unique schemes covered under various programmes in district Anantnag which are:

(a) Indra Gandhi Matritva Sahyog Yojana (IGMSY), under this scheme the pregnant ladies who avail all the doses of immunisation and prefer for institutional deliveries are provided 4,000 rupees in three instalments in their respective ICDS centres.

(b) SABLA or Rajiv Gandhi Scheme for empowerment of adolescent girls (RGSEAG). Under this scheme vocational training and education is provided to the adolescent girls.

There are no malnourished children in the area.

(vii) Previous Year Progress

Table 7.12: Progress Report, 2012

S. No.	*Beneficiaries*	*Covered in Year 2012*
1.	Boys 0-6 years	9,747
2.	Girls 0-6 years	9,067
3.	Pregnant Ladies	1,583
4.	Nursing mothers	1,671
5	Adolescent Girls	7,196

Table 7.12 indicates the progress of ICDS project Bijbehara in year 2012. According to these official records, 9,747 zero to six year boys, 9,067 zero to six years girls, 1,583 pregnant ladies, 1,671 nursing mothers, and 7,196 adolescent girls have benefited from the scheme.

4. ICDS Project Singpora (Baramulla)

(i) ***Population:*** The block level project has carried out a survey about population of project and the different ICDS services available to them. The details of this official survey reflect in the following table:

Table 7.13 Population Totals for ICDS Services

1.	Total Population in the Block	66,576
2.	Urban Population	0
3.	Schedule Tribe Population	66,576
4.	Child population 0-6 Years	11,616
5.	No. of Anganwadi Centres Functioning in the Block	161

(ii) ***Gap between Those Eligible for the Scheme and Enrolled in ICDS Centres:*** According to the official records there is a gap between actual number of deserving eligible beneficiaries for the scheme and the persons to be enrolled in ICDS centres. It is because according to the official guidelines and prevalent norms, they have to enrol only 45 beneficiaries in one Anganwadi centre. Though the population is increasing in the area, the number of ICDS centres is not increasing in the same speed, as the Table No. 7.14 below indicates:

Table 7.14: Enrolled and Eligible Beneficiaries

S. No.	*Category*	*Deserving Eligible for Scheme*	*Enrolled Because of Supply Constraints*
1.	Pregnant Ladies	591	401
2.	Nursing Mothers	1,470	396
3.	Below 6 months Boys	768	768
4.	Below 6 months Girls	702	702
5.	6 months-3 year Boys	2,537	1,233
6.	6 months-3 year Girls	2,381	1,133
7.	3-6 year Boys	2,929	887
8.	3-6 year Girls	2,289	892
9.	Adolescent Girls	3,775	1,591

According to official records, in block Singpora, in March 2013, the pregnant ladies eligible for ICDS services was 591, but they have enrolled only 401 because of constraints of the scheme. The total number of nursing mothers eligible for the scheme was 1,470 and they could enrol only 396. The total number of six months to three year boys eligible for the scheme was 2,537 and they could enrol only 1,233. The total number of six months to three years girls. eligible for the scheme was 2,381 and they could enrol only 1,133. The total number of three to six year boys eligible for the scheme was 2,939 and they could enrol only 887. The total number of three to six year girls eligible for the scheme was 2,289 and they could enrol only 892. The total number of adolescent girls eligible for the scheme was 3,775 and because of supply constraints they could enrol only 1,591.

(iii) Immunisation: Immunisation during the year 2013 in the block is satisfactory, as Anganwadi workers and helpers have motivated the beneficiaries for this timely act. According to ICDS workers, the schemes of NRHM like JSY and JSSK, which provide monetary and other benefits for timely immunisation is another motivational factor for the same. As up to March 2013 in block Singpora, 62 pregnant ladies, and 98 zero to three years children have been fully immunised, as the following official figures indicate:

(a) Pregnant Ladies Immunised	62
(b) Children 0-3 fully Immunised	98

(iv) Pre-schooling: According to ICDS officials, pre-school education is held according to the prevalent norms in all 161 Anganwadi centres, as per the official records 887 boy and 892 girl children are enrolled for the same. According to official records, these children attend minimum of 16 days in a month for pre-school education.

5. Observations and Explanation of Data

(i) Housing and Space of the Anganwadi Centres

According to ICDS guidelines, the space for the AWCs is to be donated by the community at a central location, preferably near a primary school. The AWCs should provide sufficient space for indoor and outdoor activities and also separate space for kitchen, dining and storage. However, in all the AWCs studied, it was noted that the space is provided by the Anganwadi helpers. It was rather one of the criteria that whosoever provides space would be considered for the work of Anganwadi helper.

Consequently, both the quality of space and the locational aspects of the AWCs were compromised. Usually, it was seen that AWHs devote those rooms to the AWCs which were in poor condition. Regarding the status of the building for running of AWC, it was observed that in the sample surveyed of 200 centers, 56 AWC (28.00 per cent) of the AWCs were housed in *pucca* buildings while 90 AWC (45.00 per cent) of the AWCs were housed in semi-pucca houses and another 54 AWC (27.00 per cent) were in *kalccha* houses which involved a perpetual apprehension of danger to the life of the children.

As observed, most of the AWCs (87.00 per cent) are housed in the AWHs house while only nine per cent AWCs have their own building and four per cent are rented. Majority of the AWWs complained that they do not have sufficient space for conducting different activities, storage of ration, etc. Those centres which are located in government buildings like 14 in district Anantnag and two in Budgam are having all the necessary provisions of tap water, concrete latrine and adequate space.

Kitchen is an integral part of the AWCs. However, 82.00 per cent AWCs covered under the study had no separate space for cooking purpose as cooking for AWCs was done in the AWHs personal kitchen. Other issues such as separate storage space, dining and sufficient space for indoor and outdoor activities were also compromised. This was established by the fact that only 38.00 per cent of the AWCs had separate space for storage, 55.00 per cent had separate outdoor space for recreation and 53.00 per cent had some sort of space for indoor activity.

Lack of separate storage facilities in about 38.00 per cent of the AWCs covered under the study reveals that many a time storage of various items such as utensils and records, in addition to the personal belongings of the AWH occupies the main room pushing beneficiaries to a corner. Most areas in the study witness low temperature during the winter. Delivery of services requires the beneficiaries to sit in the Centre for up to four hours a day. It was found that 80.00 per cent of the AWCs had no arrangement for heating. Consequently, the children got exposed to severe cold and viral infections like fever, cold, etc.

(ii) ***Supervision:*** Growth monitoring and promotion largely remains a neglected area. Regular weighing and keeping records, focus on malnourished children, improving the skills of mothers on child care and any concept of community based nutritional surveillance are areas of serious concern as only 41.00 per cent of the AWWs have prepared community growth chart at the time of survey. Those who have not prepared it reported that either they do not know how to prepare it or do not have relevant material for the same.

(iii) ***Enrollment of the Beneficiaries:*** Most of the beneficiaries enrolled in these centres are from the locality. However, there is a gap between the actual enrolled and the nutrition provided to the persons of the community. As informed by Anganwadi workers during the course of study, the beneficiaries include children of age zero to six years, adolescent

girls, pregnant and nursing mothers. On an average, the number of beneficiaries enrolled in these centers range from 35 to 45.

This is good as per the norms of the scheme. But, the nutrition in many of these centres is not distributed to those actually enrolled. Besides, other persons of the community are also given the supplementary nutrition. This unauthorized practice is observed in almost all the places. Both the Anganwadi worker (AWW) and community are responsible for this practice. The deserving people do not get benefited as they are not given the supplementary nutrition properly and in time. This is especially the case with the children of age group of three to six years. They are required to be provided food in two servings after some interval within the centres. But, most of the beneficiaries come around 12 pm to 1 pm and carry supplementary nutrition to their homes. This practice has become common pattern in all centers. Due to this pattern, other services of the ICDS scheme get severely affected. It has also been observed that Anganwadi workers have squeezed the scope of the scheme just to the *Daal Centre* and thus the people are not able to get benefitted from the other services.

So far as the quality or the type of food being provided to the children is concerned, the centres should have a menu, depicting the schedule for preparing a particular food item on a particular day. But no such practice is found anywhere. While asking Anganwadi workers about the calorific value of the food items and quantity of calories to be given to the beneficiaries of different age groups, they are not well versed about it. This indicates their lack of knowledge about the service of the scheme. The most valid reason behind this is the lack of orientation of the Anganwadi workers about the scheme which itself is the outcome of the poor training mechanism on behalf of concerned department. It has been observed in some (urban) areas of Srinagar city that no children are available to be admitted to the centre as there are many other institutions like creches, preparatory schools etc, catering to the purpose. Also for many there is social stigma in sending their kids to the Anganwadi centres, as for them it amounts to feeding on charity. Hence in many Anganwadi centres, they have prepared fake list of beneficiary kids (possibly those kids may be admitted in some private or government Institution). Even though many of the sincere Anganwadi workers deliver the meals to the homes of these kids, but that is not consumed by the actual beneficiary and does not serve the ultimate objective of the scheme.

(iv) Immunisation: Immunisation of pregnant women and infants protects children from various diseases. It is an important service, in which the Anganwadi worker has to play its role, as this service is mainly to be provided by the ASHA/ANM/MO. But mobilising the community and preparing them for immunisation is the role of Anganwadi worker in the community, as she is having detailed information about it and she has to act as a change agent in the community.

While analysing this service and delivering in these centres, it was found that there is lack of coordination between the Anganwadi worker and the ASHA/ANM/MO. malfunctioning this service from these centres is evident from the community's response about their awareness about the need of immunisation. It was also found by checking the immunisation cards of the infants which revealed that the irregularities, and negligence from the mothers in terms of immunisation of themselves and also of their children, especially in the areas of Budgam, Anantnag and Baramulla. As immunisation prevents the diseases that are major causes of child mortality, disability, morbidity and related malnutrition. Immunisation of pregnant women against tetanus also reduces maternal and neonatal mortality. Mobilising the community for the same is the vital responsibility of Anganwadi workers and without this the success of the scheme is unattainable.

However, it has been found that overall situation was satisfactory. This may be due to the fact that overall utilisation of immunisation services in the State are better compared to some other states in the country. Though 95.00 per cent of the beneficiary children were immunised but full immunisation rate is far from satisfactory. Only 78.00 per cent of the children had received all the doses of immunisation. Measles coverage was particularly found to be low than other vaccines and this could be because of the fact that many of the children have not attained the age of nine plus months.

(v) ***Supply of Medicine and Supplementary Nutrition:*** Supplementary nutrition includes supplementary feeding, growth monitoring and promotion, nutrition and health education, and prophylaxis against vitamin A deficiency and control of nutritional anaemia. The observations on these services are given below:

The primary objective of the ICDS is to provide supplementary nutrition to the beneficiary children. Supplementary nutrition means identifying and fulfilling the deficiencies of calories, proteins, minerals and vitamins in the existing diets, avoiding cut-backs in the family diet, and taking other measures for nutritional rehabilitation. As per the guidelines, the state government is supposed to. provide funds for supplementary nutrition. However, it was observed that there was a single ration for different target groups such as children, pregnant women and nursing mothers, which was not in accordance with the ICDS guidelines. Similarly, there should ideally be provisions of double ration for malnourished children, but it was observed that there was no such practice as no child received double diet, despite of the fact that few AWWs mentioned that certain children were suffering from malnutrition. The AWWs mentioned that they get supplies, which last for three to four months only. Once the supplies exhaust, the children stop coming to the AWCs which get virtually closed.

During the survey, most of the mothers mentioned that supplementary nutrition was not provided to their children regularly. They, however, mentioned that whenever supply of nutrition items were available at the AWCs, their children get supplementary nutrition. But the problem was that AWCs did not get enough nutrition to last for about 300 days as per norms. Many of the mothers mentioned that on an average AWCs provided supplementary nutrition for only 100 days a year. On an average the AWWs also mentioned that due to inadequate supplies, they were not in a position to provide supplementary nutrition for recommended 210 days. All the AWCs had a uniform weekly schedule for providing supplementary nutrition to the beneficiaries. The AWWs mentioned that they followed this schedule strictly when nutritional items were available.

All the AWWs also mentioned that it is not only the inadequate nutrition that affects the provision of nutrition but inadequacy of other material resource such as utensils, functional stoves and cooking fuel also contribute to it. The AWWs mentioned that sometimes they were unable to prepare supplementary nutrition, either because the stove was not in working order or the fuel was not available. The supplementary nutrition was not distributed in the utensils of the AWCs, as in most of the centers we observed the meals being served in private utensils of the beneficiaries. Supplementary nutrition was not generally consumed at the AWCs. As according to norms only, the physically challenged and sick children are allowed to take home supplementary nutrition, but, in actual practice, 90 per cent of the beneficiaries take meals to home. It was a general perception among mothers that children did not like Nutri *Pulao*. Further, *halwa* was not appreciated during winters for reason of potential throat infection. Therefore, it was required that the supplementary nutrition provided should have sensitivity to local taste and seasons.

(vi) Quality of Nutritional Items: There is a State Level Committee which is responsible for the procurement of the supplies. Quality of supplies is also monitored by this committee. Mothers of the children were asked to mention whether they were satisfied with the quality of food supplements received by their children. Almost all the respondents (98 per cent) were satisfied with the quality of supplementary nutrition received by their children from the AWCs.

AWWs mentioned that the supplies of different items were irregular and it is generally supplied in bulk for which there was an insufficient storage facility both at project and AWC level especially in tribal areas of Ringzabal, Kharian, and Chill in district Budgam. Since most of the AWCs were nothaving adequate storage facility, it affected the quality of the items when these were used after a certain period. For example *Suji* and rice used to get infested with insects in the absence of proper and adequate storage facility. It was also found that 57 per cent AWCs receive the supply of supplementaiy nutrition yearly, while 27 per cent receive it half-yearly. Seven per cent AWWs reported that they receive the supply when they need it. Two per cent AWCs have ready to eat food available at the AWC while all others give cooked food to the beneficiaries. Most of the AWCs provide different varieties of supplementary nutrition (*Khichadi, Channa, Halwa, Nutri-pulao, dalia,* etc.) to the beneficiaries on different days as per their own schedule.

(vii) Health Education: Nutrition and Health Education (NHED) is a key element of the work of the Anganwadi worker. This forms part of BCC (Behaviour Change Communication) strategy. This has the long term goal of capacity-building of women - especially in the age group of 15-45 years, so that they can look after their own health, nutrition and development needs as well as that of their children and families. This education is to be provided to the adolescent girls also. But in actual practice health education is not provided in any of the centres studied. ICDS workers held the inadequate community response responsible for the same, whereas community held ICDS workers, lack of attitude and interest responsible for it. As a result, the masses remain unaware of the health needs and facilities available from the government institutions.

(viii) Health Check-ups: This includes healthcare of children less than six years of age, antenatal care of the expectant mothers and postnatal care of nursing mothers. The various health services provided for children by Anganwadi workers and primary health centre staff includes regular health check-ups, recording of weight, immunisation, management of malnutrition, treatment of diarrhoea, distribution of free medicine etc. While analysing this service delivering by these centers, it was found that in most of the centres, no health check-up has been conducted for a year or so. ASHA has now been given some responsibilities to share. In spite of this, community is not fully benefited by these schemes and it becomes quite clear when conditions of health, and hygiene of mothers and their children, in remote rural areas or in poverty stricken family is seen. Even the weight of the new-born children is not measured properly and regularly. There is also the provision for first aid at respective ICDS centres in the scheme. But during the study, no ICDS centre reported about the availability of first aid box, and when ICDS workers were asked about it, they didn't know about the provision of the same.

(ix) ***Referral Services:*** During health check-ups and growth monitoring sick or malnourished children, in need of prompt medical attention, are to be referred to the Primary Health Centre or its sub-centre. The Anganwadi worker is also obliged to detect, disabilities in young children. She has to enlist all such cases in a special register and refer them to the medical officer of the Primary Health Centre/Sub-centre. But during the interview Anganwadi workers reported that now it is certainly responsibility of the ASHA/ANM concerned. They are not sure whether they have a dominant role about counselling for ante-natal and post-natal care to pregnant woman or not. ASHA report that a lady has to visit ICDS centre during the entire period of pre and post-delivery. So, in case of any emergency it is primarily the responsibility of ICDS worker to call for referral transport and claim the amount of same from the fund of NRHM. It was also observed during the study that, in remote areas in district Budgam like villages of Ringzabal, Konzabal, Kharian, Brass, Sutharan, etc. which are without any road connectivity there are not necessarily the provision of immunisation and first aid at respective centers.

(x) ***The Non-formal Pre-school Education (PSE):*** This component of the ICDS may well be considered the backbone of the ICDS programme, since all its services essentially converge at the Anganwadi — a village courtyard. Anganwadi Centre (AWC) — a village courtyard — is the main platform for delivering of most of these services. This is also the most joyful play-way daily activity, visibly to be sustained for three hours a day according to norms. It brings and keeps young children active at the Anganwadi centre — an activity that motivates parents and communities for availing the scheme.

The AWWs are supposed to provide pre-schooling to the children. Every center is provided pre-school teaching learning material for educating the children of age group three to six years. Teaching learning material includes books, slates, abscissa slates, pictorial charts, and alphabetic building blocks and also different kinds of toys, etc. and are provided to every centre. This service is meant to introduce the kids to formal education system. In most of the centres studied, this service is totally defunct, and even if in some rare cases pre-school education is provided but there is irregularity in the delivery of same. None of these centers were having a time table for performing different activities within these centres. According to Anganwadi workers, the non- delivering of this service in the Anganwadi centres is due to poor attendance of beneficiaries and also poor response of the community. According to them, community people just send their children for taking the supplementary nutrition from the centres. While analysing the miss management in delivering of the said service, the community blamed the Anganwadi worker, for their irregular attendance and their lack of commitment for the same. Community also claims that ICDS workers are not providing the masses; information, about the actual role, which the ICDS scheme is supposed to perform. Most of the community people treat these centres as just *Daal* Centres, as mentioned above, which are supposed to serve nutritious food to kids.

It has been observed that wherever this practice is commenced, it is undertaken only for the period when the nutrition is available in the centre. AWW mentioned that no sooner the supplementary nutrition gets exhausted in the AWC, parents stop sending their children to AWCs. Surprisingly, when mothers of the beneficiary children were asked about the range of services available at the AWCs, supplementary nutrition and pre-schooling were reported by the respondents to be the two main services available at the AWCs. Majority of the parents mentioned that the main reason for sending their children to AWCs is supplementary nutrition and pre-school education. Parents, however, are willing to send their children to AWCs for pre-schooling even if the nutrition is not available in the centre, but the problem is that AWWs prefer to close the centre in case the nutrition is not available in the centre.

6. Contribution of ICDS towards Gender Health in Kashmir

(i) Supplementary nutrition to the pregnant and lactating mothers in ICDS centers has contributed towards the fulfilment of the deficiencies of calories, proteins, minerals and vitamins in the existing diets of these beneficiaries. In lower income families in the far flung areas, it helped in avoiding cut-backs in the family diet, and taking other related measures for nutritional rehabilitation.

(ii) Immunisation especially tetanus to the pregnant woman in ICDS centre reduced maternal mortality. Immunisation of pregnant and lactating mothers also has prevented the beneficiaries from various diseases that are in later stages major causes of child and infant mortality, morbidity and related issues.

(iii) Health education and counselling has contributed for changing the attitude of the people towards the importance of gender health, as this component itself is a part of Behaviour Change Communication strategy of the programme. This has helped to achieve the long term goal of capacity building of woman— so that they can themselves look after their own health, nutrition and development needs as well as that of their children and families. The culture of family planning has also been promoted with this intervention. This strategy also helped to combat the issues like self medication, illegal abortions, etc.

(iv) During health checkups and growth monitoring the pregnant ladies in need of prompt medical attention, are being referred to the primary health centre or its sub-centre. As a pregnant lady is entitled to visit ICDS centre during the entire period of pre and post-delivery. So, in case of healthcare in general and emergency issues in particular ICDS bridges the gap between modern healthcare and common masses. In remote rural settings of district Budgam like Ringzabal, Kharian, Chill, Brass, etc., wherein the primary health centres are not easily assessable, ICDS provided the primary healthcare and first aid during pregnancy to the beneficiaries.

(v) During the period of conflict in Kashmir in 1990s, when almost all of the health interventions were in shambles, ICDS provided heed to the gender issues, as according to some Anganwadi workers, many of the women delivered in these centres with the help of local practitioners (*dais*).

(vi) Government is spending a huge allocation towards gender health by introducing various schemes like NRHM, JSY, JSSK, etc. ICDS helped to achieve the desired results of these schemes by awareness for the same through Anganwadi workers in far flung areas, so common masses will avail the benefits of the same.

(vii) Woman in Kashmir are generally differentiated, discriminated and maltreated in almost every sphere of society. Their activities especially in rural societies are restricted to the domestic jobs. This was the lack of interest among men about the health suffering of women. But ICDS workers have helped to combat this issue by the help of family level counselling.

(viii) Our health culture in remote and tribal areas is still predominantly traditional. As these people primarily attach common diseases like fever to some divine forces, e.g., *Jin* (i.e. *Kotchun* etc.). These people still practice the traditional and ineffective practices like *yezband zalun,* amulets, etc., even in complications during pregnancy. But ICDS workers have helped in changing the attitude of common masses towards scientific medicines.

7. Conclusion

The above discussion leads us to conclude that ICDS scheme is not being implemented in letter and spirit as mentioned in the guidelines of the scheme. This is quite evident by the fact that the scheme, which has an integrated approach in its implementation for the proper mental, physical and psychological development of the children, has been reduced just to Daal Center. While analysing this particular service of the scheme, the situation there, too, is not satisfactory. Various factors are responsible for the mal functioning of these centres and few have been mentioned above. In fact, the present study cannot be called macro study, as it has been carried out on a small sample of ICDS centres, but its significance for analysing the situation of the ICDS centres throughout the valley cannot be ignored. As most of the ICDS centres in the Kashmir valley are functioning in the same way. We are of the view that this study, in spite of being carried out at a micro level, can be quite helpful in conducting a research at macro level. The addressing of issues and problems prevailing in these centres in terms of their functioning is just a beginning. It needs a comprehensive strategy involving various stakeholders including government agencies, NGOs and community for eradicating these problems at the state level.

(ii) NRHM in Kashmir

(a) Introduction

National Rural Health Mission (NRHM) stands for an intervention aimed at bringing about serious and basic improvement in the health system and the health status of the people, especially those living in rural areas of the country. It seeks to provide access to equitable, affordable and quality healthcare, reduction of Infant Mortality Rate and Maternal Mortality Rate, population stabilisation and gender and demographic balance which in turn would help in achieving goals set under the National Health Policy (NHP) and the Millennium Development Goals (MDGs). J and K under this Mission is focussing on empowerment of people through effective mechanism of Rogi Kalyan Samities, decentralised planning and implementation, strengthening of physical infrastructure and ensuring fully functional facilities at the doorstep of the people not withstanding odds of topography and situational constraints. With an objective analysis of the programmes of NRHM, this study is aimed to assess the availability, adequacy and utilisation of health services in the rural areas of four districts in the valley of Kashmir, viz., Srinagar, Budgam, Anantnag and Baramulla, the role played by Accredited Social Health Activists (ASHAs) and to identify the constrains and catalyst in its implementation.

Physical Infrastructure and Medical Facilities of the Programme

(i) Physical infrastructure for NRHM in J and K comprises the following health units:

District Hospitals (DHs) 14, Community Health Centres (CHCs) 85, Primary Health Centers (PHCs) 375, Sub Centres (SCs) 1907, and health facilities 53; comprising of 14 DHs, 39 CHCs and Sub-District Hospitals (SDH) are functioning as First Referral Units (FRU). The state also has 11 Trauma Centers (TC) and eight Auxiliary Nursing Mother (ANM) Training Centres. The facility survey recommended up gradation in 70 CHCs and work started, in around 69 out of which 18 have completed the upgradation.

Physical infrastructure in terms of buildings, operation theaters, labour rooms, new-born care centres, etc., and overall development seems to be satisfactory. However, scarcity of Anesthetists and ill-functioning of Blood Storage Units (BSU) seems to be mainly responsible of underutilisation of operation theatres, lack of emergency care in DHs, SDHs and CHCs.

Human Resources in the state comprises of 142 specialists, 588 general duties Medical Officers (GDMOs) with 412 in PHCs and 176 in CHCs. About eight specialists and 176 GDMOs have been contracted under NRHM additionalities. The state has reported 28 PHCs functional with four or more doctors, 85 PHCs with three doctors and 182 PHCs with two doctors each. As per generic guidelines, PHCs are expected to be manned by only one Medical officer (MO) and thus higher strength of MOs indicates a relatively better health human resource situation in the state and that is how all the 85 PHCs are reported to be functioning on 24x7 basis. Nevertheless, 10 PHCs are yet reported to be working without a doctor and 165 SCs without ANM.

Also, we find that 452 Ayurveda, Yoga and Naturopathy, Unani, *Siddha* and Homoeopathy Systems (AYUSIT) doctors under NRHM additionalities are recruited on contract basis to supplement the gap of doctors at different health facilities centres. Thus additional contractual medical and paramedical staffs under NRHM are 375 ANMs, 13 specialists, 309 staff nurses, 221 GDMOs, and 494 paramedics. It has supplemented the human resource and seems to have filled up the gaps in the state adequately.

(ii) Case load has improved in the state such as the institutional deliveries in the state have up surged from 0.1 lakhs in 2005-06 to 1.52 lakhs in 2008-09. However, number of Janani Suraksha Yojana (JSY) beneficiaries has gone up marginally from only two lakhs to eight lakhs during the period. Bed occupancy seems not to commensurate with the infrastructure, especially of male wards/beds in DHs, SDHs, and CHCs. Case load increase in J and K does not seem to be commensurate with the increase in infrastructure and human resource. Even the beneficiaries under JSY do not depict any marked improvement. Children fully immunised were found to be only 2.7 lakhs in 2008-09, which have gone down marginally from 2.8 lakhs in 2007-08, because of different social issues and other constraints.

National Disease Control Programme seems to be working well in the state as no death due to Malaria, Kala-azar, Dengue, and Japanese Encephalitis is reported during last few years. However, as reported TB cases were 12,525 in 2008 and Blindness cases were 1,848 and only 217 malaria cases in the state. Thus, disease control activities under NRHM are working satisfactorily in the state.

(iii) Quality of health services seems to have improved because of the improvement in the overall conditions of labour rooms, new-born care corners, Operation Theaters (OTs), etc. While in some of the DHs and SDHs, it was working satisfactorily and in some others it was improper and need strengthened. Some of the facilities, especially at DHs and SDHs, the Out Patient Departments (OPDs) were overcrowded. The lack of privacy for women hampers the utilisation of obstetric and gynaecological care. Institutional delivery care in few PHCs was also without privacy, proper equipment. There was total loss of privacy of room and infection control of labour room was impossible.

Though the introduction of JSY has significantly improved these institutional deliveries, delayed payments of fund to beneficiaries need to be administered properly. Overall additionalities under NRHM and utilisation of funds under Reproductive Child Health (RCH) have improved the quality of services in the state. However, correcting imbalance in deployment of human resource and physical infrastructure can further improve the quality of these services. Some of the remote, difficult and almost inaccessible areas in Kashmir valley need proper opportunity and strengthening of the health facilities.

(iv) The number of ASHAs is 9,764 in 6,654 villages in the state and most of them have been trained and had received drug kits in the year of 2008-09. Many committed and motivated ASHAs were found working in the villages. Some of them paid even for referral services from their own pockets to send the pregnant women to the hospital for deliveries/anti natal check-ups. Few among them are tracing children due for immunisation and maintaining their records in registers. Thus, most of the ASHAs are found to be aware of their role and responsibility and are helping the community in organisation of health activities under the sub-centre. But incentive payments for ASHAs are normally getting delayed by a month.

AYUSH services are provided in majority of the PHCs (317/518) in the state. Existing infrastructure for strengthening the AYUSH services in the state comprise of three colleges and five hospitals and 588 dispensaries. There are around 3,908 RMPs in the state at present. Even earlier, it was found that around 1.3 crore budget from Ministry of Health and Family and Welfare GOI was utilised during 2007-08 and thereafter the provision of around three crores in 2007-08 and 1.8 crores in 2008-09 has been made in Personal Independence Payments (PIPs). Contractual appointments of around 371 doctors and 236 paramedics were reported by the end of 2008. Further, initiatives proposed to be materialised through AYUSH are provision of 78 mobile medical teams for the Gujjar and Bakarwal (tribal communities) in the state. Further, provision of AYUSH doctors and additional drugs as a special innovative activity for delivering services to the seasonal, temporary and shifting nomadic settlements has been suggested in PIP for 2009-10.

It was proposed to hire one AYUSH doctor and a pharmacist for every PHC in the state. Unani and Ayurveda facilities have also been provided which seem to be popular in the state. Decentralisation process under NRHM seems to be working satisfactorily. The number of ASHAs in position on the survey date was reported to be 9,764 in 6,788 villages of the state. Number of village Health and Sanitation Committees constituted are 6,788 in number with 5,215 operational joint bank accounts. Number of Village Health and Nutrition Days observed during 2008-09 was reported to be 7,5192 in the state.

(v) Number of registered Rogi Kalyan Samities (RKSs) was reported 474 with 14 in DHs, 85 in CHCs, and 375 in PHCs. Utilisation of NRHM funds in this field seem to have picked over the years but full utilisation of the funds has never been achieved. Similarly, utilisation of untied funds at different levels has also improved over the years. However, distribution of funds and equipment in different health facilities seems to be unbalanced leading to sub-optimal utilisation of the equipments in the state. Blood storage facilities need to be strengthened in First Referral Units and sub-DHs. Most of the medical staff involved in these activities was reported to be available only for day care services.

(a) The positive awareness about NRHM among the respondents was found 61.50 per cent. About ASHA, among 95.50 per cent respondents it was found that the information about the NRHM to the 89.20 per cent respondents was provided by ASHAs/ANMs. The 28.30 per cent respondents had heard from electronic media; 06.70 per cent respondents from newspapers and 00.80 per cent respondents from other sources. Thus, it may be argued that the ASHAs/ANMs played a major role in health awareness and medical facilities of the masses.

(b) It was reported by 18.40 per cent respondents that ASHA visited their houses every week, 17.30 per cent respondents reported that they visited bi-weekly, 49.10 per cent respondents reported that they visited once every month, 24.50 per cent respondents reported that they visited them once every three months and 00.70 per cent respondents reported that they never visited their houses.

(c) 70.20 per cent respondents reported that ASHAs kept kit with them while visiting their houses and 81.70 per cent responded that they provided main medicine free of cost.

(d) 81.70 per cent respondents conveyed that ASHAs usually tell them about good health especially related to practices of sanitation and hygiene. 68.40 per cent respondents said that they organise the health day in the locality/village with the help of ASHAs. The 91.80 per cent respondents reported that it was done less than three times in the previous three months.

(e) While 76.10 per cent respondents conveyed that information about safe drinking water was provided mainly by the ASHA.

(vi) 60.70 per cent respondents said that the functioning of health and sanitation committees in the villages was because of their efforts. About 02.60 per cent respondents were members of these Village Health and Sanitation Committees (VHSC).

(vii) 43.80 per cent respondents reported that VHSC contributed in supporting programs about health and hygiene conditions of the villages. The 33.60 per cent reported that health camps are organised at village level regularly.

(viii) While 95.80 per cent reported that they attended such programs, 04.20 per cent respondents reported that they could not attend such programmes.

(ix) The 91.70 per cent respondents conveyed that they became aware about the doctors visiting. While 22.80 per cent respondents said that there has been improvement in the overall healthcare system after launching the NRHM scheme in the state. The improvement got manifested in the following points:

- The 08.30 per cent respondents got the benefit of JSY/institutional deliveries.

- The 83.30 per cent respondents got regular and complete immunisation.
- The 06.60 per cent respondents reported the proper attendance of health-care workers in the professional duties.
- The 01.70 per cent respondents reported the significant improvement in the hospital infrastructure and cleanliness.

(b). Assessment of the Programme

(i) In all districts, physical infrastructure in the case of Sub Centres, PHCs, CHCs and DHs has improved to a large extent since the inception of NRHM. However, there are lesser number of cases of PHCs working on 24x7 bases. Even if some PHCs function on 24x7 basis, they lack essential facilities. They have human resource shortfall, viz., unavailability of gynaecologist, staff nurses and female doctor, electric supplies, well equippe ambulance, and continuous medicinal supply. The issue of shortage of ambulances and mobile health units is dominant factor in hampering the outreach of health care services in these remote rural settings. Even when we look at the emergency obstetric care, caesarian and other surgical intervention services, these facilities are not available at respective PHCs.

However, the condition of overall healthcare has improved with the introduction of NRHM in the state. PHC Hardipanzoo was established in the year 1985 in a two room building with no electricity and no water supply, having a meager staff of only Lab Assistant and one Pharmacist. The HC was totally in shambles till 2007, when it was covered under centrally-sponsored programme, i.e., NRHM. With the advent of this programme the condition of PHC somewhat improved as under this programme the HC received the funds of every year for the improvement of infrastructure and other basic facilities like water supply and electricity, etc. NRHM not only provided money for infrastructural development but also enabled the authorities to recruit additional staff in the PHC. With the increase in manpower and other facilities, the HC started working on 24x7 basis from 18 October, 2007.

In fact, after the advent of NRHM various facilities were made available at the HC included a labour room, laboratory for various hematological tests, dental section and has total strength of 6 beds. The PHC has one ambulance also.

According to health officials of this institution, all these facilities had been made available under NRHM programme. The total manpower available in the HC is 14 employees comprising of four doctors, three nurses, two lab assistants, one allopathic pharmacist, one ayurvedic pharmacist, one block health worker, one driver, and one sweeper. In addition to it, nine ASHAs are associated with the HC who work in different areas of Hardipanzoo. Excluding one B.D.S. doctor and one Lab Assistant, all the staff is recruited by NRHM. HC is having the facility of ECG but the technician who can operate this machine is not available. HC lacks X- ray and USG facilities which are of immense importance for providing better services, and USG is very important for diagnosing pregnancy related issues.

(ii) Ante-natal Care: Maternal and child healthcare services remain the vital and dominant mission of the NRHM. Registration of all pregnancies is reported from almost all PHC's in the first trimester (before 12th week of pregnancy) with the help of ASHAs. Although, even if a woman comes late in her pregnancy for registration she is registered and care is given to her according to gestational age. However, associated services like providing iron and folic acid tablets, injection Tetanus Toxoid, etc., is not provided as per guidelines of the programme. Doctors blame that inadequate supply of these medicines is responsible for inconvenience to the patients. As one doctor from PHC Kaiyar (Budgam) reported that only 30 tablets of iron folic acid are supplied to the centre on monthly basis, which may suffice only one beneficiary, what about others? But one cannot ignore the fact that with the advent of NRHM, minimum laboratory investigations like hemoglobin, urine albumin, sugar, etc., are available at minimum cost rates in every PHC investigated. For the ante-natal care of pregnant woman, nutrition and health counselling is provided by proper health educators and ASHAs.

(iii) Post-natal Care: With the help of mother-child tracking system of NRHM, this service has gained new momentum in the state. Now the concerned officials track the record of every pregnant woman and newly born-child and, according to health officials, a minimum of two post-partum home visits, first within 48 hours of delivery, second within seven days through sub-centre staff and ASHAs are made. The visits are meant for the initiation of early breast-feeding within half-hour of birth and imparting the education on nutrition, hygiene, contraception, new-born care, etc., and counselling for the same with the help of ASHAs and health educators, and at times through the health *melas*.

(iv) Family Planning: Education, motivation and counselling to adopt appropriate family planning methods are the vital provisions of the programme of NRHM. According to health officials, provision of contraceptives such as condoms, oral pills, emergency contraceptives, Intra-uterine Device (IUD) insertions and permanent methods like Tubal ligation and vasectomy/No-scalpel Vasectomy (NSV) are promoted in every nook and corner of Kashmiri society. But the challenge seems that most of the women related diseases and complications remain concealed because of lack of lady doctors in the health centers, as women folk don't feel comfortable in discussing their health related issues with male doctors. Thus women neglect various diseases and move to other hospitals only when the condition turn out to be more severe. Same is the case with family planning methods, even if women prefer for family planning but because of cultural constraints they cannot express before male doctors.

(v) Decentralising Health: NRHM has been envisioned as a planning process that is participatory and decentralised, starting from the village as the basic unit for planning based on community need assessment. It seeks to empower the community by placing the responsibility of health of the people on their own hands and determine the ways in which they would like to improve their health. This is the only way to ensure that health plans are truly need based. The state would only play a facilitators role. Hence, the crucial aspect which assures the success of the programme is the representation and participation of the people in this grand programme.

Decentralised planning and communitisation in NRHM, according to the health officials, encompasses capacity building in terms of training and sensitisation of ASHAs, Village Health and Sanitation Committee (VHSC) and Rogi Kalyan Samiti (RKS). The members of these committees play their role and responsibility towards proper utilisation of services, grants and funds in the best interest of the people. The common people revealed during the survey that communitisation process necessitates involvement of panchayats in the governance of VHSCs, Hospital Development Committees and District Health Societies. Though the awareness of the process of the communitisation can be adjudged in terms of constitution of VHSCs, recruitment and functioning of ASHAs, constitution of Rogi Kalyan Samities at DHs, SDHs, CHCs and PHCs, it was all done after the intervention of NRHM in J&K in all districts.

However, the role of panchayats in the initiation and maintenance of health standards seem not clear in the absence of institutions of the system. The role of these panchayat institutions has to be assessed in ideal conditions which are not possible in the prevailing conflict conditions in Kashmir.

(vi) JSY and JSSK: After the introduction and implementation of NRHM, the improvement of institutional deliveries has been recorded significantly through the JSY and JSSK schemes in J and K. These deliveries in all areas depict quantum jump as most of the health officials have highlighted this development during the course of study. They upheld that proportionate progress was experienced through institutional deliveries, covered under JSY and JSSK beneficiary scheme. However, there were some difficulties related to late payment which have resulted in inconvenience of the patients.

(vii) Immunisation: Child immunisation scheme seems to have been working in all districts under study and possibly all new born children have been immunised. But, the timely immunisation seems a concern. Most of the vaccines for immunisation need to be stored in very cold temperature in freezers and, non-availability of electricity on 24×7 bases in most of the PHCs like PHC Achabal have hampered the timely immunisation of children. It may be of interest to mention that no polio case has been reported since last one year in all districts under study.

(viii) Committees for Effective Implementation: Village Health and Sanitation Samitis at village level comprising the members of panchayat Representative/s, ANM/Multi purpose Workers, Anganwadi worker, Teacher, ASHA, Community Health Volunteers are functioning in all villages. But because of lack of coordination between these organisations these committees seldom meet to discuss various health issues of their communities. In general, the functioning of such committees is considered essential for health improvements that involve a wide range of activities, thus these committees have a central role in the organisation of Village Health and Nutrition days, Health Education and health *melas* in their respective areas. Although, under NRHM, RKS are being registered in papers in all areas, at actual level these committees are mostly non-existent. While these committees are considered as backbone for the implementation of the scheme as community participation and community management is the primary and core strategy of the programme.

(ix) ASHAs: According to the norms of NRHM scheme every village/ large habitat will have a female ASHA in order to act as the interface between the community and the public health system. Although ASHAs are recruited on need basis in all districts of Srinagar, Budgam, Anantnag and Baramulla, but in hilly and tribal areas, they are not fully conscious and active. There is also lack of co-ordination between Health Care Workers/Anganwadi Workers and ASHAs. Most of the ASHAs reported that they are not given the Drug Kit containing generic AYUSH and allopathic formulations for common ailments, which has led to some inconvenience of the patients especially in hilly areas of Budgam district where formal healthcare is not so easily accessible. A general complaint of the ASHAs was that they don't have separate waiting room and stay-arrangements at their respective PHCs and DHs at the time of accompanying pregnant woman there.

(x) Poor Implementation of the Programme: The district is the primary unit for assessment of the programme of NRHM across the country. But, in Kashmir province District Level Monitoring Cells (DLMC) have failed to achieve set targets and in supervising the scheme in its respective districts. "Most of the district officials including District Development Commissioners and Chief Medical Officers have failed to submit monthly reviews and progress reports under the NRHM". (See Greater Kashmir 11th June 2013). Even if the scheme has completed its eight years across the state, but authorities seldom take review and care of its implementation part seriously. The assessment applied to utilization of funds, progress on health front in rural areas, targets given and achieved by the State and areas and people benefited out of it.

(xi) Mainstreaming AYUSH: Making popular and revitalizing local health traditions was one of the prime strategies of the NRHM programme. Although AYUSH doctors are recruited in most of the health centers to promote this tradition, in actual terms these doctors also prescribe English medicines and promote that type of treatment for their own benefits. In one of the health centres in Baramulla, during the course of field work, one AYUSH doctor was observed prescribing English medicine because most of agencies dealing with English medicines were reportedly providing them the commission. So the need emerges to revitalise AYUSH medication.

(xii) Disparities in Pay Scales: There are reports that doctors under NRHM working in far flung areas of Jammu and Kashmir are not getting salary on equal and regular basis. Also that ISM doctors working in the same scheme are not provided the salary and allowances as admissible to them under rules (See GK 1st March, 2013). This disparity and discrimination among doctors needs to be removed.

(C) Contribution of NRHM towards Gender Health in Kashmir

(a) NRHM in Kashmir has helped to overcome the challenges faced by the state for providing equitable access to health services, across the social and geographical expansions.

(b) Equal health care to woman with the advent of this programme in far flung areas was observed during the study because in the state there is now increasing access to the decentralised public health system and establishment of new infrastructures like PHCs and SCs in deficient areas.

(c) This programme not only provided money for infrastructural development but also enabled the authorities to recruit additional staff in the health centers. With the increase in manpower and other facilities, most of the health centres started working on 24x7 basis, which helped to control increasing maternal and infant mortalities and other gender issues.

(d) NRHM has also contributed in other general maternal and child healthcare services in the state. One cannot ignore the fact that with the advent of this programme, minimum laboratory investigations like hemoglobin, urine albumin, sugar tests, etc., are available at minimum cost rates in every PHC investigated. Referral services from NRHM funds in far flung areas have also contributed to decrease maternal mortalities.

(e) For the ante-natal and post-natal care of pregnant woman nutrition and health counselling is provided by proper health educators and ASHAs.

(f) The medical losses suffered by the Kashmiri society during the period of conflict are to some extent fulfilled by the programme. But there should have been a separate provision for counselling to the conflict affected victims

(g) The culture of family planning is promoted in every nook and corner of the Kashmiri society by NRHM staff, through methods of education, motivation and counselling to woman very. Thus, it is with the advent of this programme that most of the women now adopt appropriate family planning methods.

(h) NRHM is the only health programme which seeks to empower the community by placing the responsibility of health of the people on their own hands and determine the ways in which they would like to improve their health. The committees of VHSCs, RKS, are hence empowered to execute the schemes like Total Sanitation Campaign (TSC) and Health *Melas*, which are the major contributors towards gender health in Kashmir and this also assures the success of the other health interventions.

(i) The schemes like JSY, JSSK, etc., are the major contributors for promoting institutional deliveries in the far flung areas.

(j) Immunisation of the children and pregnant mothers has contributed to control various diseases in the state. As, no case of polio was reported during last year in districts studied.

(d) Conclusion

NRHM and its sub-schemes are the only support for gender healthcare in the state. There was no special policy or programme for gender healthcare in the state. Anything noticeable done in the field of gender health is only through this programme. However, due to inefficiency on the part of the administration in the state the scheme has many lacunas in its implementation. The scheme is of less support to inhabitation in remote and far flung areas. The pressure is still on the third referral centres and hospitals. That is why in spite of this scheme we don't find satisfaction among the general public about the healthcare system. In spite of this scheme we find huge rush in the hospitals of Srinagar city. It has also been noted that due to unsatisfactory service most of the people, who can afford, shift to private nursing homes and clinics for gender healthcare also. As mentioned it has been reported in media that union government is not satisfied about the working and fund utilisation of NRHM in the state. The bureaucracy is causing many hurdles in its proper implementation. In addition to this, the addressing of issues and problems in the proper implementation of these schemes need to be dealt with in consideration to the cultural and social conditions of Kashmiri society. It needs a comprehensive strategy involving various stakeholders including government agencies, NGOs and community for eradicating these problems at state level.

8

Nature and Problems of Gender Healthcare in Kashmir

1. Gender Health Diseases in J&K

In the research investigation, an attempt was carried out to know exactly about the major and minor diseases which the women in Kashmir found often. So, we put up a particular question in this regard to the respondents. Their response has been noted in the following table:

Table 8.1: Identification of Diseases

S. No	*Q. no (3.a) Diseases Identified*	*D1 Srinagar*		*D2 Budgam*		*D3 Anantnag*		*D.4 Baramulla*		*Responses (No. and Per cent)*		
		G	*P*	*G*	*P*	*G*	*P*	*G*	*P*	*GT*	*G*	*P*
1.	Urinary Tract Infections	36.0	17.0	00.0	00.0	00.0	00.0	00.0	00.0	53.0 08.83	36.0 09.00	17.0 08.50
2.	Hysterectomy	07.0	00.0	04.0	02.0	00.0	00.0	00.0	00.0	13.0 02.16	11.0 02.75	02.0 01.00
3.	Leucorrhoea and other infections	28.0	15.0	44.0	19.0	02.0	02.0	00.0	00.0	110 18.33	74.0 18.50	36.0 18.00
4.	Analemia	39.0	16.0	71.0	39.0	40.0	27.0	67.0	50.0	349 58.16	217 54.25	132 66.00
5.	Arthritis	11.0	00.0	05.0	04.0	00.0	00.0	00.0	00.0	20.0 03.33	16.0 04.00	04.0 02.00
6.	Thyroid	11.0	10.0	18.0	19.0	17.0	16.0	45.0	34.0	170 28.33	91.0 22.75	79.0 39.50
7.	Osteoporosis	14.0	03.0	03.0	10.0	01.0	05.0	00.0	00.0	36.0 06.00	18.0 04.50	18.0 09.00

8.	Poly Cystic Ovarian Syndrome	05.0	09.0	09.0	11.0	00.0	00.0	00.0	00.0	34.0 05.66	14.0 03.50	20.0 10.00
9.	Menstrual irregularity	00.0	00.0	00.0	00.0	00.0	00.0	23.0	06.0	29.0 04.83	23.0 05.75	06.0 03.00
10.	Infertility	10.0	03.0	09.0	01.0	00.0	00.0	00.0	00.0	23.0 03.83	19.0 04.75	04.0 02.00
11.	Abortion	00.0	00.0	00.0	01.0	00.0	00.0	00.0	00.0	01.0 00.16	00.0 00.00	01.0 00.50
12.	Dysmenorrhoea	06.0	02.0	07.0	01.0	00.0	02.0	00.0	00.0	18.0 03.00	13.0 03.25	05.0 02.50
13.	Gestational diabetes	05.0	00.0	01.0	01.0	00.0	00.0	00.0	00.0	07.0 01.16	06.0 01.50	01.0 00.50
14.	Breast cancer	01.0	04.0	10.0	03.0	00.0	11.0	05.0	00.0	34.0 05.66	16.0 04.00	18.0 09.00
15.	Menorrhagia	04.0	00.0	05.0	02.0	00.0	01.0	00.0	00.0	12.0 02.00	09.0 02.25	03.0 01.50
16.	Female sexual dysfunction	03.0	01.0	00.0	00.0	00.0	00.0	00.0	00.0	04.0 00.66	03.0 00.75	01.0 00.50
17.	Depression/ Hypertension	01.0	01.0	03.0	00.0	09.0	04.0	00.0	00.0	18.0 03.00	13.0 03.25	05.0 02.25
18.	Gonorrhoea	00.0	01.0	00.0	00.0	00.0	00.0	00.0	00.0	01.0 00.16	00.0 00.0	01.0 00.0
19.	Gout	00.0	01.0	00.0	00.0	00.0	00.0	00.0	00.0	01.0 00.16	00.0 00.0	01.0 00.50
20.	Fibroids	02.0	00.0	03.0	05.0	00.0	05.0	00.0	00.0	15.0 02.50	05.0 01.25	10.0 05.00
21.	Backache/ pain	13.0	00.0	12.0	01.0	02.0	00.0	00.0	00.0	28.0 04.66	27.0 06.75	01.0 00.50
22.	Malnutrition	00.0	00.0	02.0	01.0	30.0	07.0	07.0	04.0	51.0 08.50	39.0 09.75	12.0 06.00
23.	Pre and post-delivery complications	00.0	00.0	11.0	06.0	07.0	00.0	00.0	00.0	24.0 04.00	18.0 04.50	06.0 03.00
24.	Urinary Tract Infections and Sexually Transmitted Diseases	00.0	00.0	26.0	40.0	08.0	17.0	68.0	39.0	198 33.00	102 25.50	96.0 48.00
25.	Cervical cancer	00.0	00.0	00.0	00.0	01.0	00.0	00.0	00.0	01.0 00.16	01.0 00.25	00.0 00.00
26.	Jaundice	00.0	00.0	00.0	00.0	00.0	01.0	00.0	00.0	01.0 00.16	01.0 00.25	00.0 00.00
27.	Polymorgia	00.0	00.0	00.0	00.0	00.0	01.0	00.0	00.0	01.0 00.16	00.0 00.00	01.0 00.50
28.	Gynaecological disorders	00.0	00.0	00.0	00.0	00.0	02.0	00.0	00.0	02.0 00.33	00.0 00.00	02.0 01.00
29.	Ovarian cancer	00.0	00.0	00.0	00.0	00.0	01.0	00.0	00.0	01.0 00.16	00.0 00.00	01.0 00.50

30.	Genital herpes	00.0	00.0	00.0	00.0	00.0	01.0	00.0	00.0	01.0 00.16	00.0 00.00	01.0 00.50
31.	Hepatitis A/B	00.0	00.0	00.0	00.0	00.0	02.0	00.0	00.0	02.0 00.33	00.0 00.00	02.0 01.00
32.	Syphilis	00.0	00.0	00.0	00.0	00.0	02.0	00.0	00.0	02.0 00.33	00.0 00.00	02.0 01.00
33.	Menstrual disorders	00.0	00.0	00.0	00.0	01.0	06.0	00.0	00.0	07.0 01.16	01.0 00.00	06.0 03.00
34.	Endometriosis	00.0	00.0	00.0	00.0	00.0	02.0	00.0	00.0	02.0 00.33	00.0 00.00	02.0 01.00
35.	Pelvic pain	00.0	00.0	00.0	00.0	04.0	02.0	00.0	00.0	02.0 00.33	00.0 00.00	02.0 01.00
36.	Heart problems	00.0	00.0	00.0	00.0	04.0	01.0	23.0	17.0	45.0 07.50	27.0 06.75	13.0 09.00
37.	Hormonal imbalances	00.0	00.0	00.0	00.0	00.0	00.0	10.0	04.0	14.0 02.33	10.0 02.50	04.0 02.00

The above table reveals the following points:

1. Anaemia as gender health disease was reported by 217/400 (54.25 per cent) respondents from the general category and 132/200 (66.00 per cent) respondents from the professional category. A total of 349/600 (58.16 per cent) respondents reported it as an important health need. This response composes of the following district-wise responses. In district Srinagar, 28 respondents reported it from general category while 15 respondents from professionals. In district Budgam, 44 respondents from general category and 19 respondents from professional category reported it. In district Anantnag, two respondents from general category and two respondents from professional category reported it. Respondents from above mentioned districts reported it as the most required health need.

2. UTI and STD as gender health diseases were reported by 102/400 (25.50 per cent) respondents from the general category and 96/200 (48.00 per cent) respondents from the professional category. A total of 198/600 (33.00 per cent) respondents reported them as an important issue. This response composes of the following district-wise responses. In district Budgam, 26 respondents from general category and 40 respondents from professional category reported it. In district Anantnag 08 respondents from general category and 17 respondents from professional category reported it. In district Baramulla, 68 respondents from general category and 39.0 respondents from professional category reported it. Respondents from above mentioned districts reported it as the most required health issue.

3. Thyroid as gender health disease was reported by 91/400 (22.75 per cent) respondents from the general category and 79/200 (39.50 per cent) respondents from the professional category. A total of 170/600 (28.33 per cent) respondents reported it as an important health problem. This response composes of the following district-wise responses. In district Srinagar, 11 respondents reported it from general category where as 10 respondents reported it from professionals. In district Budgam 18 respondents from general category and 19 respondents from professional category reported it. In district Anantnag, 17 respondents from general category and 16 respondents from professional category reported it. In district Baramulla, 45 respondents from general category and 34 respondents from professional category reported it. Respondents from above mentioned districts reported it as the most required health need.
4. Menstrual disorders as gender health disease was reported by 91/400 (22.75 per cent) respondents from the general category and 79/200 (39.50 per cent) respondents from the professional category. A total of 170/600 (28.33 per cent) respondents reported it as an important health issue. This response composes of the following district-wise responses. In district Srinagar, 11 respondents reported it from general category whereas 10 respondents reported it from professionals. In district Budgam, 18 respondents from general category and 19 respondents from professional category reported it. In district Anantnag, 17 respondents from general category and 16 respondents from professional category reported it. In district Baramulla, 45 respondents from general category and 34 respondents from professional category reported it. Respondents from above mentioned districts reported it as the most required health need.
5. Menorrhagia as gender health disease was reported by 09/400 (22.75 per cent) respondents from the general category and 03/200 (39.50 per cent) respondents from the professional category. A total of 12/600 (28.33 per cent) respondents reported it as an important health need. This response composes of the following district-wise responses. In district Srinagar, four respondents reported it from general category. In district Budgam , five respondents from general category and two respondents from professional category reported it. In district Anantnag, one respondent from professional category reported it. Respondents from above mentioned districts reported it as the most required health need.
6. Jaundice as gender health disease was reported by 91/400 (22.75 per cent) respondents from the general category and 79/200 (39.50 per cent) respondents from the professional category. A total of 170/600 (28.33 per

cent) respondents reported it as an important health issue. This response composes of the following district-wise responses. In district Anantnag, one respondent from professional category reported it. Respondents from above mentioned districts reported it as the most required health issue.

7. Leucorrhoea and other infections as gender health diseases were reported by 74/400 (18.50 per cent) respondents from the general category and 36/200 (18.00 per cent) respondents conveyed it from the professional category. A total of 110/600 (18.33 per cent) respondents as an important health need. This response composes of the following district-wise responses. In district Srinagar, 28 respondents reported it from general category 15 respondents reported it from professionals. In district Budgam, 44 respondents from general category and 19 respondents from professional category reported it. In district Anantnag, two respondents from general category and, two respondents from professional category reported it. Respondents from above mentioned districts reported it as the most required health need.

8. Malnutrition as gender health disease was reported by 39/400 (09.75 per cent) respondents from the general category and 12/200 (06.00 per cent) respondents from the professional category. A total of 51/600 (08.50 per cent) respondents reported it as an important health need. This response composes of the following district-wise responses. In district Budgam, two respondents from general category and one respondent from professional category reported it. In district Anantnag, 30 respondents from general category and seven respondents from professional category reported it. In district Baramulla, seven respondents from general category and four respondents from professional category reported it. Respondents from above mentioned districts reported nourishment as the most required health need.

9. UTI as gender health disease was reported by 36/400 (09.00 per cent) respondents from the general category and 17/200 (08.50 per cent) respondents from the professional category. A total of 53/600 (08.38 per cent) respondents reported it as an important health need. This response composes of the following district-wise responses. In district Srinagar, 36 respondents reported it from general category and 17 respondents from professional category. Respondents from above mentioned district reported it as the most required health need.

10. Heart problem as gender health disease was reported by 27/400 (06.75 per cent) respondents from the general category and 18/200 (09.00 per cent) respondents from the professional category. A total of 45/600 (07.50 per cent) respondents reported it as an important health issue. This response

composes of the following district-wise responses. In district Anantnag, four respondents from professional category reported it. In district Baramulla, one respondent from general category and 23 respondents from professional category reported it. Respondents from above mentioned districts reported it as the most required health issue.

11. Backache/pain as gender health disease were reported by 27/400 (06.75 per cent) respondents from the general category and 01/200 (00.50 per cent) respondent from the professional category. A total of 28/600 (04.66 per cent) respondents reported it as an important health need. This response composes of the following district-wise responses. In district Srinagar, 13 respondents reported it from general category. In district Budgam,12 respondents from general category and one respondent from professional category reported it. In district Anantnag,two respondents from general category. Respondents from above mentioned districts reported it as the most required health need.
12. Menstrual irregularity as gender health disease was reported by 23/400 (05.75 per cent) respondents from the general category and 6/200 (03.00 per cent) respondents from the professional category. A total of 29/600 (04.83 per cent) respondents reported it as an important health need. This response composes of the following district-wise responses. In district Baramulla, 23 respondents from general category and six respondents from professional category reported it. Respondents from above mentioned districts reported it as the most required health need.
13. Infertility as gender health disease was reported by 19/400 (04.75 per cent) respondents from the general category and 4/200 (02.00 per cent) respondents from the professional category. A total of 23/600 (03.88 per cent) respondents reported it as an important health need. This response composes of the following district-wise responses. In district Srinagar, 10 respondents reported it from general category whereas three respondents reported it from professionals. In district Budgam,nine respondents from general category and 11 respondents from professional category reported it. Respondents from above mentioned districts reported it as the most required health need.
14. Osteoporosis as gender health disease was reported by 18/400 (04.50 per cent) respondents from the general category and 18/200 (09.00 per cent) respondents from the professional category. A total of 36/600 (06.00 per cent) respondents reported it as an important health need. This response composes of the following district-wise responses. In district Srinagar, 14 respondents reported it from general category whereas three respondents

reported it from professionals. In district Budgam, three respondents from general category and 10 respondents from professional category reported it. In district Anantnag, one respondent from general category and five respondents from professional category reported it. Respondents from above mentioned districts reported it as the most required health need.

15. Pre/post-delivery complications were reported by 18/400 (04.50 per cent) respondents from the general category and 06/200 (03.00 per cent) respondents from the professional category. A total of 24/600 (04.00 per cent) respondents reported it as an important health need. This response composes of the following district-wise responses. In district Budgam, 11 respondents from general category and six respondents from professional category reported it. In district Anantnag, seven respondents from general category reported it. Respondents from above mentioned districts reported it as the most required health need.

16. Breast cancer as gender health disease was reported by 16/400 (04.00 per cent) respondents from the general category and 18/200 (09.00 per cent) respondents from the professional category. A total of 34/600 (05.66 per cent) respondents reported it as an important health need. This response composes of the following district-wise responses. In district Srinagar, one respondent reported it from general category four respondents reported it from professionals. In district Budgam, 10 respondents from general category and three respondents from professional category reported it. In district Anantnag, 11 respondents from professional category reported it. In district Baramulla, five respondents from general category. Respondents from above mentioned districts reported it as the most required health need.

17. Arthritis as gender health disease was reported by 16/400 (04.00 per cent) respondents from the general category and 4/200 (02.00 per cent) respondents from the professional category. A total of 20/600 (03.33 per cent) respondents reported it as an important health need. This response composes of the following district-wise responses. In district Srinagar, 11 respondents reported it from general category. In district Budgam,five respondents from general category and four respondents from professional category reported it. Respondents from above mentioned districts reported it as the most required health need.

18. PCOD as gender health disease was reported by 14/400 (03.50 per cent) respondents from the general category and 20/200 (1.0.00 per cent) respondents from the professional category. A total of 34/600 (05.66 per

cent) respondents reported it as an important health need. This response composes of the following district-wise responses. In district Srinagar, five respondents reported it from general category whereas nine respondents reported it from professionals. In district Budgam, nine respondents from general category and 11 respondents from professional category reported it. Respondents from above mentioned districts reported it as the most required health need.

19. Dysmenorrhoea as gender health disease was reported by 13/400 (03.25 per cent) respondents from the general category and 05/200 (02.50 per cent) respondents from the professional category. A total of 18/600 (03.00 per cent) respondents reported it as an important health need. This response composes of the following district-wise responses. In district Srinagar, six respondents reported it from general category while as two respondents reported it from professionals. In district Budgam, seven respondents from general category and one respondent from professional category reported it. In district Anantnag, two respondents from professional category reported it. Respondents from above mentioned districts reported it as the most required health need.
20. Depression/hypertension as gender health diseases were reported by 13/400 (03.25 per cent) respondents from the general category and 05/200 (02.25 per cent) respondents from the professional category. A total of 18/600 (03.00 per cent) respondents reported it as an important health need. This response composes of the following district-wise responses. In district Srinagar, one respondent reported it from general category while as one respondent reported it from professionals. In district Budgam, three respondents from general category reported it. In district Anantnag, nine respondents from general category and four respondents from professionals reported it. Respondents from above mentioned districts reported it as the most required health need.
21. Hysterectomy as gender health disease was reported by 11/400 (02.75 per cent) respondents from the general category and 2/200 (01.00 per cent) respondents from the professional category. A total of 13/600 (02.16 per cent) respondents reported it as an important health need. This response composes of the following district-wise responses. In district Srinagar, seven respondents reported it from general category. In district Budgam, four from general category and two respondents from professional category reported it. Respondents from above mentioned district reported it as the most required health need.

22. Hormonal imbalance as gender health issue was reported by 02.00 (02.50 per cent) respondents from the general category and 79/200 (02.00 per cent) respondents from the professional category. A total of 170/600 (02.33 per cent) respondents reported it as important health issue. This response composes of the following district-wise responses. In district Baramulla, 10 respondents from general category and four respondents from professional category reported it. Respondents from above mentioned district reported it as the most required health issue.
23. Gestational diabetes as gender health disease was reported by 6/400 (01.50 per cent) respondents from the general category and 1/200 (00.50 per cent) respondent from the professional category. A total of 7/600 (00.16 per cent) respondents reported it as an important health need. This response composes of the following district-wise responses. In district Srinagar, five respondents reported it from general category. In district Budgam, one respondent from general category and one respondent from professional category reported it. Respondent from above mentioned districts reported it as the most required health need.
24. Fibroids as gender health disease was reported by 05/400 (01.25 per cent) respondents from the general category and 10/200 (05.00 per cent) respondents from the professional category. A total of 15/600 (02.50 per cent) respondents reported it as an important health need. This response composes of the following district-wise responses. In district Srinagar, two respondents reported it from general category. In district Budgam, three respondents from general category and five respondents from professional category reported it. In district Anantnag, five respondents from professional category reported it. Respondents from above mentioned districts reported it as the most required health need.
25. Gynaecological disorders as gender health disease was reported by 02/200 (01.00 per cent) respondents from the professional category. A total of 02/600 (00.33 per cent) respondents reported them as important health issues. This response composes of the following district-wise responses. In district Anantnag, two respondents from professional category reported it. Respondents from above mentioned districts reported it as the most required health issue.
26. Endometriosis as gender health disease was reported by 02/200 (01.00 per cent) respondents from the professional category. A total of 02/600 (00.33 per cent) respondents reported it as an important health issue. This

response composes of the following district-wise responses. In district Anantnag, two respondents from professional category reported it. In district Baramulla, six respondents from general category reported it. Respondents from above mentioned districts reported it as the most required health issue.

27. Pelvic pain as gender health disease was reported by 02/200 (01.00 per cent) respondents from the professional category. A total of 02/600 (00.33 per cent) respondents reported it as an important health issue. This response composes of the following district-wise responses. In district Anantnag, four respondents from professional category reported it. In district Baramulla, two respondents from general category. Respondents from above mentioned districts reported it as the most required health issue to be addressed.
28. Female sexual dysfunction as gender health disease was reported by 03/400 (00.75 per cent) respondents from the general category and 01/200 (00.50 per cent) respondent from the professional category. A total of 04/600 (00.66 per cent) respondents reported it as an important health need. This response composes of the following district-wise responses. In district Srinagar, 11 respondents reported it from general category whereas 10 respondents reported it from professionals. In district Budgam,18 respondents from general category and 19 respondents from professional category reported it. In district Anantnag, 17 respondents from general category and 16 respondents from professional category reported it. In district Baramulla, 45 respondents from general category and 34 respondents from professional category reported it. Respondents from above mentioned districts reported it as the most required health need.
29. Ovarian cancer as gender health disease was reported by 01/200 (00.50 per cent) respondent from the professional category. A total of 01/600 (00.16 per cent) respondent reported it as an important health issue. This response composes of the following district-wise responses. In district Anantnag, one respondent from professional category reported it. Respondents from above mentioned district reported it as most required health issue.
30. Gonorrhoea as gender health disease was reported by 1/200 (00.50 per cent) respondent from the professional category. A total of 1/600 (00.16 per cent) respondent reported it as an important health need. This response composes of the following district-wise responses. In district Srinagar, one respondent reported it from professionals. Respondents from above mentioned district reported it as the most required health need.

31. Genital herpes as gender health disease was reported by 01/200 (00.50 per cent) respondent from the professional category. A total of 01/600 (00.16 per cent) respondent reported it as an important health issue. This response composes of the following district-wise responses. In district Anantnag, one respondent from professional category reported it. Respondents from above mentioned districts reported it as the most required health issue.
32. Abortion was reported by 01/200 (00.50 per cent) respondents from the professional category. A total of 1/600 (00.16 per cent) respondent reported it as an important health need. This response composes of the following district wise responses. In Budgam, respondent from professional category reported it.
33. Hepatitis A/B as gender health disease were reported by 02/200 (00.50 per cent) respondents from the professional category. A total of 02/600 (00.16 per cent) respondents reported it as an important health issue. This response composes of the following district-wise responses. In district Anantnag, two respondents from professional category reported it. Respondents from above mentioned districts reported it as the most required health issue.
34. Gout as gender health disease was reported by 01/200 (00.50 per cent) respondent from the professional category. A total of 01/600 (00.16 per cent) respondent reported it as an important health need. This response composes of the following district-wise responses. In district Srinagar, 11 respondents reported it from general category while as 10 respondents reported it from professionals. In district Budgam, 18 respondents from general category and 19 respondents from professional category reported it. In district Anantnag, 17 respondents from general category and 16 respondents from professional category reported it. In district Baramulla, 45 respondents from general category and 34 respondents from professional category reported it. Respondents from above mentioned districts reported it as the most required health need.
35. Syphilis as gender health disease was reported by 02/200 (00.50 per cent) respondents from the professional category. A total of 02/600 (00.33 per cent) respondents reported it as an important health issue. This response composes of the following district wise responses. In district Anantnag, two respondents from professional category reported it. Respondents from above mentioned districts reported it as the most required health issue.

36. Polymorgia as gender health disease was reported by 1/200 (00.50 per cent) respondent from the professional category. A total of 01/600 (00.16 per cent) respondent reported it as an important health issue. This response composes of the following district-wise responses. In district Anantnag, one respondent from professional category reported it. Respondents from above mentioned districts reported it as the most required health issue.

37. Cervical cancer as gender health disease was reported by 01/400 (00.25 per cent) respondent from the general category A total of 01/600 (00.16 per cent) respondent reported it as an important health issue. This response composes of the following district-wise responses. In district Anantnag, one respondent from general category reported it. Respondents from above mentioned districts reported it as the most required health issue.

(2.) Other Gender Health Care Problems in Kashmir

Like the first question, we put another related question to all respondents regarding the general health problems which the women face in their family, community, class and group. Their responses are noted in the following table:

Table 8.2: Other Problems of Gender Health in Kashmir

	Problems	D1 Srinagar		D2 Budgam		D3 Anantnag		D.4 Baramulla		Responses (No. and per cent)		
S. No		G	P	G	P	G	P	G	P	GT	G	P
1.	Late marriages	15.0	07.0	00.0	00.0	00.0	01.0	00.0	00.0	23.0 03.83	15.0 03.75	08.0 04.00
2.	Communication Gap	30.0	32.0	00.0	00.0	06.0	04.0	56.0	44.0	112 18.66	62.0 15.50	50.0 25.00
3.	Illiteracy	30.0	02.0	00.0	30.0	03.0	02.0	00.0	00.0	07.0 01.16	03.0 00.75	04.0 02.00
4.	Lack of funding schemes	11.0	01.0	00.0	00.0	01.0	00.0	00.0	00.0	13.0 02.16	12.0 03.00	01.0 00.50
5.	Lack of facilities	12.0	02.0	32.0	06.0	07.0	04.0	00.0	00.0	63.0 12.75	10.50 12.0	51.0 06.00
6.	Gender Bias	10.0	04.0	16.0	09.0	08.0	01.0	00.0	00.0	48.0 08.50	08.00 14.0	34.0 07.00
7.	Less Preventive Education	00.0	00.0	06.0	07.0	00.0	00.0	00.0	00.0	13.0 01.50	02.16 07.0	06.0 03.50
8.	Female (specialised doctors) not available	00.0	00.0	38.0	04.0	13.0	00.0	00.0	00.0	56.0 09.33	52.0 13.00	04.0 02.00
9.	Less Educated	00.0	00.0	04.0	07.0	00.0	00.0	00.0	00.0	11.0 01.00	01.83 07.0	04.0 03.50

10.	Expensive Treatment	00.0	00.0	04.0	00.0	01.0	00.0	00.0	00.0	05.0 01.25	00.33 00.0	05.0 00.00
11.	Too Many Children	00.0	00.0	01.0	05.0	00.0	00.0	00.0	00.0	06.0 0.25	01.00 05.0	01.00 02.50
12.	Hectic Work Schedule	00.0	00.0	13.0	20.0	02.0	01.0	00.0	00.0	07.0 01.25	01.16 02.0	05.0 01.00
13.	Less Family Support	00.0	00.0	13.0	01.0	02.0	01.0	00.0	00.0	17.0 03.75	02.83 01.0	15.0 00.50
14.	Cultural Restrictions	00.0	00.0	15.0	07.0	16.0	06.0	68.0	38.0	150 24.75	25.00 51.0	99.0 24.75
15.	Unhygienic Environment	00.0	00.0	08.0	07.0	03.0	00.0	00.0	00.0	18.0 02.75	03.00 07.0	11.0 03.50
16.	Negligence by Doctors	00.0	00.0	09.0	00.0	00.0	00.0	00.0	00.0	09.0 02.25	01.50 00.0	09.0 00.00
17.	Poverty	00.0	00.0	04.0	03.0	04.0	02.0	00.0	00.0	13.0 02.00	02.16 05.0	08.0 02.50
18.	Self-medication	00.0	00.0	05.0	00.0	01.0	00.0	00.0	00.0	04.0 01.00	00.66 00.0	04.0 00.00
19.	Programmes not Implemented Properly	00.0	00.0	05.0	01.0	00.0	04.0	00.0	00.0	10.0 01.25	01.65 05.0	05.0 02.25
20.	Lack of Supervision and Accountability	00.0	00.0	00.0	04.0	02.0	01.0	00.0	00.0	08.0 00.75	01.33 05.0	03.0 02.50
21.	Violence against Women	00.0	00.0	00.0	01.0	01.0	00.0	00.0	00.0	02.0 00.25	00.33 01.0	01.0 01.00
22.	Complications during and After Pregnancy	00.0	00.0	00.0	02.0	00.0	00.0	00.0	00.0	02.0 00.00	00.33 02.0	00.0 01.00
23.	Shyness among Women	00.0	00.0	01.0	03.0	00.0	00.0	00.0	00.0	04.0 01.00	00.66 03.0	00.0 01.50
24.	Drug Abuse	00.0	00.0	01.0	00.0	00.0	00.0	00.0	00.0	01.0 01.00	00.16 00.0	27.0 00.00
25.	Accessibility to PHCs	00.0	00.0	00.0	00.0	00.0	00.0	44.0	27.0	71.0 11.00	11.83 27.0	22.0 13.50
26.	Transportation	00.0	00.0	00.0	00.0	00.0	00.0	34.0	22.0	56.0 08.50	09.33 22.0	02.0 11.00

The above table conveys that:

1. Cultural restrictions as gender health care problem was reported by 99/400 (24.75 per cent) respondents from the general category and 51/200 (25.50 per cent) respondents from the professional category. A total of 150/600 (25.00 per cent) respondents reported it as an important health care need. This response composes of the following district-wise responses. In district Budgam, 15 respondents reported it from general category while as seven

respondents reported it from professionals. In district Anantnag, 16 respondents from general category and six respondents from professional category reported it. In district Baramulla, 68 respondents from general category and 38 respondents from professional category reported it. Respondents from above mentioned districts reported it as a problem involved in gender health care.

2. Communication gap as gender health care problem was reported by 62/400 (15.50 per cent) respondents from the general category and 50/200 (25.00 per cent) respondents from the professional category. A total of 112/600 (18.66 per cent) respondents reported it as an important health care need. This response composes of the following district-wise responses. In district Srinagar, two respondents reported it from professionals. In district Anantnag, six respondents from general category and four respondents from professional category reported it. In district Baramulla, 56 respondents from general category and 44 respondents from professional category reported it. Respondents from above mentioned districts reported it as a problem involved in gender health care.

3. Accessibility to modern healthcare as gender healthcare problem was reported by 44/400 (11.00 per cent) respondents from the general category and 27/200 (13.50 per cent) respondents from professionals reported it. A total of 71/600 (11.83 per cent) respondents reported it as an important healthcare need. This response composes of the following district-wise responses. In district Baramulla, 44 respondents reported it from generals where as 27 respondents reported from professionals. Respondents from above mentioned district reported it as a problem involved in gender health care.

4. Lack of Specialised female personnel as gender healthcare problem was reported by 52/400 (13.00 per cent) respondents from the general category and 4/200 (02.00 per cent) respondents from the professional category. A total of 56/600 (09.33 per cent) respondents reported it as an important health care need. This response composes of the following district-wise responses. In district Budgam, 13 respondents reported it from general category. In district Anantnag, 13 respondents from general category reported it. Respondents from above mentioned districts reported it as a problem involved in gender healthcare.

5. Lack of relevant facilities as gender healthcare problem was reported by 51/400 (12.75 per cent) respondents from the general category and 12/200 (06.00 per cent) respondents from the professional category. A. total

of 63/600 (10.50 per cent) respondents reported it as an important healthcare need. This response composes of the following district-wise responses. In district Srinagar, 12 respondents reported it from general category while as two respondents from professionals reported it. In district Budgam, 32 respondents from general category and six respondents from professional category reported it. In district Anantnag, seven respondents from general category and four respondents from professional category reported it. Respondents from above mentioned districts reported it as a problem involved in gender healthcare.

6. Gender bias as a gender healthcare problem was reported by 34/400 (08.50 per cent) respondents from the general category and 14/200 (07.00 per cent) respondents from the professional category. A total of 48/600 (08.00 per cent) respondents reported it as an important healthcare need. This response composes of the following district-wise responses. In district Srinagar, 10 respondents from general category and four respondents reported it from professionals. In district Budgam, 15 respondents from general category and nine respondents from professional category reported it. In district Anantnag, eight respondents from general category and one respondent from professional category reported it. Respondents from above mentioned districts reported it as a problem involved in gender health care.

7. Late marriages as gender healthcare problem were reported by 15/400 (03.25.25 per cent) respondents from the general category and 08/200 (04.00 per cent) respondents from the professional category. A total of 23/600 (03.83 per cent) respondents reported it as an important healthcare need. This response composes of the following district-wise responses. In district Srinagar, 15 respondents reported it from general category whereas seven respondents reported it from professionals. In district Anantnag, one respondent from professional category reported it. Respondents from above mentioned districts reported it as a problem involved in gender health care.

8. Affordability to modern healthcare as gender healthcare problem was reported by 24/400 (06.00 per cent) respondents from the general category and 2/200 (01.00 per cent) respondents from professionals reported it A total of 26/600 (04.33 per cent) respondents reported it as an important healthcare need. This response composes of the following district-wise responses. In district Baramulla, 24 respondents reported it from generals whereas two respondents reported from professionals. Respondents from above mentioned district reported it as a problem involved in gender care health.

9. Awareness of modern health care as gender healthcare problem was reported by 20/400 (05.00 per cent) respondents from the general category and 1/200 (01.00 per cent) respondent from professionals reported it. A total of 21/600 (03.50 per cent) respondents reported it as an important health need. This response composes of the following district-wise responses. In district Baramulla, 20 respondents reported it from generals while as one respondent reported from professionals. Respondents from above mentioned districts reported it as a problem involved in gender healthcare.
10. Transportation as. gender health care problem was reported by 34/400 (08.50 per cent) respondents from the general category and 22/200 (11.00 per cent) respondents from professionals reported it. A total of 56/600 (09.33 per cent) respondents reported it as an important healthcare need. This response composes of the following district-wise responses. In district Baramulla, 34 respondents reported it from generals whereas 22 respondents reported from professionals. Respondents from above mentioned districts reported it as a problem involved in gender healthcare.
11. Unhygienic environment as gender healthcare problem was reported by 11/400 (02.75 per cent) from the general category and 7/200 (03.50 per cent) respondents from the professional category. A total of 18/600 (03.00 per cent) respondents reported it as an important health need. This response composes of the following district-wise responses. In district Budgam, eight respondents reported it from general category whereas seven respondents reported it from professionals. In district Anantnag, three respondents from general category reported it. Respondents from above mentioned districts reported it as a problem involved in gender health.
12. Less family support as gender healthcare problem was reported by 15/400 (03.75 per cent) respondents from the general category and 1/200 (00.50 per cent) respondent from the professional category. A total of 17/600 (02.83 per cent) respondent reported it as an important healthcare need. This response composes of the following district-wise responses. In district Budgam, 13 respondents reported it from general category where as one respondent reported it from professionals. In district Anantnag, two respondents from general category and one respondent from professional category reported it. Respondents from above mentioned districts reported it as a problem involved in gender healthcare.
13. Poverty as gender health problem was reported by 8/400 (02.00 per cent) respondents from the general category and 5/200 (02.50 per cent) respondents

from the professional category. A total of 13/600 (02.16 per cent) respondents reported it as an important healthcare need. This response composes of the following district-wise responses. In district Budgam, four respondents reported it from general category whereas three respondents reported it from professionals. In district Anantnag, four respondents from general category and two respondents from professional category reported it. Respondents from above mentioned districts reported it as a problem involved in gender healthcare.

14. Less preventive education as gender healthcare problem was reported by 06/400 (01.50 per cent) respondents from the general category and 07/200 (03.50 per cent) respondents from the professional category. A total of 13/600 (02.16 per cent) respondents reported it as an important healthcare need. This response composes of the following district-wise responses. In district Budgam, six respondents reported it from general category whereas seven respondents reported it from professionals. Respondents from above mentioned districts reported it as a problem involved in gender healthcare.

15. Illiteracy as gender healthcare problem was reported by 3/400 (00.75 per cent) respondents from the general category and 4/200 (02.00 per cent) respondents from the professional category. A total of 7/600 (01.16 per cent) respondents reported it as an important healthcare need. This response composes of the following district-wise responses. In district Srinagar, two respondents reported it from professionals. In district Baramulla, three respondents from general category and two respondents from professional category reported it. Respondents from above mentioned districts reported it as a problem involved in gender health.

16. Programmes not implemented fully as gender healthcare problem was reported by 5/400 (01.25 per cent) respondents from the general category and 5/200 (02.25 per cent) respondents from professionals reported it. A total of 5/600 (01.66 per cent) respondents reported it as an important healthcare need. This response composes of the following district-wise responses. In district Budgam, four respondents reported it from professionals. Respondents from above mentioned district reported it as a problem involved in gender healthcare.

17. Lack of supervision and accountability as gender healthcare problem was reported by 3/400 (00.75 per cent) respondents from the general category and 5/200 (02.50 per cent) respondents from professionals reported it. A total of 8/600 (01.33 per cent) respondents reported it as an important healthcare need. This response composes of the following district-wise

responses. In district Budgam, four respondents reported it from professionals. In district Anantnag, one respondent reported it from general. Respondents from above mentioned districts reported it as a problem involved in gender healthcare.

18. Drug abuse and Self-medication as gender healthcare problem was reported by 4/400 (01.00 per cent) respondents from the general category. A total of 4/600 (00.66 per cent) respondents reported it as an important health need. This response composes of the following district-wise responses. In district Budgam, 15 respondents reported it from general category whereas 10 respondents reported it from professionals. In district Anantnag, two respondents from general category and four respondents from professional category reported it. Respondents from above mentioned district reported it as a problem involved in gender health- care.

19. Violence against women as gender healthcare problem was reported by 1/400 (00.25 per cent) respondent from the general category and 1/200 (00.50 per cent) respondent from professionals reported it. A total of 2/600 (00.33 per cent) respondents reported it as an important healthcare need. This response composes of the following district-wise responses. In district Budgam, one respondent reported it from professionals. In district Anantnag, one respondent reported it from generals. Respondents from above mentioned district reported it as a problem involved in gender health care.

20. Complications during and after pregnancy as gender healthcare problem was reported by 2/200 (06.00 per cent) respondents from professionals reported it. A total of 17/600 (02.80 per cent) respondents reported it as an important health need. This response composes of the following district-wise responses. In district Budgam, two respondents reported it from professionals. Respondents from above mentioned districts reported it as a problem involved in gender healthcare.

21. Lack of funding schemes as gender healthcare problem was reported by 12/400 (03.00 per cent) respondents from the general category and 1/200 (00.50 per cent) respondent from the professional category. A total of 13/600 (02.16 per cent) respondents reported it as an important healthcare need. This response composes of the following district-wise responses. In district Srinagar, 11 respondents reported it from general category whereas one respondent reported it from professionals. In district Anantnag, one respondent from general category reported it. Respondents

from above mentioned districts reported it as a problem involved in gender healthcare.

22. Hectic work schedule and negligence by women as gender healthcare problem was reported by 17/400 (04.25 per cent) respondents from the general category and 14/200 (07.00 per cent) respondents from the professional category. A total of 31/600 (05.16 per cent) respondents reported it as an important healthcare need. This response composes of the following district-wise responses. In district Budgam, 13 respondents reported it from general category whereas 20 respondents reported it from professionals. In district Anantnag, two respondents from general category and one respondent from professional category reported it. Respondents from above mentioned districts reported it as a problem involved in gender healthcare.

23. Expensive treatment as gender health care problem was reported by 5/400 (01.25 per cent) respondents from the general category. A total of 05/600 (00.83 per cent) respondents reported it as an important healthcare need. This response composes of the following district-wise responses. In district Budgam, four respondents reported it from general category. In district Anantnag, one respondent from general category reported it. Respondents from above mentioned districts reported it as a problem involved in gender healthcare.

24. Less education as gender healthcare problem was reported by 04/400 (01.00 per cent) respondents from the general category and 07/200 (03.50 per cent) respondents from the professional category. A total of 11/600 (01.83 per cent) respondents reported it as an important healthcare need. This response composes of the following district-wise responses. In district Budgam, four respondents reported it from general category whereas seven respondents reported it from professionals. Respondents from above mentioned districts reported it as a problem involved in gender healthcare.

25. Too many children as gender healthcare problem was reported by 1/400 (00.25 per cent) respondent from the general category and 5/200 (02.50 per cent) respondents from the professional category. A total of 6/600 (01.00 per cent) respondents reported it as an important healthcare need . This response composes of the following district-wise responses. In district Budgam, one respondent reported it from general category whereas five respondents reported it from professionals. Respondents from above mentioned districts reported it as a problem involved in gender healthcare.

3. Gender Healthcare and Child Health

Finally, our investigation focussed on the nature of relationship between gender health and child health as the latter contributes (positively and negatively) to the former. Our respondents conveyed the following responses regarding this important relationship:

Table No 8.3: Relationship between Gender Healthcare and Child Health

S. No	Problems	D/ Srinagar G	D/ Srinagar P	D2 Budgam G	D2 Budgam P	D3 Anantnag G	D3 Anantnag P	D.4 Baramulla G	D.4 Baramulla P	Responses (No. & per cent) GT	Responses (No. & per cent) G	Responses (No. & per cent) P
1.	Interdependent	90.0	45.0	58.0	14.0	82.0	36.0	00.0	00.0	325 54.16	230 57.50	95.0 47.50
2.	Totally dependent	07.0	00.0	17.0	31.0	00.0	00.0	45.0	19.0	119 19.83	69.0 17.25	50.0 25.00
3.	Healthy mother can give birth to healthy child	00.0	00.0	25.0	00.0	07.0	07.0	00.0	00.0	39.0 06.50	32.0 08.00	07.00 3.50
4.	Post-marital counselling is important	00.0	00.0	00.0	01.0	00.0	00.0	00.0	00 .0	01.0 00.00	00.16 01.0	00.0 00.50
5.	Nutritional Dependency	00.0	00.0	00.0	00.0	05.0	02.0	44.0	24.0	75.0 12.25	12.50 26.0	49.0 13.00
6.	Mutual Relationship	00.0	00.0	00.0	00.0	05.0	05.0	00.0	00.0	10.0 02.50	01.66 05.0	05.0 01.25
7.	Important for Survival	00.0	00.0	00.0	00.0	00.0	00.0	11.0	07.0	18.0 02.75	03.00 07.0	11.0 03.50
	No response	03.0	05.0	00.0	04.0	01.0	00.0	00.0	00.0	13.0 01.00	02.16 09.0	04.0 04.50

The above table reveals the following points:

1. Relation between child health and gender healthcare as interdependent was reported by 230/400 (57.50 per cent) respondents from the general category and 95/200 (47.50 per cent) respondents from professional category.A total of 325/600 (54.16 per cent) respondents reported the relationship. This response composes of the following district-wise responses. In district Srinagar, 90 respondents reported it from general category whereas 45 respondents reported it from professional category. In district Budgam, 58 respondents reported it from general category while 14 respondents reported it from professionals. In district Anantnag, 82 respondents from general category and 36 respondents from professional category reported

it. Respondents from above mentioned districts reported the relationship between child health and gender healthcare as interdependent.

2. Relation between child health and gender healthcare as totally dependent was reported by 69/400 (17.25 per cent) respondents from the general category and 50/200 (25.00 per cent) respondents from professional category. A total of 119/600 (19.83 per cent) respondents reported the relationship. This response composes of the following district-wise responses. In district Srinagar, seven respondents reported it from general category. In district Budgam, 17 respondents reported it from general category while 31 reported it from professionals. In district Baramulla, 45 respondents from general category and 19 respondents from professional category reported it. Respondents from above mentioned districts reported the relationship between child health and gender healthcare as interdependent.

3. Nutritional dependency as the relation between child health and gender healthcare was reported by 49/400 (12.25 per cent) respondents from the general category and 26/200 (13.00 per cent) respondents from professional category. A total of 75/600 (12.50 per cent) respondents reported the relationship. This response composes of the following district-wise responses. In district Anantnag, five respondents from general category and four respondents from professional category reported it. In district Baramulla, 48 respondents from general category and 12.25 respondents from professional category reported it. Respondents from above mentioned districts reported the relationship between child health and gender healthcare as interdependent.

4. Healthy mother can give birth to healthy baby as response was reported by 32/400 (08.00 per cent) respondents from the general category and 7/200 (03.50 per cent) respondents from professional category. A total of 39/600 (06.50 per cent) respondents reported the relationship. This response composes of the following district-wise responses. In district Budgam, 25 respondents reported it from general category. In district Anantnag, seven respondents from general category and seven respondents from professional category reported it. Respondents from above mentioned districts reported the relationship between child health and gender health-care as highly interdependent.

5. Relation between child health and gender healthcare important for survival was reported by 11/400 (02.75 per cent) respondents from the general category and 07/200 (03.50 per cent) respondents from professional category. A total

of 18/600 (03.00 per cent) respondents reported the relationship. This response composes of the following district-wise responses. In district Baramulla, 11 respondents from general category and seven respondents from professional category reported it. Respondents from above mentioned districts reported the relationship between child health and gender healthcare as interdependent and important for survival.

6. Post- marital counselling is important was reported by 01/200 (00.50 per cent) respondent from professional category. A total of 1/600 (00.16 per cent) respondent reported it. This response composes of the following district-wise responses. In district Budgam, one respondent reported it from professionals. Respondents from above mentioned districts reported the relationship between child health and gender healthcare as interdependent.

7. Mutual relation between child health and gender healthcare was reported by 05/400 (01.25 per cent) respondents from the general category and 05/200 (02.50 per cent) respondents from professional category. A total of 10/600 (01.66 per cent) respondents reported the relationship. This response composes of the following district-wise responses. In district Anantnag, five respondents from general category and five respondents from professional category reported it. Respondents from above mentioned districts reported the relationship between child health and gender healthcare as mutual.

Two Case Studies

[i] Lal Ded Maternity Hospital, Srinagar.

[ii] G. B. Pant Children Hospital, Srinagar

(i) Lal Ded Maternity Hospital, Srinagar: An Assessment Report

1. Introduction

[i] History of the Hospital: Like other states in the country, the allopathic healthcare system got introduced in late eighteenth or early nineteenth century in Kashmir. The first modern health centre in Kashmir was started by the missionaries in Rainawari, Srinagar, an area dominated by the Kashmiri Pandits. This health institute has seen ups and downs and stands at present as functional major healthcare centre of sub-district status with the name of Jawaharlal Nehru Hospital. Subsequently, the biggest hospital with all healthcare facilities and services was established in the name of S.M.H.S. Hospital in interior city of Srinagar in early twentieth century by the then Dogra ruler. This hospital was the central place in Kashmir for overall healthcare and all governmen efforts were aimed at to develop, expand and make it an ideal place for multidisciplinary treatment in healthcare. After 1947, several organised and planned efforts were made by the government to make it an effective agency to fulfill all basic health needs of the people.

[ii] Functioning of the Hospital: However, women's health was not identified as a separate field to be concentrated upon. It was partly because there was no proper consciousness in this regard and partly because there was no formal initiative regarding gender healthcare separately. It was only in the early 1970s that the state government took the initiative for the establishment of special maternity hospital to provide specialist services and facilities for women, especially at the time of their delivery. Several other measures and schemes started by the Central government in the J&K state were adopted in order to provide all medical help to women suffering from major and minor diseases. Thus the Lal Ded Maternity Hospital was established in 1974 in order to provide specialised services and facilities and relevant expertise for pre-natal and post-natal care of pregnant mothers and to provide all medical help at the time of delivery. This was the first formal step towards the problem of gender healthcare in Kashmir. It still stands as the sole hospital in the Kashmir region for maternity treatment and other related medical facilities.

[iii] Facilities at the Hospital: While the maternity hospital was started with 100 bed capacity, it was upgraded to 300 beds in 1980-81 and later to 500 beds in 1985. In the last few years, a new block has been added to it and the bed-strength may go up to 600 beds. Our observation revealed that while the strength of the hospital is 500, two patients per bed were sharing in every ward. Even the labour rooms were not different. The only exception is the post-operative ward, where patients find a bed each just for a day post-operation.

The labour section is the most important part of the hospital. It consists of 13 smaller labour rooms each comprising of four single beds. Each bed is shared by two patients. Contrary to normal expectations, the labour section seems chaotic and each room contains four beds, eight patients and 16 attendants [two for each patient], two pregnant women, bearing the pain of their life, on a single bed. The post-operative ward is the only ward in the entire hospital where patients are provided with a single bed, at least for a day. It was reported that "there are three operation tables in the hospital for the critical patients, one each for emergency, post-emergency and SOS, which is agonising for patients who need to be operated upon immediately. The situation is grimmer during night hours when only two operation tables remain functional due to insufficient theatre strength [See *Greater Kashmir*, Srinagar, 22nd June, 2013].

The maternity hospital is attended by patients from nearby as well as from far flung areas. The records in the hospital confirm that on an average, the out-patient department [OPD] receives 600-700 obstretics and gynaecological cases daily [see *Kashmir* Reader, Srinagar, 23rd August, 2013]. According to another source, Lal Ded hospital has an average number of 350-400 patients in the OPD daily with 250 obstretics and 150 gynaecological patients. About 115 patients are admitted everyday as IDPs with about 80 obstretics and 35 gynaecological ailments. The hospital performs 45 major and 30 minor surgeries daily. About 20 deliveries and 40-45 lower segment caesarean operations are performed daily. The hospital has all necessary and modern equipments in the labortary, radiology section, laundry, blood bank, and anaesthesia. Another report says that this hospital has the distinction of having the highest number of caesarean operations. As per official sources, about 80-100 children are born in the hospital. Officials confirm that nearly half of these births are caesarean.

[iv] Staff of the Hospital: The official records show the following number of professional, semi-professional and administrative staff in the hospital:

Professional Staff		*Semi-professional Staff*		*Administrative Staff*	
Medical Superintendent	[01]	Asstt. Accounts Officer	[01]	Boiler Operator	[04]
Pathologist	[01]	Head Assistant	[01]	Electrician	[03]
Radiologist	[01]	Med. Rec. Supervisor	[01]	Telephone Operator	[02]
Asstt. Professor	[01]	Senior Assistants	[04]	Driver	[08]
Junior Anesthetist	[01]	Junior Assistant	[03]	Asstt. Matron	[01]
Paediatrician	[01]	Med. Rec. Tech.	[02]	Nursing Supervisor	[16]
Nursing Superintendent	[01]	Ticket writer	[02]	Nurses	[30 + 67]
M. O. Stores	[01]	Receptionist	[03]	ANMs	[54]
Radiologist	[01]	Histo. Path. Tech.	[01]	Dais	[14]
Blood Bank Officer	[01]	B. Bank Tech.	[01]	Nursing Orderly	[52]
Registrar	[05]	Clinical Path Tech.	[03]	Sweepers	[92]
Asstt. Surgeon	[03]	Labortary Tech.	[02]	Theatre boy	[14]
				Other class IV	[44]

2. The OPD Facilities

[i] The OPD of Lal Ded hospital is of great importance because it caters to the entire rush of such women patients in the valley. It has been observed that such patients from all areas, urban, rural and hilly, come to this hospital. It was reported that, because of this heavy rush of patients, most of them and their attendants faced several problems. They have to wait for hours and days [and

even weeks] for their turn in the que for check up, consultation, etc. Some pregnant women faced several problems by wasting so much time in waiting in the que. It was reported that the hospital is always jam-packed as it is thronged by patients from across the valley. Every day around 120 patients are admitted to the hospital. Under such circumstances, it is not possible to provide a bed for each patient. Thus, overcrowding in the hospital in general and OPD in particular tells upon the working of the staff as well as the health of patients. The overload of work decreases the efficiency of all medicos, non-medical staff and others involved. It also led to short-cut practices in the hospital on the part of doctors. It was also conveyed that in such a situation some doctors, male and female, were influenced by power or money.

3. The IPD Facilities

[i] Since Lal Ded hospital is sole medical centre for providing maternity related treatment, all gender ailments are taken care of here. Different gender related medicinal and surgical ailments are treated in the hospital. It was observed that various needed medical facilities and services were provided in the IPD. It was also observed that doctors, para-medical personnel, attendants and maids took full care of the problems of the patients in different wards.

4. Supply of Medicines

[i] In all government hospitals in the state, all basic and necessary drugs are provided to the patients. But in Lal Ded hospital, this is not the practice. Patients, particularly in-patients, are provided the cheapest analgesic and antibiotic tablets but not the important and life saving and costly drugs even the drugs which are supplied to the patients were reportedly found fake and spurious. In the recent years, several scams and frauds related to fake drug supply were unearthed by the authorities in different hospitals in the valley, including this hospital. It was found that this had happened because of the involvement of health administrators, bureaucrats and politicians. It has also been reported that there remain shortage of even these are drugs in the hospital, though these funded by the budget allocations.

5. Child Delivery in the Hospital

[i] The main function of this hospital is to deal with child delivery. Till some time back when the district and sub-district status hospitals [having maternity facilities and expertise] and several private nursing homes were not in all areas in the valley, this hospital was the only medical centre to take care of deliveries. Now, the rush has decreased but overcrowding still exists in this

hospital. At present, above 90 per cent female deliveries are medically treated here.

[ii] Since the awareness about institutional deliveries has increased tremendously, there has also been proportionate increase in the rush for deliveries in this central place of maternal health facilities. According to experts, the proportion of caesarean surgeries in Lal Ded hospital was per 100 deliveries which stands undesirable and reflects the non-professional treatment at the hands of doctors. The huge rush of delivery cases in every stage of treatment makes the ideal treatment for deliveries difficult. As a result of this kind of treatment, frequent death of pregnant mothers and their unborn children take place. This inhuman treatment of women in Lal Ded hospital has increased significantly in the previous years, especially after 2008. At that time, several deaths were reported in this hospital at the hands of negligent and irresponsible doctors. This led to mass protests against these practices in the hospital and demand was made for efficient treatment of women during delivery.

6. Corruption in the Hospital

[i] The financial corruption is common in Lad Ded hospital. In fact, it is considered as one of the grave non-medical problems in the hospital which deteriorates and degenerates the social environment in the hospital. Though this trend is common among the non-medical and class IV staff members, the doctors cannot absolve themselves from this charge absolutely. Many of them are doing private practice like any other business. They do this practice even during office hours. In this way, they have commercialised this profession and dehumanised the sacred practice.

[ii] Moreover, there prevails corruption in this hospital in different forms and at different stages. *First,* the drug companies, called the drug *mafia* here, consistently approach the doctors and health administrators and present their gifts and commissions and get their fake and sub-standard drugs approved in the government hospitals and circulate in the markets also for selling to the needy people. This entire work is carried out in league and encouragement of the health administration and politicians.

[ii] *Second,* the Lal Ded hospital is famous for looting the relatives of the women[who have delivered a child, especially the male child] at the time of new-born baby. At that time, the entire para-medical staff and class IV staff members bounce upon relatives and virtually loot them financially. They grab everything in their pockets on the name of *'chai'* and *'bakhshish'.*

[iii] *Third,* Lal Ded hospital is notorious for smuggling or stealing the new-born male babies at the time of their birth. The practice is that the para-medical staff member with the passive or silent support of her/his support smuggle/

steal the babies inside or outside the hospital and hand over to the needed persons who pay them hefty amounts. Hundreds of such cases have been reported every month and every year in the local print media.

[iv] Some sad but real stories of this situation can be heard in any section of this hospital. In this connection, a local daily gave the relevant details of this stealing of the child in the hospital [see *Greater Kashmir,* Srinagar, 30 April, 2013].

7. Conflict and the Hospital

[i] The Lal Ded hospital was a reputed medical institution during the decades of 1970s and 1980s for its functioning, services, and facilities. But the deviation from standard practices, violation of norms, and degeneration of human values and behaviour became common in the hospital after the militancy started in Kashmir in 1989-1990. It generally led to a downward trend in every health sector and field. But militants and security forces violated the sanctity of the hospital and used it for their interests and gains. Nobody, insider or outsider, could stop that steep deterioration from bad to worse situation in the health and hospital culture. This led to a critical situation in which the hospital practices, services and facilities faced extreme exploitation and misuse and touched their lowest standards. The doctors and para-medical staff preferred to be silent or absent from duty and the government or its role was not visible anywhere. This also led to the destruction of infrastructure in the hospital and no new technology could be introduced here.

[ii] However, from mid-1990s, the situation started improving in the hospital and universal values, norms and standards of health and hospital could be maintained again, though slowly. But, the important fact is that, during the decades of militancy and afterwards, the processes of deterioration and degeneration were institutionalised and it was difficult to root them out completely and immediately. Thus, though the ideal practices, values and norms related to health and hospital culture could be revived, some problems became chronic and continue in one form or the other. These problems included the following:

- Violation of values and norms,
- Absence from duty of medical and para-medical staff,
- Carelessness and irresponsibility of hospital administration and health administration,
- Institutionalisation of practices of corruption in all health sectors, sections and fields,
- Emergence of the practice of child theft at the time of birth of new babies,

- Disorientation of all services and facilities,
- Increased deaths at the time of delivery, and
- Supply of fake and sub-standard medicines to all government hospitals in league with health professionals and health administrators.

8. Hospital Management

[i] The affairs of the hospital from the professional point of view is messy. It is in shambles and nobody is accountable here. The norms of medical decency, governance and work culture were flouted in broad day light and with full consciousness. Thus, existing situation can be characterised as *'chaos'* and 'crisis'. It needs complete and radical change at every stage and in every area and section. In order to make this hospital a place of decent place for gender healthcare, a group of eminent experts and professionals must guide this grand effort of radical transformation.

(ii.) G.B. Pant Children Hospital: An Assessment Report

1. Introduction and Development

[i] Kashmir had no separate and specific healthcare centre exclusively for children till the recent past. It was only in the mid-1970s that a particular children hospital was established in Srinagar by the state government. This was a humble formal state initiative towards the child healthcare in the state. This new hospital was located in the close neighbourhood building of Lal Ded Maternity hospital which made the approach to the former more easy and fast. It was because all newly born cases in the maternity hospital which developed any kind of complication or abnormality were referred to and immediately taken to the children hospital. They could be treated by the concerned expert doctors. This initial effort for the child healthcare on the part of the state government of J&K had small accommodation. But, with the little infrastructure and other lesser facilities, number of child healthcare facilities and services increased and this hospital treated all children who were taken there for treatment.

[ii] In 1985, the Children hospital was shifted to another place in the city, i.e., Sonawar by the government mainly because of lesser

space and accommodation available at the earlier place. However, this decision with good intentions and objectives didn't prove purposeful because of three major reasons. *First,* the new area was a congested area in comparison to the earlier one, so was not more suitable for the hospital. *Second,* the new area fell within the cantonement area of the city, which is generally controlled by the army with no local administration's intervention. *Third,* this led to the problem of 'dual control' of the hospital, one the state authorities and second the army authorities. In this type of situation, the hospital at the new place could not prosper and developed the features of mis-management, mal-administration, no accountability and so on in the hospital. The cumulative effect of this situation was felt in the deterioration in the practices of treatment, facilities and services. This all reflected in the increasing number of infant deaths in the recent years, for which this hospital became notorious.

2. Facilities in the Hospital

[i] It is clear that this hospital for children exclusively started functioning with lesser infrastructure and medical facilities. In this limited framework, the hospital could not increase and expand its services. However, it performed some basic and important functions related to child healthcare, particularly the following three:

[a] It provided all possible–available treatment to all children who were victims of dreaded and acute diseases;

[b] It provided all possible-available important and necessary healthcare to children who were referred to it from maternity hospital and other district level hospitals. In actuality, most of the children born in Lal Ded Maternity Hospital were taken to this hospital if they developed some abnormality.

[c] Some children who were the vicitims of dreaded and acute diseases were admitted and treated for shorter period. This treatment was not available at any other hospital in the valley.

[ii] In totality, the hospital did not perform the role of an ideal healthcare institution because of its limitations in the fields of medical facilities and finances. This situation of the children hospital could not be improved after it was shifted to the new place in the

cantonement area. It was reported that these conditions led to deterioration in all standard practices in the hospital. This particularly reflected in the

[a] Decrease of the strength of the hospital patients– 185 in 1975 in the old place to 135 in 1985 in the new place; and

[b] Highest number of infant deaths in the hospital which raised the infant mortality rate to the alarming level in previous few years.

3. Staff Strength of the Hospital

[i] According to the official records of the hospital, it maintains the following professional staff on its roll at present:

- Professors 03
- Associate Professors 04
- Assistant Professors 04
- Lecturers 05

[ii] The hospital had following gazette staff members:

- Medical Superintendent 01
- Deputy Medical Superintendent 01
- Resident Medical Officer 01
- Radiologist 01
- Registrar 03
- Assistant Surgeon 03
- Matron 01

[iii] The hospital had the superior staff as mentioned below:

• Head Assistant	01	Junior Stenographer	01
• Account Assistant	01	Junior Assistant	03
• Senior Assistant	03	Med. Rec. Technician	03
• G. S. Keeper	01	X-Ray Technician	02
• X-Ray Assistant	02	Drivers	04

•	S. Inspector	01	Th. Sister	01
•	Junior Electrician	02	Lady Receptionist	01
•	Head Pharmacist	01	Sup Pharmacist	02
•	Sr. Pharmacist	01	JR. Pharmacist	05
•	Lab. Tech	02	Lab Asstt	08
•	Asstt. Matron	01	N/supervisors	04
•	Senior Gr. Nurses	09	Junior Gr. Nurses	29
•	ANM	27		

[iv] The hospital has the following inferior staff members on its rol:

•	Carpenter	01	Dhobi	02
•	Sr. Plumber	01	Jr. Plumber	01
•	Tailor	01	Lab Boy	02
•	B. Boy	01	Barber	01
•	Cook	02	Dresser	01
•	Hallporter	02	Tel. Boy	02
•	X-Ray Boy	01	Gardner	01
•	Lineman	02	Cleaner	02
•	Chowkidar	02	Orderly	05
•	N/orderly	31	Sweeper	34

[v] The hospital has following additional plan staff:

•	Child Psychologist	01	Health Educator	01
•	Social Worker	01	Med Rec Tech.	01

4. Supply of Sub-standard Drugs

[i] One of the grave problems which the hospital faces at present is the supply of sub-standard drugs in the form of fake and spurious drugs which are supplied to the patients. This problem has two major aspects which follow:

[a] these drugs are continuously supplied to patients in the hospital. They have no choice except to accept these medicines, which have negative impact in child patients, from doctors and para-medical staff; and

[b] these drugs are supplied to the hospital without any break despite extreme criticism from civil society and the media.

These drugs are supplied with the support of health professionals and administrators in the hospital. In fact, some of them are in league with representatives of drug companies, called *'drug mafia'*. Thus all three sections share the responsibility of the supply of sub-standard drugs to the children hospital and to other hospitals and health centres also. Even these drugs are not supplied regularly to the patients. It was reported that the financial assistance for purchase of life saving drugs under JSSK scheme is not provided to them.

It has been observed that this problem of fake drugs supply has been highlighted by the civil society, professionals and local media. But, the government of the state has not been able to control the menace effectively. Several inquiries after the exposure of drug scams in the hospital have been ordered by the government, but no major effect was reportedly experienced.

5. Highest Number of Infant Deaths

[i] Another grave problem faced by the hospital is alarming number of infant deaths in recent years. According to recent reports, the dangerous level of infant deaths in the hospital was going on for several years [see reports about infant deaths in G.B. Pant Hospital, Greater Kashmir, Srinagar; June, 2013]. The media reports revealed the following relevant information:

- In 2012, nine infant deaths took place in just 24 hours in the children hospital,
- During the same year, 41 deaths in the month of May in the children hospital were registered,
- 32 infant deaths were reported in the children hospital in first 15 days of May 2012,
- 480 infant deaths were registered in the year 2012 in the children hospital,
- Total number of 400 infant deaths were recorded in last 12 months in children hospital, and

- Total number of 3,800 infant deaths was recorded since 2008 in the children hospital.

It was also reported that State Human Rights Commission and civil society organisations took strong notice of mass infant deaths and asked the concerned authorities to stop it immediately. Even the Chief Minister of the state ordered an inquiry into this huge number of infant deaths in the children hospital [*Ibid*].Thus, this hospital became notorious for infant deaths in huge numbers and so it was labeled as 'killer hospital'.

Thus, the existing situation clearly reveals that G. B. Pant Children hospital has experienced highest number of infant deaths in J&K. The hard fact stands that this grave situation has occurred because of the following factors:

- Complete negligence of health professionals, i.e., doctors, experts and other professionals towards child patients;
- Complete neglect of rules, laws, values and norms by the health administration at all levels;
- Continuous supply of sub-standard drugs to the hospital on the one hand and to the patients on the other, i. e., children who are the only victim of this practice; and
- Total apathy of concerned authorities in the hospital and in the government for a long time.

6. Corruption Practices

Another grave problem faced by the children hospital is the practice of corruption. It exists at all levels, in all areas, in all sections, and at all times. The entire ethos of the hospital has been corrupted. It was reported in the local media that there are two types of corruption in the hospital which are:

[a] corrupt practices related to commission and gifts to doctors and others in the hospital; and

[b] corrupt practices related to the compulsion for paying for various services and facilities in the hospital.

Our observation revealed that this situation prevails in the hospital in extreme form. As sincere, committed and honest people are not available in the hospital, the corruption increases and gets strong roots. This situation has certainly led to extreme form of deterioration and degeneration. In the recent past, the government tried to overhaul the entire top administration, but it has not led to serious change.

7. Critical Conditions in the Hospital

In addition to the above-mentioned problems, the children hospital faces some other conditions which have made the situation more abnormal and dangerous. The consequences of the present situation have undermined the role of standard practices in the hospital. This situation reveals in the following functional conditions:

[i] ***Absence of Work Culture:*** The most undesirable social condition which has emerged in the hospital during last three decades is directly related to the maintenance of healthcare is the absence of work culture which has polluted the whole environment. It crudely reflects in the–

[a] Negligence of child patients by doctors and others,

[b] Irresponsibility of the hospital administration,

[c] Absenteeism of semi-professional and administrative staff, and

[d] Complete apathy of the concerned official authority.

The lack of work culture prevails in every section and every field and has created a situation of normlessness. This has also led to the rise of pathological situation of non-accountability and non-responsiveness in the hospital and has marred its proper functioning.

[ii] ***Private Practice of the Professional Staff:*** It has been reported in the local media repeatedly and was also observed that a significant number of doctors and semi-professional staff members are engaged in private practice in their private clinics. It has also been observed that some of them do this practice even during office hours which is totally illegal and immoral. But, nobody has bothered to warn and stop them from this act of devastating impact on child healthcare. In actuality, it has negatively affected the ideal practices of healthcare in the sole children hospital in the valley.

[iii] ***Non-availability and Non-issue of Medicines:*** The condition of supply of sub-standard drugs was explained in this report earlier. Even these medicines are reportedly not available as per the needs of patients. So, most patients are compelled to purchase these medicines from the open market.

[iv] ***No Proper Ambulances:*** It was reported that there was lack of proper and up-to-date ambulances with the children hospital, though it composed one of the primary component parts of child healthcare system. It was reported that every child patient suffers because these ambulances lack some basic facilities and services such as stretcher, first aid box, gas cylendars and integrated super-speciality kit. It was also reported that most of these vehicles were not found useful and purposeful due to lack of these basic medical facilities.

[v] ***Non-performance of the Diagonastic Laboratory:*** Though the hospital has a diagonastic lab with little facilities and services, it has not proved purposeful absolutely. Reportedly, it was either found without necessary and up to date technology for tests or these machines were often found defunct and these were not repaired for months and years together. In this grim situation, the attendants of child patients were compelled to go to the nearby market for diagonstic tests, which were carried out at the private clinics owned by the doctors and para-medical staff of the hospital.

[vi] ***The Oxygen Plant:*** This hospital has one oxygen plant which is supposed to fulfill the concerned needs of the hospital. But as was reported, it faces the threat of becoming non-functional mainly due to overloading. The information gained in this regard is that this plant at present is overloaded with 22,000 oxygen point and 14 ventilators are functional in different wards of the hospital. The fact is that the plant has the capacity of 446 litres per minute, but it is forced to supply 1,000 litres per minute to meet the emergency services and facilities. As revealed by the technical engineering section of this hospital, there is the possibility of its collapse at any time in future.

8. Conflict and the Hospital

It is correct that like other hospitals and health centres in Kashmir, this hospital too faced the negative implications of conflict during last two decades which led to deterioration in its services and facilities. But, at the same time, it is argued by experts and professionals here that all abnormalities in the hospital, like other hospitals in the valley, cannot be related exclusively with the conflict impact. In actuality, there are other factors of equal importance, which need to be identified, so that a proper perspective of the problems faced by the hospital could be understood and later on resolved. All present day problems of this hospital can also be related to the negligence of doctors and professionals, irresponsible attitude and behaviour of hospital administration, absence of work culture among para-medical and administrative staff members, selfish and corrupt approach of the class IV employees, complete apathetic attitude of state functionaries, non-intervention of the government in the hospital affairs, and others responsible for steep deterioration and degeneration.

Section - C

Perceptions, Suggestions and Conclusions

9

Major Gender Healthcare Issues

After observing various responses of the respondents, these could be summed up in six major GHC issues, whose explanation is given below:

1. Family Planning

(i) Family planning is less preferred has been told by 40/600 (06.66 per cent) respondents. The response has been revealed by 40/100 general respondents of district Srinagar. In a male dominated society where woman is subjugated, is left with one more burden of family planning due to which mainly Tubectomy is preferred as a permanent method of family planning. This has been revealed by 39/600 (06.50 per cent) respondents. In district Budgam, 08/100 and 08/50 general and professional respondents respectively are of the view that Tubectomy is preferred among people as a family planning method. In district Anantnag, 12/100 general respondents and 11/50 professionals are of the same view.

(ii) Education and awareness regarding family planning methods is very essential for reproductive and child health has been revealed by 36/600 (06.00 per cent) respondents. In district Budgam, 10/100 general respondents and 06/50 professionals are of the same view. In district Anantnag, 18/100 general respondents and 02/50 professional respondents revealed that improving education in this regard is very important.

(iii) Contraceptive pills are being used as a family planning method or child spacing method among women has been revealed by 20/600 (03.33 per cent). In district Budgam, 07/50 professionals reveal that contraceptive pills are being used among women. In district Anantnag, 13/100 general respondents reveal that women use the same for avoiding pregnancies.

(iv) Following religious practices are considered important for production of children. In Islam, using family planning methods is not considered a good practice due to which many people don't go for it. This response has been conveyed by 13/600 (02.16 per cent) respondents. In district Budgam, 04/100 general respondents and 09/100 general respondents of district Anantnag have given the same response.

(v) People usually go for family planning methods after having three children has been revealed by 10/600 (01.66 per cent) respondents. This response has been taken from 10/100 general respondents of district Srinagar only.

(vi) Due to ongoing armed conflict in the valley, many families have lost their children and rendered various parents childless, which created a fear psychosis among people, so people preferred more children, especially rural people where intensity of conflict was more. This response has been put forth by 07/600 (01.16 per cent) respondents. In district Budgam, 01/100 general respondents and 03/50 professionals have revealed this response and in district Anantnag, 03/100 general respondents are of the same view.

(vii) Various policies and programmes started by government related to providing of incentives to families which follow the two child norm and go for permanent family planning methods (Tubectomy and vasectomy) after having two healthy children is considered desirable. This response has been put forth by 05/600 (00.83 per cent) respondents who belong to general respondents of district Anantnag.

2. Gender Sex Ratio

The sex ratio is the number of males and females for every 100 females in a population. Sex ratio affects various aspects of social life, including the availability of potential marriage partners and the composition of the labour force. Sex ratios among newborn is typically around 105 males per 100 females; however that changes considerably at older ages because women outlive men. The response related to this and other matters conveyed by respondents is explained as follows;

(i) The sex ratio in Kashmir is normal has been revealed by 132/600 (22.00 per cent) respondents. In district Srinagar, 60/100 general respondents have revealed that sex ratio is normal in state. In district Budgam, 58/100 general respondents and 10/50 professionals have given the same response. In district Anantnag, 04/100 general respondents are of the same view.

(ii) The female sex ratio in state has declined to a larger extent as per census 2011 was revealed by 34/600 (05.66 per cent) respondents in all the four districts. In district Srinagar, 20/100 general respondents have revealed that there is a decline in female sex ratio. In district Budgam, 05/100 general respondents and 01/50 professionals are of the same view. In district Anantnag, 04/100 general respondents and 04/50 professionals have given the same response.

(iii) Extensive moral and religious education can help in bringing a balance in population has been revealed by 30/600 (05.00 per cent) respondents who compose of 22/400 (05.50 per cent) general respondents and 08/200 (04.00 per cent) of professionals. The response has been revealed by 22/100 general respondents and 08/50 professionals in district Anantnag.

(iv) Proper legislative measures are very important for bringing a population control in the society. The view that enforce strict laws to prevent illegal abortions has been put forth by 26/600 (04.33 per cent) respondents who compose of 22/400 (05.50 per cent) general respondents and 04/200 (02.00 per cent) professional respondents. The response has been put forth by 22/100 general respondents and 04/50 professionals in district Anantnag.

(v) 07/600 (01.16 per cent) respondents have revealed that the NRHM, which is central level programme, has a greater influence in all the areas of women and child health. MCTS (mother child tracking system) in NRHM system has curbed more population has been revealed by 07/600 (01.16 per cent) respondents who compose of 02/400 (00.50 per cent) general respondents and 05/200 (02.50 per cent) professionals. This response has been given by 02/100 general respondents and 05/50 professionals in district Anantnag.

(vi) 01/600 (00.16 per cent) respondents have given the responses that like inadequate facilities in health centrs is a reason for such negative gender issues. This response has been revealed by 01/100 general respondent in district Anantnag. Decline in sex ratio is an emerging issue nowadays has been revealed by 01/50 professional respondent in district Baramulla. Empowerment of women is necessary to tackle this issue has been revealed by 01/100 general responde of district Anantnag. Dowry has become the main reason for emergence of such issues has been revealed by 01/100 general respondent in district Anantnag.

3. Female Foeticide

Female foeticide means sex selective abortion which is the practice of terminating a pregnancy based upon the predicted sex of the baby. The selective abortion of female foetuses is most common in areas where cultural norms value male children over female children. Sex selective abortion can affect the human sex ratio. In this regard, the following responses were conveyed by respondents in this study:

(i) Female foeticide is being illegally done at many places has been revealed by a 153/600 (25.50 per cent) respondents, who consist of 110/400 (27.50 per cent) general and 43/200 (21.40 per cent) professional respondents. In district Srinagar, 30/100 general respondents have given the same response. In district Anantnag, 23/100 general respondents and 14/50 professionals have responded in the same way. In district Baramulla, 57/100 general respondents and 29/50 professionals have given the same response.

(ii) Female foeticide is not much common nowadays due to the ban imposed on any such practice has been put forth by 78/600 (13.00 per cent) respondents, who compose of 48/400 (12.00 per cent) general respondents and 30/200 (15.00 per cent) professionals. In district Budgam, 04/50 professionals have given this response. In district Anantnag, 05/100 general respondents and 07/50 professionals have given the above response. In district Baramulla, 43/100 general respondents and 19/50 professionals are of the same view.

(iii) Strict law enforcement is important for bringing control in population has been revealed by 26/600 (04.33 per cent) respondents, composing of 16/400 (04.00 per cent) general respondents and 10/200 (05.00 per cent) professionals in total. In district Budgam, the same response has been highlighted by 11/100 general respondents and 07/50 professionals. In district Anantnag, 05/100 general respondents and 03/50 professionals are of the same view.

(iv) Awareness regarding this type of abortion needs to be changed and improved has been revealed by 24/600 (04.00 per cent) respondents, composing of 11/400 (02.75 per cent) general and 13/200 (06.50 per cent) professional respondents. In district Budgam, 01/50 professional respondents have given the same response. In district Anantnag, 11/100 general respondents and 12/50 professionals are of the same view.

(v) Social evils like dowry is mainly responsible for such crime has been revealed by 21/600 respondents who belong to general category. In district Srinagar, 20/100 general respondents have given the same response. In district Anantnag, 01/100 general respondents are of the same view.

(vi) Private and unregistered clinics are mainly responsible for carrying out such tests has been revealed by 20/600 (03.33 per cent) respondents who compose of 11/400 (02.75 per cent) general respondents and 09/200 (04.50 per cent) professionals. The response has been put forth also by 11/100 general respondents and 09/50 professionals in district Budgam.

(vii) NRHM a centrally sponsored scheme is aimed to curb such practices by MCTS as one of its components, has been revealed by 17/600 (02.83 per cent) respondents, of whom 12/400 (03.00 per cent) compose from general category and 05/200 (02.50 per cent) professionals. The response has also revealed by 12/100 general respondents and 05/50 professionals in district Budgam.

(viii) Even if the case of female foeticide occur people usually do not report about it, the response has been put forth by 15/600 (02.50 per cent) respondents, Out of whom 13/400 (03.25 per cent) respondents belong to general category and 02/200 (01.00 per cent) are professional respondents. The response has also been revealed by 13/100 general respondents and 02/50 professionals in district Budgam.

(ix) Moral and religious education need to be imparted to curb this practice has been revealed by 11/600 respondents of whom 05/400 are general respondents and 06/200 professionals. In district Budgam, 02/50 professionals have given the same response. In district Anantnag, 05/100 general respondents and 04/50 professionals are of the same view.

(x) Gender bias is responsible for such practices has been revealed by 08/600 respondents, of whom all are the respondents belonging to general category. The response has been put forth also by 08/100 general respondents from district Anantnag.

(xi) A total number of 02/600 (00.33 per cent) respondents have given the response like, female foeticide mainly take place in case of unwanted pregnancies, who consist of 01/400 (00.25 per cent) general respondent and 01/200 (00.50 per cent) professionals. The response has been given by 01/100 general respondent and 01/50 professionals from district Budgam.

4. Maternal Mortality (MM)

Maternal death is the death of a woman while pregnant or within 42 days of termination of pregnancy, irrespective of the duration and site of the pregnancy, from any cause related to or aggravated by the pregnancy or its management but not from accidental or incidental causes. The responses conveyed by our respondents during investigation are as follows:

(i) Institutional deliveries have reduced MM has been revealed by 143/600 (23.83 per cent) respondents, of whom 90/400 (22.50 per cent) are general respondents and 53/200 (26.50 per cent) professionals. In district Budgam, 05/100 general respondents and 03/50 professionals have given the above response. In district Anantnag, 08/50 professionals were of the same view. In district Baramulla, 85/100 general respondents & 42/50 professionals have given the same response.

(ii) MM has reduced to a larger extent has been revealed by 89/600 (14.83 per cent) respondents who composed of 65/400 (16.25 per cent) general respondents and 24/200 (12.00 per cent) professionals. In district Srinagar, 40/100 general respondents have given the same response. In district Budgam, 15/100 general respondents and 14/50 professionals are of same view. In district Anantnag, 10/100 general respondents and 10/50 professionals have revealed that maternal mortality has reduced. The main reason of MM is inadequate facilities and weak referral system was put forth by 55/600 (09.16 per cent) respondents, of whom 40/400 (10.00 per cent) are of general category and 15/200 (07.50 per cent) professionals. In district Budgam, 25/100 general respondents and 06/50 professional respondents have given the above response. In district Anantnag, 15/100 general respondents and 09/50 professionals were of the same view.

(iii) Unavailability of specialised maternity hospitals is one of the reasons for MM has been revealed by 41/600 (06.83 per cent) respondents, of whom 31/400 (07.75 per cent) are of general category and 10/200 (05.00 per cent) are professional respondents. The response has been revealed by 31/100 general respondents and 10/50 professionals in district Budgam.

(iv) Mass awareness religious and moral education can help in curbing this problem has been revealed by 23/600 (03.83 per cent) respondents, of whom 15/400 (03.75 per cent) are of general category and 08/200 (04.00 per cent) professionals. The response has been revealed by 15/100 general respondents and 08/50 professionals in district Anantnag.

(v) Recruiting female counsellors and their active role can help in addressing the problem of MM has been revealed by 04/600 (00.66 per cent) respondents who were of professional category. The response has been put forth by 04/50 professional respondents in district Anantnag.

5. Cultural Restrictions

(i) Cultural restrictions had contributed to gender bias due to which women are being less cared in the field of healthcare. The response has been given by

59/600 (09.83 per cent) respondents, of whom 38/400 (09.50 per cent) were of general category and 21/200 (10.50 per cent) were professional respondents. In district Budgam, 27/100 general respondents and 08/50 professionals have given the same response. In district Anantnag, 11/100 general respondents and 13/50 professionals have given the same response.

(ii) Cultural restrictions on GHC are more prevalent in far flung areas, the response has been put forth by 22/600 (03.66 per cent) respondents. The respondents compose of 15/400 (03.75 per cent) general respondents and 07/200 (03.50 per cent) professionals. The response has been given by 15/100 general respondents and 07/50 professionals in district Budgam.

(iii) Less importance is generally given to gender healthcare has been revealed by 10/600 (01.66 per cent) respondents, of whom 08/400 (02.00 per cent) are general respondents and 02/200 (01.00 per cent) professionals. The response has been revealed by 08/100 general respondents and 02/50 professionals in district Anantnag.

(iv) To overcome cultural restrictions, gender specialised treatment is needed, the response has been given by 172/600 (28.66 per cent) respondents These respondents compose of 105/400 (26.25 per cent) general respondents and 67/200 (33.50 per cent) professionals. In district Budgam, 01/50 professionals have given the same response. In district Anantnag, 11/100 general respondents and 16/50 professionals are of the same view. In district Baramulla, 94/100 general respondents and 50/50 professionals have given the same response.

(v) There is a great need of stopping negative affects and cultural restrictions, has been put forward by 150/600 (25.00 per cent) respondents. They compose of 100/400 (25.00 per cent) general respondents and 50/200 (25.00 per cent) professionals. The response has been revealed by 100/100 general respondents and 50/50 professionals in district Baramulla.

(vi) Cultural restrictions have reduced now to larger extent have been put forth by 05/600 (00.83 per cent) respondents which belong to general category. In district Budgam, 03/100 general respondents have given the same response. In district Anantnag, 02/100 general respondents are of the same view.

(vii) Less education and inadequate facilities led to cultural restrictions has been revealed by 03/600 (00.50 per cent) respondents belonging to general category. The response has been given by 03/100 general respondents of district Budgam.

10

Gender Healthcare System – Positive Point of View

After studying various aspects, dimensions, problems and issues of Gender-negative healthcare system through our empirical investigation, we now turn to the explanation of Gender-positive healthcare system and its features, needs and problems. It is healthcare system which does not allow gender differentiation and discrimination and fulfill all just health needs of women. This new healthcare system demands dropping of certain obsolete practices and processes and adoption of new practices and processes. In other words, we enquire in this study what is lacking in the existing healthcare system which needs to be restored in order to serve health interests of women in a better way. It is also to be probed how government and the private sector can provide help in evolving such a gender-equity healthcare system. Moreover, the important matter in this regard is how the medical and paramedical staff can be trained to work for the creation, evolution and development of the gender positive health care system. Our investigation in this regard gave the responses as noted below:

1. Limitations of Present Healthcare System

As has been explained, the present day healthcare system has some serious limitations for the gender healthcare in general, various things are lacking in this system which come as a big halt as far as gender health needs are concerned. Our enquiry in this regard gave us the responses noted in the following table;

Table 10.1: What is Lacking in Health Care System?

S. No.	*Lacking in Present Health Care System*	*D1 Srinagar*		*D2 Budgam*		*D3 Anantnag*		*D4 Baramulla*		*Responses (No. and Per cent)*		
		G	*p*	*G*	*P*	*G*	*P*	*G*	*p*	*GT*	*G*	*P*
1.	Female Gynaecologists/Doctors	61.0	25.0	75.0	19.0	66.0	32.0	78.0	39.0	395 (65.83)	280 (70.00)	115 (57.50)
2.	Concerned Facilities and infrastructure	97.0	35.0	80.0	34.0	54.0	13.0	32.0	25.0	370 (61.67)	263 (65.75)	107 (53.50)
3.	Separate hospitals for women	00.0	02.0	00.0	00.0	14.0	06.0	40.0	15.0	77.0 (12.83)	54.0 (13.50)	23.0 (11.50)
4.	Concerned Policies and Programmes	32.0	00.0	00.0	00.0	00.0	00.0	00.0	00.0	32.0 (05.33)	00.0 (00.00)	32.0 (16.00)
5.	Medical Attention	49.0	07.0	00.0	00.0	00.0	00.0	00.0	00.0	56.0 (09.33)	49.0 (12.25)	07.0 (03.50)
6.	Adultered drugs/ Medicines	55.0	01.0	00.0	00.0	00.0	00.0	00.0	00.0	56.0 (09.33)	55.0 (13.75)	01.0 (00.50)
7.	Funds availability	04.0	00.0	00.0	00.0	00.0	00.0	00.0	00.0	04.0 (00.66)	00.0 (00.00)	04.0 (02.00)
8.	Meager Facilities In PHC's	00.0	01.0	00.0	00.0	00.0	00.0	00.0	00.0	01.0 (00.16)	01.0 (00.25)	00.0 (00.00)
9.	Less HealthEducation/ Educators and Awareness	00.0	01.0	08.0	00.0	12.0	05.0	00.0	00.0	26.0 (04.33)	20.0 (05.00)	06.0 (03.00)
10.	No Special Gender Treatment	00.0	02.0	00.0	00.0	00.0	00.0	48.0	29.0	81.0 (13.50)	50.0 (12.50)	31.0 (15.50)
11.	No Privacy of Women in Health Centres.	00.0	01.0	00.0	00.0	00.0	00.0	00.0	00.0	01.0 (00.16)	00.0 (00.00)	01.0 (00.50)
12.	No 24 X 7 Services for Women	00.0	00.0	01.0	01.0	00.0	00.0	00.0	00.0	02.0 (00.33)	01.0 (00.25)	01.0 (00.50)
13.	No Drug Quality	00.0	00.0	10.0	00.0	01.0	00.0	00.0	00.0	11.0 (01.83)	00.0 (00.00)	11.0 (05.50)
14.	Supply of Medicines	00.0	00.0	11.0	12.0	34.0	14.0	00.0	00.0	71.0 (11.83)	45.0 (11.25)	26.0 (13.00)
15.	No Fair Price Medical Shops	00.0	00.0	04.0	02.0	00.0	00.0	00.0	00.0	06.0 (01.00)	04.0 (01.00)	02.0 (01.00)
16.	No Blood Banks at PHC's	00.0	00.0	10.0	04.0	07.0	07.0	00.0	00.0	28.0 (04.66)	17.0 (04.25)	11.0 (05.50)
17.	No Well-equipped Ambulances	00.0	00.0	06.0	04.0	28.0	07.0	00.0	00.0	45.0 (07.50)	34.0 (08.50)	11.0 (05.50)
18.	No Referral Service	00.0	00.0	08.0	01.0	12.0	10.0	00.0	00.0	31.0 (05.16)	20.0 (05.00)	11.0 (05.50)
19.	Negligence of Doctors	00.0	00.0	09.0	00.0	00.0	00.0	00.0	00.0	09.0 (01.50)	00.0 (00.00)	09.0 (04.50)
20.	Proper implementation of Programme	00.0	00.0	04.0	00.0	00.0	00.0	00.0	00.0	04.0 (00.66)	04.0 (01.00)	00.0 (00.00)
21.	Supervision and Motivation	00.0	00.0	05.0	02.0	00.0	00.0	00.0	00.0	07.0 (01.16)	05.0 (01.25)	02.0 (01.00)
22.	Counselling centres.	00.0	00.0	02.0	00.0	10.0	07.0	00.0	00.0	19.0 (03.16)	12.0 (03.00)	07.0 (03.50)
23.	Proper Allocation of Funds	00.0	00.0	00.0	00.0	04.0	02.0	00.0	00.0	06.0 (01.00)	04.0 (01.00)	02.0 (01.00)
24.	Incentives for Working in Far flung Areas	00.0	00.0	00.0	00.0	00.0	01.0	00.0	00.0	01.0 (00.16)	00.0 (00.00)	01.0 (00.50)
25.	Specialised Labs for Testing	00.0	00.0	00.0	00.0	02.0	01.0	00.0	00.0	03.0 (00.50)	02.0 (00.50)	01.0 (00.50)
26.	Heating System in Winters	00.0	00.0	00.0	00.0	04.0	00.0	00.0	00.0	04.0 (00.66)	04.0 (01.00)	00.0 (00.00)

In response to this question what is lacking in the present health care system of Kashmir valley from gender point of view, varied kind of responses have been put forth by people as well as professionals in all the four districts. The main responses are as under:

(i) In all four districts 395/600, (65.83 per cent) respondents who compose of 280/400 (70.00 per cent) general respondents and 115/200 (57.50 per cent) professionals have revealed that health centres lack the availability of female gynaecologists/specialised doctors in the entire valley. In district Srinagar, 61/100 general respondents and 25/50 professionals have given this response. In district Budgam, 75/100 general respondents and 19/50 professionals were of the same view. In district Anantnag, 66/100 general respondents and 32/50 professionals have given the above response. In district Baramulla, 78/100 general respondents and 39/50 professionals have given the above response.

(ii) The healthcare system of the valley lacks proper facilities, adequate infrastructure and specialised gender treatment required for gender health has been revealed by 370/600 (61.66 per cent) respondents, of which 263/400 (65.75 per cent) were of general category and 107/200 (53.50 per cent) were professionals. In district Srinagar, 97/100 general respondents and 35/50 professionals have given the above response. In district Budgam, 80/100 general respondents and 34/50 professionals have revealed the above response. In district Anantnag, 54/100 general respondents and 13/50 professionals were of the same view. In district Baramulla, 32/100 general respondents and 25/50 professionals have given the above response.

(iii) The health centres of the valley lack proper staff both doctors as well as paramedics has been revealed by 87/600 (14.50 per cent) respondents, who compose of 45/400 (11.25 per cent) general respondents and 42/200 (21.00 per cent) professionals. In district Budgam, 18/50 professionals have given the same response. In district Anantnag, 25/100 general respondents and 14/50 professionals have revealed the same response. In district Baramulla, 20/100 general respondents and 10/50 professionals were of the same view.

(iv) There is no separate hospital for women has been put forth by 77/600 (12.83 per cent) respondents, who consist of 54/400 (13.50 per cent) general respondents and 23/200 (11.50 per cent) professionals. In district Srinagar, 02/50 professionals have given the same response. In district Anantnag, 14/100 general respondents and 06/50 professionals have revealed the same response. In district Baramulla, 40/100 general respondents and 15/50 professionals were of the same view.

(v) Inadequate supply of medicines in the hospitals has been revealed by 71/600 (11.83 per cent) respondents, from whom 45/400 (11.25 per cent) were from general category and 26/200 (13.00 per cent) were professionals. In district Budgam, 11/100 general respondents and 12/50 professionals have given the same response. In district Anantnag, 34/100 general respondents and 14/50 professionals were of the same view.

(vi) Proper medical attention for women is lacking in the entire healthcare system of the valley has been revealed by 56/600 (09.33 per cent) respondents, of whom 49/400 (12.25 per cent) are from general category and 07/200 (03.50 per cent) are professionals. The response has been put forth by 49/100 general respondents and 07/50 professionals from district Srinagar.

(vii) The ambulances in the hospitals are not well equipped has been revealed by 45/600 (07.50 per cent) respondents, of whom 34/400 (08.50 per cent) were general respondents and 11/200 (05.50 per cent) professionals. The response has been given by 06/100 general respondents and 04/50 professionals from district Budgam. In district Anantnag, 28/100 general respondents and 07/50 professionals have given the same response.

(viii) In rural areas, there is very less accessibility to healthcare units has been put forth by 33/600 (05.50 per cent) respondents, of whom 30/400 (07.50 per cent) were from general category and 03/200 (01.50) were professionals. In district Anantnag, 20/100 general respondents have given the same response. In district Baramulla, 10/100 general respondents and 03/50 professionals have revealed the same response.

(ix) The healthcare system of the valley lack proper governmental policies and programmes have been put forth by 32/600 (05.33 per cent) respondents who were of general category. The response has been given by 32/100 general respondents of district Srinagar.

(x) Healthcare system of the valley lacks proper referral services has been revealed by 31/600 (05.61 per cent) respondents, who compose of 20/400 (05.00 per cent) general respondents and 11/200 (05.50 per cent) professionals. In district Budgam, 08/100 general respondents and 01/50 professional have given the same response. In district Anantnag, 12/100 general respondents and 10/50 professionals are of the same view.

(xi) Majority of PHC's in the valley lack the facility of blood banks has been revealed by 28/600 (04.66 per cent) respondents, of whom 17/400 (04.25 per cent) were general respondents and 11/200 (05.50 per cent) professionals. In district Budgam, 10/100 general respondents and 04/50 professionals have given the same response. In district Anantnag, 07/100 general respondents and 07/50 professionals were of the same view.

(xii) Lack of health educators and awareness programmes has been revealed by 26/600 (04.33 per cent) respondents, of whom 20/400 (05.00 per cent) were from general category and 06/200 (03.00 per cent) professionals. In district Srinagar, 01/50 professional respondents have given the same response. In district Budgam, 08/100 general respondents were of the same view. In district Anantnag, 12/100 general respondents and 05/50 professionals have given the same response.

(xiii) Healthcare system of the valley lack proper counseling centres as revealed by 19/600 (03.16 per cent) respondents, of whom 11/400 (03.00 per cent) were from general category and 07/200 (03.50 per cent) were professionals. In district Budgam, 02/100 general respondents have given the same response. In district Anantnag, 10/100 general respondents and 07/50 professionals were of the same view.

(xiv) Negligent behaviour of doctors towards their services has been revealed by 09/600 (01.50 per cent) respondents belonging to the general category. The response has been given by 09/100 general respondents of district Budgam.

(xv) The healthcare system of the valley lack the services of fair price medical shops has been revealed by 06/600 (01.00 per cent) respondents, from whom 04/400 (03.00 per cent) were from general category and 02/200 (01.00 per cent) professionals. The response has been given by 04/100 general respondents and 02/50 professionals of district Budgam. Hospitals lack proper allocation of funds has been put forth by 06/600 (01.00 per cent) respondents, of whom 04/400 (01.00 per cent) were from general category and 02/200 (01.00 per cent) professionals. The response has been given by 04/100 general respondents and 02/50 professionals of district Anantnag.

(xvi) Lack of proper implementation of programmes makes the whole system defunct has been put forth by 04/600 respondents belonging to general category. The response has been given by 04/100 general respondents of district Budgam. Hospitals lack heating arrangement in winters has been revealed by 04/600 (00.66 per cent) respondents belonging to general category. The response has been given by 04/100 general respondents of district Anantnag.

(xvii) Majority of healthcare units in valley lack specialised laboratories as revealed by 03/600 (00.50 per cent) respondents, of whom 02/400

(00.50 per cent) were from general category and 01/200 (00.50 per cent) from professionals. The response has been given by 02/100 general respondents and 01/50 professional of district Anantnag.

(xviii) Many healthcare units in Kashmir valley lack 24x7services has been revealed by 02/600 (00.33 per cent) respondents, of whom 01/400 (00.25 per cent) was from general category and 01/200 (00.50 per cent) from professionals. The response has been given by 01/100 general respondent and 01/50 professional from district Budgam.

(xix) Lack of privacy in healthcare units has been revealed by 01/600 (00.16 per cent) respondent, who was from professional category. The response has been given by 01/50 professional respondents in district Srinagar. Hospitals lack proper screening facilities was revealed by 01/600 (00.16 per cent) total respondent, who are from professional category. The response has been given by 01/50 professional respondent of district Anantnag. The healthcare system of the valley lack the facility of providing incentives to healthcare providers for working in far flung areas has been revealed by 01/600 (00.16 per cent) respondent, who from professional category. The response has been given by 01/50 professional respondent of district Anantnag.

2. Role of the State

After knowing about limitations of the existing healthcare system, we enquired about the creation of positive healthcare system, the role to be played by government and private sectors. The response in this regard was as follows:

Table 10.2 reveals that:

(i) The biggest role state can play in making the healthcare system in the valley more gender effective is through the availability of female doctors in all healthcare units. It has been revealed by 133/600 (21.16 per cent) respondents, of whom 83/400 (20.75 per cent) were general respondents and 50/200 (25.00 per cent) are professionals. In district Srinagar, the same response has been given by 04/100 general respondents and 02/50 professional respondents. In district Anantnag, 18/100 general respondents and 17/50 professionals have given the same response. In district Baramulla, 61/100 general respondents and 31/50 professional respondents were of the same view.

(ii) The state should improve healthcare facilities related to women health has been revealed by 124/600 (20.66 per cent) respondents, who compose of 85/400 (21.25 per cent) general respondents and 39/200 (19.50 per cent) professionals. In district Srinagar, same response has been revealed by

Table 10.2: Role of the State

S. No.	Role of the State	D1 Srinagar		D2 Budgam		D3 Anantnag		D4 Baramulla		Responses (No. and Per cent)		
		G	P	G	P	G	P	G	P	GT	G	P
1.	Provision of Female Doctors	04.0	02.0	00.0	00.0	18.0	17.0	61.0	31.0	133 (22.16)	83.0 (20.75)	50.0 (25.00)
2	Strenghen Infrastructure	25.0	09.0	07.0	15.0	29.0	09.0	00.0	00.0	94.0 (15.66)	61.0 (15.25)	33.0 (16.50)
4.	Improve Health Facilities	12.0	23.0	58.0	09.0	00.0	00.0	15.0	07.0	124 (20.66)	85.0 (21.250	39 (19.50)
5.	Make Drug Laws Strict	10.0	03.0	00.0	01.0	00.0	00.0	00.0	00.0	14.0 (02.330	10.0 (02.50)	04.0 (02.00)
6.	Maintain Needed Doctor Patient Ratio	06.0	05.0	14.0	05.0	00.0	00.0	00.0	00.0	30.0 (05.00)	20.0 (05.00)	10.0 (05.00)
8.	Ban on Private Practice	00.0	02.0	00.0	02.0	00.0	04.0	00.0	00.0	08.0 (01.33)	00.0 (00.00)	08.0 (04.00)
9.	Check Adulteration in Medicines	12.0	08.0	00.0	01.0	00.0	00.0	00.0	00.0	21.0 (03.50)	12.0 (03.00)	09.0 (04.50)
10.	Check Corruption	04.0	03.0	00.0	03.0	00.0	00.0	00.0	00.0	10.0 (01.66)	04.0 (01.00)	06.0 (03.00)
11.	Mission Based Planning by the Government	00.0	02.0	27.0	00.0	04.0	00.0	00.0	00.0	33.0 (05.50)	31.0 (07.75)	02.0 (01.00)
12.	Check Doctors Stagnation	06.0	04.0	00.0	00.0	00.0	00.0	00.0	00.0	10.0 (01.66)	06.0 (01.50)	04.0 (02.00)
13.	Provide Free Medical Supplies	22.0	02.0	02.0	03,0	11.0	02.0	00.0	00.0	42.0 (07.00)	35.0 (08.75)	07.0 (03.50)
14.	Stress on Preventive Care	00.0	00.0	02.0	00.0	00.0	00.0	00.0	00.0	02.0 (00.33)	02.0 (00.50)	00.0 (00.00)
16.	Increase Gender Health Education	00.0	00.0	10.0	00.0	00.0	00.0	00.0	00.0	10.0 (01.66)	10.0 (02.50)	00.0 (00.00)
17.	24x7 Gender Healthcare Services	00.0	00.0	04.0	04.0	04.0	05.0	00.0	00.0	17.0 (02.83)	08.0 (02.00)	09.0 (04.50)
18.	Fair Price Medical Shops	00.0	00.0	08.0	04.0	00.0	00.0	00.0	00.0	12.0 (02.00)	08.0 (02.00)	04.0 (02.00)
19.	Proper Established Referral System	00.0	00.0	04.0	03.0	03.0	00.0	00.0	00.0	10.0 (01.66)	07.0 (01.75)	03.0 (01.50)
22.	Reduce Over-crowdedness in Hospitals	00.0	00.0	04.0	00.0	00.0	00.0	00.0	00.0	04.0 (00.66)	04.0 (01.00)	00.0 (00.00)
23.	Introduce Blood Banks at PHC's	00.0	00.0	02.0	01.0	00.0	00.0	00.0	00.0	03.0 (00.50)	02.0 (00.50)	01.0 (00.50)
24	Proper Implementation of Policy and Programmes	00.0	00.0	15.0	05.0	01.0	03.0	00.0	00.0	24.0 (04.00)	16.0 (04.00)	08.0 (04.00)
25.	More Special Maternity Hospitals	00.0	00.0	00.0	01.0	04.0	00.0	00.0	00.0	05.0 (00.83)	04.0 (01.00)	01.0 (00.50)
28.	Ambulance Services	00.0	00.0	00.0	02.0	00.0	00.0	05.0	05.0	12.0 (02.00)	05.0 (01.25)	07.0 (03.50)
29.	Proper use of Funds	00.0	00.0	00.0	03.0	00.0	02.0	00.0	00.0	05.0 (00.83)	00.0 (00.00)	05.0 (02.50)
30.	Educate the Women about their Health	00.0	00.0	00.0	00.0	12.0	01.0	35.0	09.0	57.0 (09.50)	47.0 (11.75)	10.0 (05.00)
32.	Incentives to Work in Far Flung Areas	00.0	00.0	00.0	00.0	00.0	01.0	00.0	00.0	01.0 (00.16)	00.0 (00.00)	01.0 (00.50)
34.	Hospital Accessibility in Far Flung Areas	00.0	00.0	00.0	00.0	01.0	04.0	40.0	27.0	72.0 (12.00)	41.0 (10.25)	31.0 (15.50)
35.	Free Healthcare to Women	00.0	00.0	00.0	00.0	06.0	00.0	00.0	00.0	06.0 (01.00)	06.0 (01.50)	00.0 (00.00)
38.	Autonomous Monitoring Cell	00.0	00.0	00.0	00.0	06.0	00.0	00.0	00.0	06.0 (01.00)	06.0 (01.50)	00.0 (00.00)

12/100 general respondents and 23/50 professionals. In district Budgam, the above response has been put forth by 58/100 general respondents and 09/50 professionals. In district Baramulla, 15/100 general respondents and 07/50 professionals have revealed the above response.

(iii) Proper supervision, inspection and monitoring by state authorities can help in improving this health sector's functioning has been put forth by 105/600 (17.50 per cent) total respondents, of whom 83/400 (20.75 per cent) were general respondents and 22/200 (11.00 per cent) are professionals. In district Srinagar, 33/100 general respondents and 14/50 professionals have given the same response. In district Budgam, 48/100 general respondents and 06/50 professionals were of the same view. In district Anantnag, 02/100 general respondents and 02/50 professionals have given the same response.

(iv) The role of the state would be in strengthening infrastructure of healthcare units has been revealed by 94/600 (15.66 per cent) respondents, who compose of 61/400 (15.25 per cent) general respondents and 33/200 (16.50 per cent) professionals. In district Srinagar, 25/100 general respondents and 09/50 professionals have revealed the same response. In district Budgam, 07/100 general respondents 15/50 professionals were of the same view. In district Anantnag, same response has been given by 29/100 general respondents and 09/50 professionals.

(v) The state should improve hospital accessibility in far flung areas has been revealed by 72/600 (12.00 per cent) respondents, which consist of 41/400 (10.25 per cent) general respondents and 31/200 (15.50 per cent) professionals. In district Anantnag, the same response has been given by 01/100 general respondent and 04/50 professionals. In district Baramulla, same response has been given by 40/100 general respondents and 27/50 professionals.

(vi) The state should frame strong gender health policy to provide better facilities has been put forth by 51/600 (08.50 per cent) respondents, of whom 38/400 (09.50 per cent) were general respondents and 14/200 (07.00 per cent) were professionals. In district Anantnag, the same response has been given by 08/100 general respondents and 01/50 professional. In district Baramulla, 30/100 general respondents and 12/50 professionals have given the above response.

(vii) State should recruit well trained and adequate staff in the hospitals to provide better services for women healthcare, has been put forth by 49/600 (08.16 per cent) respondents, who compose of 34/400 (08.50 per cent) general respondents and 15/200 (07.50 per cent) professionals. In district Srinagar, 04/100 general respondents and 06/50 professionals have given the above response. In district Budgam, 30/100 general respondents and 09/50 professionals have revealed the above response.

(viii) Short term courses for paramedic staff must be organised to update their knowledge and skills has been revealed by 43/600 (07.16 per cent) respondents, of whom 35/400 (08.75 per cent) were general respondents and 08/200 (04.00 per cent) were professionals. The response has been given by 35/100 general respondents and 08/50 professionals of district Baramulla.

(ix) The state should provide free medical supplies to people especially poor and underprivileged women has been put forth by 42/600 (07.00 per cent) respondents, who composed of 35/400 (08.75 per cent) general respondents and 07/200 (03.50 per cent) professionals. In district Srinagar, 22/100 general respondents and 02/50 professionals have given the same response. In district Budgam 02/100 general respondents and 03/50 professionals were of the same view. In district Anantnag, 11/100 general respondent and 02/50 professionals have given the same response.

(x) Efforts need to be taken by state to maintain needed doctor-patient ratio in hospitals to prevent overcrowding and help in improving services has been revealed by 30/600 (05.00 per cent) respondents, who compose of 20/400 (05.00 per cent) general respondents and 10/200 (05.00 per cent) professionals. In Srinagar, district the same response has been revealed by 06/100 general respondents and 05/50 professional respondents. In district Budgam, 14/100 general respondents and 05/50 professionals were of the same view.

(xi) Proper implementation of programmes by state can help in providing better services has been put forth by 24/600 (04.00 per cent) respondents, who compose of 16/400 (04.00 per cent) general respondents and 08/200 (04.00 per cent) professionals. In district Budgam, 15/100 general respondents and 05/50 professionals of district Budgam have given the same response. In district Anantnag, 01/100 general respondent and 03/50 professionals were of the same view.

(xii) The state should have a proper check on quality of drugs has been put forth by 23/600 (03.83 per cent) respondents, of who 18/400 (04.50 per cent) general respondents and 05/200 (02.50 per cent) professionals. In district Budgam, 14/100 general respondents and 05/50 professionals have revealed the same response. In district Anantnag, 04/100 general respondents have given the above response.

(xiii) The state should take measures to make 24x7 services related to GHC available for women in health centres to provide better services has been put forth by 17/600 (02.83 per cent) respondents, who compose of 08/400 (02.00 per cent) general respondents and 09/200 (04.50 per cent) professionals. In district Budgam, 04/100 general respondents and 04/50 professionals have given the same response. In district Anantnag, 04/100 general respondents and 05/50 professionals were of the same view.

(xiv) Fair price medical shops must be introduced in all the healthcare units has been put forth by 12/600 (02.00 per cent) respondents, of whom 08/400 (02.00 per cent) general respondents and 04/200 (02.00 per cent) professionals. The response has been given 08/100 general respondents and 04/50 professionals of district Budgam. The state should provide better ambulance services to people has been revealed by 12/600 (02.00 per cent) respondents, of which 05/400 (01.25 per cent) general respondents and 07/200 (03.50 per cent) were professionals. In district Budgam, 02/50 professionals have given the same response. In district Anantnag, 05/100 general respondents and 05/50 professionals were of the same view.

(xv) The problem of corruption need to be curbed first to improve the healthcare services has been revealed by 10/600 (01.66 per cent) respondents, of whom 04/400 (01.00 per cent) are from general category and 06/200 (03.00 per cent) were professionals. In district Srinagar, 04/100 general respondent and 03/50 professionals have given the same response. In district Budgam, same response has been put forth by 03/50 professional respondents.

(xvi) The state should check doctor's stagnation in service to improve service records especially in far flung areas has been revealed by 10/600 (01.66 per cent) respondents, of whom 06/400 (01.50 per cent) are general respondents and 04/200 (02.00 per cent) were professionals. The response has been given by 06/100 general respondents and 04/50 professionals of district Srinagar. The response has been given by 10/100 general respondents of district Budgam. The state should work on proper referral system to provide adequate services to people has been revealed by 10/600 (01.66 per cent) respondents, who compose of 07/400 (01.75 per cent) general respondents and 03/200 (01.50 per cent) professional respondents. In district Budgam, 04/100 general respondents and 03/50 professionals have given the same response. In district Anantnag, 03/100 general respondents have revealed the above response.

(xvii) Ban on private practice can help in improving the gender health services provided by government hospitals has been revealed by 08/600 (01.33 per cent) respondents who were from professional category. In district Srinagar, the above response has been given by 02/50 professional respondents. In district Budgam, same response has been revealed by 02/50 professional respondents. In district Anantnag, 04/50 professional respondents were of the same view.

(xviii) To provide better services in far flung areas, PHCs must be strengthened has been conveyed by 06/600 (01.00 per cent) respondents belonging to professional category. The response has been given by 02/50 professionals of district Budgam, and 04/50 professionals of district Anantnag. Free healthcare services should be provided to women in these areas to improve their health conditions has been revealed by 06/600 (01.00 per cent) respondents, belonging to general category. The response has been given by 06/100 general respondents of district Anantnag.

(xix) The government should establish more maternity hospitals to provide better services to women in rural and urban areas has been revealed by 05/600 (00.83 per cent) respondents, of whom 04/400 (01.00 per cent) were general respondents and 01/200 (00.50 per cent) is professional The response has been given by 01/50 professionals of district Budgam and 04/100 general respondents of district Anantnag. Moreover, proper utilisation of funds can help in providing better services have been said by 05/600 (00.83 per cent) respondents, who are from professional category. The response has been given by 03/50 professionals from district Budgam and 02/50 professionals from district Anantnag.

(xx) The health authorities should check over crowdedness in hospitals and try to solve this problem has been revealed by 04/600 (00.66 per cent) respondents belonging to general category. The response has been given by 04/100 general respondents of district Budgam.

(xxi) Blood banks should be established at every PHC for GHC has been put forth by 03/600 (00.50 per cent) respondents, of whom 02/400 (00.50 per cent) are from general category and 01/200 (00.50 per cent) professional. The response has been given by 02/100 general respondents and 01/50 professional from district Budgam.

(xxii) The doctors should stress on early diagnosis of the gender diseases to tackle these issues as early as possible has been revealed by 02/600 (00.33 per cent) total respondents of whom 01/400 (00.25 per cent) is from general category and 01/200 (00.50 per cent) from professionals. The response has been given by 01/100 general respondent and 01/50 professional from district Budgam.

(xxiii) To provide better GHC services, the government should keep a check on private health institutions has been revealed by 01/600 (00.16 per cent) respondent, who is from professional category. This response has been given by 01/50 professional respondent from district Budgam.

Table 10.3: Role of the Private Sector

S. No.	Role of Private Sector	SRC D1		BUD D2		ANA D3		BAR D4		Responses (No. and Per cent)		
		G	P	G	P	G	P	G	P	GT	G	P
	YES	51	21.0	44.0	25.0	44.0	23.0	100	50.0	358 (59.66)	239 (59.75)	119 (59.50)
1.	Establishing Private Women Clinics and Hospitals	47.0	10.0	26.0	18.0	20.0	13.0	00.0	00.0	134 (22.33)	93.0 (23.25)	41.0 (20.50)
2.	Encourage PPP's in Health sector	04.0	11.0	00.0	00.0	00.0	00.0	00.0	00.0	15.0 (02.50)	04.0 (01.00)	11.0 (05.50)
3.	Engage NGOs and Counsellors	00.0	00.0	01.0	03.0	22.0	10.0	60.0	30.0	126 (21.00)	83.0 (20.75)	43 (21.50)
4.	Start Nursing Homes for Women Exclusively.	00.0	00.0	11.0	01.0	00.0	00.0	00.0	00.0	12.0 (02.00)	11.0 (02.75)	01.0 (00.50)
5.	Start Mobile Medical Units	00.0	00.0	01.0	00.0	00.0	00.0	00.0	00.0	01.0 (00.16)	01:0 (00.25)	00.0 (00.00)
6.	Engage Private Business Organisation in GHC Programmes.	00.0	00.0	00.0	00.0	00.0	00.0	15.0	09.0	24.0 (04.00)	15.0 (03.75)	09.0 (04.50)
	NO	37.0	09.0	56.0	24.0	56.0	27.0	00.0	00.0	209 (34.83)	149 (37.25)	60.0 (30.00)
1.	Strengthen Government Hospital Only	15.0	03.0	13.0	09.0	06.0	06.0	00.0	00.0	52.0 (08.66)	34.0 (08.50)	18.0 (09.00)
2.	Limited Resources Available in GHC Sector	05.0	03.0	00.0	00.0	00.0	00.0	00.0	00.0	08.0 (01.33)	05.0 (01.25)	03.0 (01.50)
3.	Poor People Can't Afford Private Healthcare Sector	00.0	00.0	36.0	15.0	48.0	18.0	00.0	00.0	117 (19.50)	84.0 (21.00)	33.0 (16.50)
4.	Private Clinics Work only for Money	00.0	00.0	07.0	00.0	02.0	03.0	00.0	00.0	12.0 (02.00)	09.0 (02.25)	03.0 (01.50)

3. Role of the Private Sector

Subsequently, we enquired about the role which the private sector in Kashmir can play in establishing the gender healthcare system. Our investigation in this regard got the following responses:

Table 10.3 reveals following points of positive and negative response:

In response to this question, 358/600 (59.66 per cent) respondents, of whom 239/400 (59.75 per cent) were general respondents and 119/200 (59.50 per cent) professionals have given the positive response. The district-wise distribution of these respondents is as follows: In district Srinagar, 51/100 general respondents 21/50 professionals are of the view that private healthcare sector can play a good role in providing better facilities to people. In district Budgam, 44/100 general respondents and 25/50 professionals have given the same response. In district Anantnag, 44/100 general respondents and 23/50 professionals were of the same view. In district Baramulla, 100/100 general respondents and 50/50 professionals have given the positive response.

(i) Private clinics and hospitals can play a good role in providing better healthcare facilities to women has been revealed by 134/600 (22.33 per cent) respondents, of whom 93/400 (23.25 per cent) general respondents and 41/200 (20.50 per cent) were professionals. In district Srinagar, the same response has been given by 47/100 general respondents and 10/50 professionals. In district Budgam, 26/100 general respondents and 18/50 professionals have given the same response. In district Anantnag, 20/100 general respondents and 13/50 professionals were of the same view.

(ii) Non-governmental organisations and counsellors can play a better role in providing effective services has been revealed by 126/600 (21.00 per cent) respondents, who composed of 83/400 (20.75 per cent) general and 43/200 (21.50 per cent) professional respondents. In district Budgam, the above response has been given by 01/100 general and 03/50 professionals respondents. In district Anantnag, 22/100 general respondents and 10/50 professionals were of the same view. In district Baramulla, 60/100 general respondents and 30/50 professionals have given the same response.

(iii) Private business organizations can help in improving healthcare facilities in the valley has been revealed by 24/600 (04.00 per cent) respondents, of whom 15/400 (03.75 per cent) are general and 09/

200 (04.50 per cent) professional respondents. The response has been given by 15/100 general respondents and 09/50 professionals of district Baramulla.

(iv) To improve healthcare sector public-private partnerships should be encouraged has been put forth by 15/600 respondents, who comprise of 04/400 general respondents and 11/200 professionals. The response has been given by 04/100 general respondents and 11/50 professionals of district Srinagar.

(v) Nursing homes for women specialised treatment can play a good role in providing better services to women's health has been revealed by 12/600 (02.00 per cent) respondents, who compose of 11/400 (02.75 per cent) general respondents and 01/200 (00.50 per cent) professionals. The response has been given by 11/100 general respondents and 01/50 professional of district Budgam.

(vi) Mobile Medical units can help in providing better services for women patients has been put forth by 01/600 (00.16 per cent) respondents belonging to general category. The response has been given by 01/100 general respondents of district Budgam.

In response to the same question 209/600 (34.83 per cent) respondents, which compose of 149/400 (37.25 per cent) general respondents and 60/200 (30.00 per cent) professionals, gave negative response. The district-wise distribution is as follows: In district Srinagar, 37/100 general respondents and 09/50 professionals have given the negative response. In district Budgam, 56/100 general respondents and 24/50 professionals were of the same view. In district Anantnag, 56/100 general respondents and 27/50 professionals have given the negative view. In support of the negative response by respondents the various reasons put forth by them are mentioned as below:

(i) Poor people especially their women can't afford the costs of healthcare services in private sector has been revealed by 117/600 (19.50 per cent) respondents, of whom 84/400 (21.00 per cent) are general respondents and 33/200 (16.50 per cent) professionals. In district Budgam, the response has been given by 36/100 general respondents and 15/50 professionals. In district Anantnag, 48/100 general respondents and 18/50 professionals have given the same response.

(ii) Governmental hospitals need to be strengthened for providing better services has been put forth by 52/600 (08.66 per cent) respondents, of whom 34/400 (08.50 per cent) are general respondents and 18/200 (09.00 per cent) professionals. In district Srinagar, 15/100 general respondents and 03/50 professionals have given the same response. In district Budgam, 13/100 general respondents and 09/50 professionals are of the same view. In district Anantnag 06/100 general respondents and 06/50 professionals have revealed the same response.

(iii) Limited resources in government sector need to be expanded has been put forth by 08/600 (01.33 per cent) respondents, of which 05/400 (01.25 per cent) are general and 03/200 (01.50 per cent) professional respondents. The response has been given by 05/100 general respondents and 03/50 are professionals of district Srinagar.

(iv) Private clinics are mainly for money-making has been revealed by 12/600 (02.00 per cent) respondents, who compose of 09/400 (02.25 per cent) general and 03/200 (01.50 per cent) professional respondents. In district Budgam, 07/100 general respondents have given the same response. In district Anantnag, 02/100 general respondents and 03/50 professionals are of the same view.

4. Level of Awareness Among Respondents

In this series of questions, we also enquired about the level of awareness among respondents regarding positive gender health care system. The respondents gave positive and negative responses which are noted below.

If the level of awareness regarding positive gender health system is not satisfactory, we enquired from them what needs to be done so that positive gender healthcare system is established. They gave the answers registered in Table 10.4

Table 10.4: Satisfactory Level of Awareness

S. No.	*Satisfactory Level of Awareness*	*D1 Srinagar*		*D2 Budgam*		*D3 Anantnag*		*D4 Baramulla*		*Responses (No. and Per cent)*		
		G	*P*	*G*	*P*	*G*	*P*	*G*	*P*	*GT*	*G*	*P*
1.	Yes	59.0	15.0	18.0	08.0	06.0	04.0	00.0	00.0	110 (18.33)	83.0 (20.75)	27.0 (13.50)
2.	No	41.0	25.0	82.0	42.0	94.0	46.0	100	50.0	480 (80.00)	317 (79.25)	163 (81.50)
	If no, what need to be done											
1.	Planned Programs to be Started	00.0	03.0	00.0	00.0	00.0	00.0	00.0	00.0	03.0 (00.50)	00.0 (00.00)	03.0 (01.50)
2.	Counselling must be Carried out in an Organised Way	20.0	02.0	00.0	00.0	02.0	00.0	00.0	00.0	24.0 (04.00)	22.0 (05.50)	02.0 (01.00)
3.	Imparting Health Education to Raise Awareness	02.0	06.0	08.0	12.0	00.0	00.0	00.0	00.0	28.0 (04.66)	10.0 (02.50)	18.0 (09.00)
4.	Taking Preventive Measures for GHC	07.0	01.0	00.0	00.0	00.0	00.0	00.0	00.0	08.0 (01.33)	07.0 (01.75)	01.0 (00.50)
5.	Organising Health Camps and *melas*	00.0	00.0	11.0	06.0	15.0	04.0	00.0	00.0	36.0 (06.00)	26.0 (06.50)	10.0 (05.00)
6.	Role of NGO's must be Established	00.0	00.0	00.0	00.0	07.0	09.0	10.0	03.0	29.0 (04.83)	17.0 (04.25)	12.0 (06.00)
7.	ICDS workers and ASHA's Help must be Sought	00.0	00.0	00.0	00.0	11.0	01.0	00.0	00.0	12.0 (02.00)	11.0 (02.75)	01.0 (00.50)
8.	Cooperation of Various Agencies of Development	00.0	00.0	00.0	00.0	03.0	03.0	35.0	17.0	58.0 (09.66)	38.0 (09.50)	20.0 (10.00)
9.	Religious Scholars should be Involved	00.0	00.0	00.0	00.0	04.0	02.0	00.0	00.0	06.0 (01.00)	04.0 (01.00)	02.0 (01.00)
10.	Panchayat has a Positive Role in GHC Programme	00.0	00.0	00.0	00.0	02.0	00.0	00.0	00.0	02.0 (00.33)	02.0 (00.50)	00.0 (00.00)
11.	Organising Seminars and Workshops	00.0	00.0	00.0	00.0	05.0	00.0	00.0	00.0	05.0 (00.83)	05.0 (01.25)	00.0 (00.00)

The Positive response has been given by 110/600 (18.33 per cent), who compose of 83/400 (20.75 per cent) general respondents and 27/200 (13.50 per cent) professionals. They believe that their exists satisfactory level of awareness about GHC among people. In district Srinagar, 59/100 general respondents and 15/50 professionals have given the positive response. In district Budgam, 18/100 general respondents and 08/50 professionals are of the same view. In district Anantnag, 06/100 general respondents and 04/50 professionals have revealed the above response.

In direct opposition to it, 480/600 (80.00 per cent) respondents, of whom 317/400 (79.25 per cent) were general respondents and 163/200 (81.50 per cent) professionals have given the negative response i.e, there was not sufficient awareness about GHC among respondents. In district Srinagar, 41/100 general respondents and 25/50 professionals have given the negative response. In district Budgam, 82/100 general respondents and 42/50 professionals are of the same view. In district Anantnag, 94/100 general respondents and 46/50 professionals have given the above response. In district Baramulla, 100/100 general respondents and 50/50 professionals have revealed the same response. As per their option, there is not satisfactory level of awareness among people and the various measures need to be taken in this regard. These measures are as follows:

(i) Awareness programmes need to be started everywhere, especially in far flung areas has been revealed by 152/600 (25.33 per cent) respondents, who compose of 99/400 (24.75 per cent) general respondents and 53/200 (26.50 per cent) professionals. In district Srinagar, the above response has been given by 12/100 general respondents and 13/50 professionals. In district Budgam, 61/100 general respondents and 27/50 professionals have given the same response. In district Anantnag, 26/100 general respondents and 13/50 professionals were of the same view.

(ii) Cooperation between various agencies of the government like schools, *mohalla* committees, etc, which can help in spreading awareness has been revealed by 58/600 (09.66 per cent) respondents, of whom 38/400 (09.50 per cent) were general respondents and 20/200 (10.00 per cent) from professional category. In district Anantnag, 03/100 general respondents and 03/50 professionals have given the above response. In district Baramulla, 35/100 general respondents and 20/50 professionals are of the same view.

Organisation of health camps and *melas* can help in spreading awareness message among people has been revealed by 36/600 (06.00 per cent) respondents, of whom 26/400 (06.50 per cent) are general respondents and 10/200 (05.00 per cent) professionals. In district Budgam, 11/100 general respondents and 06/50 professionals have given the same response. In district Anantnag, 15/100 general respondents and 04/50 professionals were of the same view.

(iii) Imparting of health education needs to be carried out has been revealed by 32/600 (05.33 per cent) respondents, of whom 24/400 (06.00 per cent) are general respondents and 08/200 (04.00 per cent) professionals. In district Budgam, 07/100 general respondents and 07/50 professionals have given the above response. In district Anantnag, 07/100 general respondents have given the same response. In district Baramulla, 10/100 general respondents and 01/50 professionals are of the same view.

(iv) NGO's need to be engaged which can help in spreading awareness among people has been revealed by 29/600 (04.83 per cent) respondents, of whom 17/400 (04.25 per cent) are general respondents and 12/200 (06.00 per cent) professionals. In district Anantnag, the above response has been revealed by 07/100 general respondents and 09/50 professionals. In district Baramulla, 10/100 general respondents and 03/50 professionals have given the above response.

(v) Counselling programmes need to be started in hospitals which can help in creating GHC awareness among people has been put forth by 24/600 (04.00 per cent) total respondents, who compose of 22/400 (05.50 per cent) general respondents and 02/200 (01.00 per cent) professionals. In district Srinagar, the response has been given by 20/100 general respondents and 02/50 professionals. In district Anantnag, same response has been given by 02/100 general respondents.

(vi) ICDS workers and ASHAs involvement can help in effective awareness GHC programmes has been revealed by 12/600 (02.00 per cent) respondents, who composed of 11/400 (02.75 per cent) general respondents and 01/200 (00.50 per cent) professionals. The response has been given by 11/100 general respondents and 01/50 professionals of district Anantnag.

(vii) Awareness regarding preventive measures need to be increased has been revealed by 08/600 (01.33 per cent) respondents who composed of 07/400 (01.75 per cent) general respondents and 01/200 (00.50 per cent)) professional. In district Srinagar, the same response has been revealed by 07/100 general respondents and 01/50 professionals.

(viii) Seminars and workshops must be organised repeatedly for healthcare providers so that they can forward information to common masses has been revealed by 05/600 (00.83 per cent) respondents, who are from general category. The response has been given by 05/100 general respondents of district Anantnag.

(ix) Panchayats can play an effective role in creating awareness among rural people related to various GHC services provided by the government has been

Table 10.5: Training to Medicos and Paramedics

		D1		*D2*		*D3*		*D4*				
	Training to Medicos	*Srinagar*		*Budgam*		*Anantnag*		*Baramulla*		*Responses (No. and per cent)*		
S. No.	*and Paramedics*	*G*	*P*	*G*	*P*	*G*	*P*	*G*	*P*	*GT*	*G*	*P*
1.	Organising Short Training Courses during Service	43.0	06.0	13.0	11.0	64.0	22.0	30.0	24.0	213 (35.50)	150 (37.50)	63.0 (31.50)
2.	Organising Seminars and Workshops	29.0	15.0	05.0	16.0	18.0	19.0	23.0	03.0	128 (21.33)	75.0 (18.75)	53.0 (26.50)
3.	Starting Refresher Courses	18.0	14.0	21.0	14.0	07.0	02.0	00.0	00.0	76.0 (12.66)	46.0 (11.50)	30.0 (15.00)
4.	Keeping Supervision of the Staff Continuously	07.0	04.0	09.0	01.0	00.0	00.0	00.0	00.0	21.0 (03.50)	16.0 (04.00)	05.0 (02.50)
5.	Introducing Awareness Programmes	01.0	02.0	00.0	00.0	00.0	00.0	00.0	00.0	03.0 (00.50)	01.0 (00.25)	02.0 (01.00)
6.	Make Active Participation Possible	00.0	02.0	00.0	00.0	00.0	00.0	00.0	00.0	02.0 (00.33)	00.0 (00.00)	02.0 (01.00)
7.	Trainings on the Basis of new Technology	00.0	00.0	21.0	05.0	02.0	02.0	00.0	00.0	30.0 (06.00)	23.0 (05.75)	07.0 (03.50)
8.	Training as per Gender Needs	00.0	00.0	07.0	01.0	00.0	00.0	00.0	00.0	08.0 (01.33)	07.0 (01.75)	01.0 (00.50)
9.	Cultural Training in Health Practices	00.0	00.0	00.0	00.0	02.0	01.0	00.0	00.0	03.0 (00.50)	02.0 (00.50)	01.0 (00.50)

revealed by 02/600 (00.33 per cent) respondents belonging to general category. The response has been given by 02/100 general respondents of district Anantnag.

5. Training to Medicos and Paramedical Staff

It was seriously felt that, in order to establish a gender positive healthcare system in Kashmir, the relevant training to medicos and paramedics was necessary. It will serve the basic purpose and help the women's health in many ways. When we put this question to the respondents, their response is noted in Table 10.5 below:

(i) Short training courses during service was suggested by 213/600 (35.50 per cent) respondents, who compose of 150/400 (37.50 per cent) general respondents and 63/200 (31.50 per cent) professionals. In district Srinagar, 43/100 general respondents and 06/50 professionals have given the same response. In district Budgam, 13/100 general respondents and 11/50 professionals are of the same view. In district Anantnag, 64/100 general respondents and 22/50 professionals have given the same response. In district Baramulla, 30/100 general respondents and 24/50 professionals suggested the same.

(ii) Seminars and workshops must be organised to update healthcare providers information has been suggested by 128/600 (21.33 per cent) respondents, of whom 75/400 (18.75 per cent) are general respondents and 53/200 (26.50 per cent) professionals. In district Srinagar, 29/100 general respondents and 15/50 professionals have give the same response. In district Budgam, the same response has been revealed by 05/100 general respondents and 16/50 professionals. In district Anantnag, 18/100 general respondents and 19/50 professionals were of the same view. In district Baramulla, 23/100 general respondents and 03/50 professionals have given the same response.

(iii) Refresher courses for medicos and paramedics can help in improving their skills and knowledge as per current requirements has been put forth by 76/600 (12.66 per cent) respondents, who compose 46/400 (11.50 per cent) general respondents and 30/200 (15.50 per cent) were professionals. In district Srinagar, the above response has been given by 18/100 general respondents and 14/50 professionals. In district Budgam, same response has been revealed by 21/100 general respondents and 14/50 professionals. In district Anantnag, 07/100 general respondents and 02/50 professionals are of the same view.

(iv) Trainings as per new technology must be imparted to healthcare givers has been suggested by 30/600 (05.00 per cent) respondents, who composed of 23/400 (05.75 per cent) general respondents and 07/200 (03.50 per cent) professionals. The same response has been given by 21/100 general respondents and 05/50 professionals of district Budgam. In district Anantnag, 02/100 general respondents and 02/50 professionals have revealed the same response.

(v) Proper supervision can help in better GHC service delivery has been revealed by 21/600 (03.50 per cent) respondents, of whom 16/400 (04.00 per cent) are general respondents and 05/200 (02.50 per cent)) professionals. In district Srinagar, the above response has been given by 07/100 general respondents and 04/50 professionals. In district Budgam, 09/100 general respondents and 01/50 professionals are of the same view.

(vi) Training should be given as per gender requirements has been revealed by 08/600 respondents, of whom 07/400 general respondents and 01/200 professionals. The response has been given by 07/100 general respondents and 01/50 professional of district Budgam.

(vii) Introduction of awareness programmes for Gender healthcare providers is important for updating their knowhow has been revealed by 03/600 (00.50 per cent) respondents, of which 01/400 (00.25 per cent) are from general category and 02/200 (01.00 per cent) from professionals. The response has been given by 01/100 general respondent and 02/50 professionals from district Srinagar. Trainings should be given as per cultural norms has been revealed by 03/600 respondents, from which 02/400 were general respondents and 01/200 was professional. The response has been given by 02/100 general respondents and 01/50 were professionals of district Anantnag.

(viii) Active participation of healthcare providers is very important has been put forth by 02/600 (00.33 per cent) respondents, belonging to professional category. The response has been given by 02/50 professional respondents of district Srinagar.

11

Suggestions for Positive Gender Healthcare

After the necessary questions about gender health care were posed to the respondents, they were approached to make some realistic suggestions for establishment, promotion and improvement of its system in J&K. They responded by making several suggestions which we later on categorised into three types on the basis of their direction. Moreover, these suggestions have some policy and administrative implications for the government and other multi-sector implications of other organisations. Thus, these suggestions were directed:

[i] to the government in J & K,

[ii] to the Non-Governmental Organisations [NGOs] in J & K, and

[iii] to the civil society in J & K.

The respondents put forward their suggestions for three collective institutions keeping in view their crucial role and functioning in the broader framework. These were aimed to provide a guiding framework for helping the gender health sufferers in Kashmir. These practical, purposeful and pointed suggestions were mentioned as follows:

1. Suggestions for the Government in J & K

[i] The first set of suggestions put forward by the respondents was for official institutions, organisations, agencies and other collectivities. These suggestions included:

[a] ***Formulation and Implementation of Gender Health Policy:*** It follows that the government at the initiation must think in terms of formulation of the policy towards women's health. It must be formulated after taking into consideration the basic needs of women living in the state. Minimum health standards in the present day society must be considered while determining the variables of the gender health policy. The next step demands that the policy has to be implemented in complex social, cultural, and economic conditions. While this policy must be relevant, realistic and purposeful, it must be implemented by the government agencies with missionary zeal and total commitment, for which necessary steps have to be taken. These suggestions were presented by 25/600 [04.16 per cent] respondents who composed of 16/200 [08.00 per cent] professional and 09/400 [02.25 per cent] general respondents.

[b] ***Expansion and Improvement in Gender Health Services:*** Gender health services are neither complete nor of high standard in the J&K state. So, there was immediate need of two important steps. *First,* these services must be expanded heavily and, second, ideal facilities must be provided to all needy, especially in rural and hilly areas, and at the time of pregnancy and delivery. Thus, the respondents suggested that overall improvement in gender health can be brought by improving and upgrading the related health services and facilities at all levels and in all areas. This suggestion was given by 75/600 [12.50 per cent] respondents who comprised of 36/200 [18.00 per cent] professional and 16/400 [04.00 per cent] general respondents.

[c] ***Introduction of Mission-based Planning:*** The respondents expressed that the government, particularly its policy makers, must develop a radical view of their ideas related to gender health. They must also feel ideologically committed to the ideals of gender healthcare and system. This suggestion was given by 05/600 [00.83 per cent] respondents who belonged to professional [03/200, 01.50 per cent] and general [02/400, 00.50 per cent] categories of respondents.

[d] There was very important suggestion that number of female medical staff must be increased significantly in order to provide solace and satisfaction to a majority of gender patients. This, according to them, was necessary because of cultural, religious, psychological and personal factors. The entire medical staff must compose of lady-specialist doctors, Para-medicos, nurses and others at all levels and in all areas. This suggestion was made by 24/600 [04.00 per cent] respondents who belonged to professional and general categories in the proportion of

18/200 [09.00 per cent] and 06/400 [01.50 per cent] respondents respectively.

[e] ***Increase in the Level of Infrastructure:*** Since the existing health infrastructure in the state was neither according to the present needs nor according to the present standards, there seems an absolute need to increase the level of infrastructure in the health sector in J&K. This suggestion of basic importance had two aspects. First, to shun and stop the use of obsolete and out of date technology and to install modern technology in this medical specialty of gender health. This suggestion was put forth by 59/600[09.83 per cent] respondents who represented two sub-groups of professional [34/200, 17.00 per cent] and general [23/400, 05.75 per cent] categories.

[f] ***Coordination between Different Departments:*** It was held by the respondents that most of the government organisations working for same gender heath cause are not well co-ordinated. In some cases, these organisations were not aware even about other organisations and agencies working for the same cause. So, there emerges a basic need of strong coordination between various state agencies in J&K. This suggestion was made by 02/600[00.33 per cent] respondents who all belonged to the professional category.

[g] ***Mass Awareness Campaign:*** It was suggested by many that a strong, continuous, and contextual awareness campaign is necessarily needed in order to make every woman conscious about her health needs, rights and responsibilities. So, they suggested a formal and organised campaign in this regard with all formal and informal means of communication to be utilised for this purpose. This was suggested by 2/600 [00.33 per cent] respondents who belonged to professional and general categories in the proportion of 01/200 [00.50 per cent] and 01/400 [00.25 per cent] respondents.

[h] ***Gender Health Investigation:*** It was suggested that actual reality about gender health situation in not known widely. So, there must be serious academic efforts to investigate about facts directly related to gender health in Kashmir. In order to know about basic problems of this health, survey type of investigation/research must be carried out and its findings must be widely circulated and decimated through social media. This broader academic suggestion was made by 13/600[02.16 per cent] respondents who included 10/200 [05.00 per cent] professional and 03/400 [00.75 per cent] general respondents.

[i] ***All Facilities at All Times:*** All gender health facilities and services must be provided in all health centres at all levels, especially at village/

block level, to ensure all gender needy persons 24 x 7. This suggestion was made by 04/600 [00.66 per cent] respondents who belonged to professional and general categories in the proportion of 03/200[01.50 per cent] and 01/400 [00.25 per cent] respectively.

[j] ***Relevant Training to Medicos:*** A significant number of respondents, i.e., 13/600 [02.16 per cent] suggested that training in gender health issues is necessary and it must not be avoided. They emphasised two of its aspects. The first was related to train the medicos and para-medicos in the rural background where larger number of gender health patients live The second was related to training of medicos in the problems of people of villages in the state. This must be followed by developing a system of monitoring and accountability of medicos and others. These suggestions were conveyed by 07/200 [03.50 per cent] professional and 06/400 [01.50 per cent] general respondents.

[k] ***Establishment of Blood Banks:*** Since many deaths have taken place in the past mainly because of absence of blood facility at different health centres, especially at the time of delivery of women, the respondents suggested that 'blood banks' must be established at every possible level of healthcare. This was supported by 01/600 [00.16 per cent] respondent who belonged to professional category.

[l] ***Availability of Funds:*** The respondents felt that most of the health centres faced the shortage of funds for gender health drugs, facilities and services. So, they suggested every healthcare centre must be provided sufficient funds through legal means for purchasing necessary drugs. This was suggested by 03/600[00.50 per cent] respondents who were from professional [02/200,01.00 per cent] and general [01/400,00.25 per cent] categories.

[m] ***Increase the Availability of Quality Drugs:*** Since the practice of fake drugs is very common in Kashmir, the women, too, have become victims of this menace. So, the respondents suggested that every effort must be carried out to stop this practice through formal measures. They also suggested that this is the prime responsibility of the government which it must fulfill necessarily. These suggestions were put forth by 02/600 [00.33 per cent] respondents who were all from professional category.

[n] ***Control and curbing Corruption:*** Since corruption has been a common phenomenon in Kashmir, the health sector has also fallen prey to this evil practice. The respondents suggested that government must uproot the basis of corruption with people's support in the most sacred area of human life. Corruption among the medicos, para-medicos and health administrators must also be rooted out through formal laws. This suggestion was made by

16/600 [02.66 per cent] respondents who were professional [09/200, 04.50 per cent] and general [07/400, 01.75 per cent] respondents.

[o] ***Doctors' Care and Patients' Treatment:*** This type of suggestion was made about the role of doctors, their service conditions and their medical treatment of people. The first suggestion was that there should be proper inspection or supervision of doctors who evade their duties in the health centres and go for private practice in their clinics during the office hours. They must be dealt with strictly and even punished for their illegal acts. This was suggested by 25/600 [04.16 per cent] respondents who belonged to professional [15/200, 07.50 per cent] and general [10/40002.50 per cent] categories.

The second suggestion was related to the service stagnation of many doctors and para-medical staff. They suggested that every effort must be attempted to give total service satisfaction to them and resolve their chronic problems. This suggestion was made by 05/600 [00.83 per cent] respondents who were from professional [04/200, 02.00 per cent] and general [01/400, 00.25 per cent] categories.

The third suggestion was related to the busy schedule of doctors in health centres due to huge rush of female patients who exhausts them and affect the quality of treatment. So, in specific words, the respondents suggested that there, must be realistic ratio between doctors and patients. In other words, they suggested that more number of doctors must be recruited and deputed to health centres where there is heavy rush of gender health patients. This suggestion was made by 12/600 [02.00 per cent] respondents who belonged to professional [09/200, 04.50 per cent] and general [03/400, 00.75 per cent] categories.

[p] ***Proper Care of Pregnancy and Delivery:*** Since the gender health stands as most important and most crucial, particularly at times of pregnancy and delivery, there was suggestion that there should be proper aid and services available to women in all areas on priority basis. That is the minimum what a democratic government can do. This suggestion was made by 01/600 [00.16 per cent] respondent who belonged to professional category.

[q] ***Increase in the Number of Women/Maternity Hospitals:*** In the context of acute shortage of gender health care services and facilities, the respondents suggested that maximum number of women's hospitals and other related healthcare centres must be established. In the present situation, there is sole maternity hospital in the Kashmir province which is always flooded with women patients. So, the necessity of establishing women/maternity hospitals increases manifold. This suggestion was presented by 17/600 [02.83 per cent] respondents who belonged to professional [14/200, 07.00 per cent] and general [03/400, 00.75 per cent] categories.

[r] ***Establishment of Fair Price Medical Shops:*** Since fake medicines are available in large numbers in Kashmir, the respondents suggested that all necessary, life saving and gender drugs must be made available in the hospitals through fair price shops and on affordable prices. They also suggested that these shops must be under the government's control. This was suggested by 01/600 [00.16 per cent] respondent who belonged to the professional category.

[s] ***Proper Treatment of Female Mental Health Patients:*** Since Kashmir has comparatively a large number of female mental health patients; they must be provided specialized experts, hospitals, and latest technology to deal properly with their health problems. More and more rehabilitation and psychiatry centres must be opened for them. This suggestion was presented by 02/600 [00.33 per cent] respondents who included 01/200 [00.50 per cent] professional and 01/400 [00.25 per cent] general respondents.

[t] ***Gender Healthcare Services to Far Flung Areas:*** The respondents, particularly from hilly areas, suggested that all necessary and basic gender healthcare facilities and services must be made available in far flung areas [which are not approachable during winter season] and in advance before the arrival of winter season. This suggestion was conveyed by 13/600 [02.16 per cent] respondents who included 07/200 [03.50 per cent] and 06/400 [01.50 per cent] professional and general categories of respondents respectively.

[u] ***Provision for Ambulances:*** It was suggested that modern ambulances well equipped with all gender healthcare emergency facilities and services must be made available at every tehsil/block level health centre. These vehicles must be utilized by the people easily and without many formalities. This suggestion was presented by 12/600 [02.00 per cent] who composed of 02/200 [01.00 per cent] professional and 10/400 [02.50 per cent] general respondents.

[v] ***Mass Health Education:*** It was strongly upheld by the respondents that a general mass movement about various aspects of health education must be started formally as well as informally. They felt that if general awareness about basic needs of gender healthcare is carried out, it will certainly contribute to grand success of gender healthcare. This suggestion was conveyed by 04/600 [00.66 per cent] respondents who were from professional [03/200,01.50 per cent] and general [01/400,00.25 per cent] categories.

2. Suggestions For Non-Governmental Organisations [NGOs]

The second set of suggestions presented by respondents was meant for the NGOs and their role *vis-à-vis* gender healthcare and its problems in Kashmir. The major suggestions in this regard are as follows:

[a] ***Active Role of NGOs:*** The respondents suggested that NGOs can play effective role in developing and maintaining the gender health care standard practices. These organisations have been playing this role and can ensure the fulfillment of its objectives. This suggestion about active role of NGOs was conveyed by the following respondents:

- Total number of respondents 290/600 [48.33 per cent]
- Number of professional respondents 196/200 [98.00 per cent]
- Number of general respondents 95/400 [23.75 per cent]

[b] ***Highlighting All Problems:*** It was suggested by respondents that NGOs must always highlight all major and minor problem of gender health care in Kashmir for the government and the gender health sufferers. This, according to respondents, was the first objective of NGOs working in this field. This suggestion was put forth by the following respondents:

- Total number of respondents 22/600 [03.66%]
- Number of professional respondents 12/200 [06.00%]
- Number of general respondents 10/400 [02.590%]

[c] ***Follow Mission-based Policy:*** The respondents suggested that NGOs must adopt ideas and ideals of gender health like a policy and follow it with a missionary zeal. These ideas were suggested by the following respondents:

- Total number of respondents 05/600 [00.83 per cent]
- Number of professional respondents 04/200 [02.00 per cent]
- Number of general respondents 01/400 [00.25 per cent]

[d] ***Organisation of Gender Health Camps and Melas:*** The respondents suggested that number of gender health camps and 'melas' must be organised by the NGOs with two specific objectives: to demonstrate gender health care plans and programmes and to present actual medical help to the sufferers. This suggestion was presented by the following respondents:

- Total number of respondents 15/600 [02.50 per cent]

- Number of professional respondents 13/200 [06.50 per cent]
- Number of general respondents 02/400 [00.50 per cent]

[e] ***Family Counselling:*** The respondents suggested that regular sessions of family counselling must be held for ensuring the minimum standards of gender health to be maintained in the state. This is more important in rural areas and lower socio-economic classes and culturally unexposed groups and communities. This suggestion was made by the following respondents:

- Total number of respondents 17/600 [02.83 per cent]
- Number of professional respondents 15/200 [07.50 per cent]
- Number of general respondents 02/400 [00.50 per cent]

[f] ***Health Surveys:*** In order to enquire about problems and issues related to gender health care in Kashmir province, the respondents suggested that regular and standard research- based surveys must be carried out by the experts. This will help to understand the problems and to put suggestion for their effective resolution. This suggestion was presented by the following respondents:

- Total number of respondents 18/600 [03.00 per cent]
- Number of professional respondents 17/200 [08.50 per cent]
- Number of general respondents 01/400 [00.25 per cent]

[g] ***Helping the Poor:*** The respondents suggested that special efforts must be carried out by the NGOs to help those patients of gender health who belong to lower economic sections and are not in a position to get the requisite facilities and services and medicines, even on lesser prices. This suggestion was formulated by the following respondents:

- Total number of respondents 09/600 [01.50 per cent]
- Number of professional respondents 05/200 [02.50 per cent]
- Number of general respondents 04/400 [01.00 per cent]

[h] ***Supporting the Preventive Measures:*** The respondents suggested that the NGOs are in a better position to convince people about benefits of preventive healthcare, especially in case of female healthcare. So, these organizations must always emphasise to adopt measures which will treat gender health care problems in effective preventive framework. This suggestion was made by the following respondents:

- Total number of respondents 04/600 [00.66 per cent]

- Number of professional respondents 03/200 [01.50 per cent]
- Number of general respondents 01/400 [00.25 per cent]

[i] ***Work in Co-ordination:*** The respondents also suggested that NGOs working in the field of gender healthcare must always show readiness for coordination which must be carried out at two levels, one, at the level of between these specialised NGOs and, two, between the NGOs and government agencies and organisations. This suggestion was presented by the following respondents:

- Total number of respondents 26/600 [04.33 per cent]
- Number of professional respondents 14/200 [07.00 per cent]
- Number of general respondents 12/400 [03.00 per cent]

[j] ***Promote Health Culture:*** In order to provide the permanence to the ideas and ideals of gender healthcare, the respondents suggested that evolution and maintenance of the relevant healthcare in the state. This needs wider social support at every level and sector of gender healthcare. This was suggested by the following respondents:

- Total number of respondents 01/600 [00.16 per cent]
- Number of professional respondents 01/200 [00.50 per cent]
- Number of general respondents 00/400 [00.00 per cent]

3. Suggestion for Civil Society

The respondents of this study also put forth some specific suggestions for the consideration of civil society groups and individuals. These suggestions were as follows:

[a] ***Awareness about Gender Healthcare:*** The respondents suggested that there should be organised mass campaign about gender health and its major problems in the Kashmir context. The role and importance of this campaign must also be highlighted. The civil society through its functional organs must play a central role in this campaign. It was also suggested that there seems complete consonance between objectives of gender healthcare and civil society. These views were presented by following respondents:

Total Respondents	Professional Respondents	General Respondents
47/600 [07.83 per cent]	37/200 [18.50 per cent]	10/400[02.50 per cent]

[b] ***Co-operation with Government:*** There must be complete cooperation between governmental institutions organisations and civil society organs-

agencies in relation to the implementation of gender health care schemes and programmes and make these purposeful and successful. This seems necessary for the functional dynamics of gender healthcare activities. This suggestion was presented by the following respondents:

Total Respondents	Professional Respondents	General Respondents
06/600 [01.00 per cent]	03/200 [01.50 per cent]	03/400 [00.75 per cent]

[c] ***Popularising Health Education:*** The respondents suggested that health education with special focus on gender health education must be popularised, which will certainly lead to mass awareness about its problems and issues. They also suggested that it is only through education that this mass level awareness can be raised, so that they can prove careful towards their health needs. These views were suggested by the following respondents:

Total Respondents	Professional Respondents	General Respondents
08/600 [01.33 per cent]	05/200 [02.50 per cent]	03/400 [00.75 per cent]

[d] ***Utilisation of All Resources:*** The respondents suggested that the facilities and services provided by the governmental institutions and organisations must be utilised properly and carefully, so that their effects are more extensive and deeply felt. The civil society cari do a lot in this regard through its organs and agencies. This was expressed by the following respondents:

Total Respondents	Professional Respondents	General Respondents
35/600[05.83 per cent]	22/200 [11.00 per cent]	13/400 [03.25 per cent]

[e] ***Check Corruption Seriously:*** The respondents felt the civil society of Kashmir is aware of the problem of corruption, so it must help the people to come out of this undesirable situation. The health institutions must be completely free from corruption. This suggestion was made by the following number of respondents:

Total Respondents	Professional Respondents	General Respondents
01/600 [00.16 per cent]	01/200 [00.50 per cent]	00/400 [00.00 per cent]

[f] ***Self-care by Respondents:*** The civil society has a decisive role in the healthcare of individuals. It can emphasise upon them to adopt all concerned facilities and services and take full care of themselves, especially by women. This suggestion was presented by the following number of respondents:

Total Respondents	Professional Respondents	General Respondents
36/600 [06.00 per cent]	27/200 [13.50 per cent]	09/400[02.25 per cent]

[g] *Attention Towards Preventive Care:* The respondents suggested that civil society in Kashmir must carry out all actions of related programmes in order to draw women's attention to positive aspects of preventive healthcare which are comparatively more beneficial. This suggestion was made by the following number of respondents:

Total Respondents	Professional Respondents	General Respondents
03/600 [00.50 per cent]	01/200 [00.50 per cent)	02/400 [00.50 per cent]

[h] *Stop Self-medication:* As the practice of self-medication is very common in Kashmir, the civil society groups can play a significant role in convincing people to desist from this practice as it has long term disastrous consequences for gender health. This suggestion was made by the following respondents:

Total Respondents	Professional Respondents	General Respondents
03/600 [00.50 per cent]	02/200 [01.00 per cent]	01/400[00.25 per cent]

[i] *Health Needs and Doctor's Advice:* The respondents felt that the civil society can effectively work for convincing the people regarding their needs and ask them to consult specialised doctors and follow their advice strictly. This critical role of the civil society was suggested by the following number of respondents:

Total Respondents	Professional Respondents	General Respondents
06/600 [01.00 per cent]	04/200 [02.00 per cent]	02/400 [00.50 per cent]

[j] *Highlight Gender Health Care Issues:* One of the important functions of civil society is to highlight the basic issues of general/gender health care repeatedly and at all levels of the government. In order to fulfill this purposeful role, the civil society must focus on all issues of gender healthcare before the government and before the people. This suggestion was put forth by the following respondents:

Total Respondents	Professional Respondents	General Respondents
91/600 [15.16 per cent]	46/200 [23.00 per cent]	45/400 [11.25 per cent]

[k] *Helping by Counselling:* The other way civil society can help gender health victims is through organising counselling sessions for all women at the individual, family and community levels. This suggestion was put forth by the following respondents:

Total Respondents	Professional Respondents	General Respondents
15/600 [02.50 per cent]	13/200 [06.50 per cent]	02/400 [00.50 per cent]

12

Critique and Conclusion

1. GHC and Conflict in J&K

(i) The Kashmir society had a deeper and wider experience of the armed conflict from 1989. As a result of this, the entire society was engulfed in its dynamics and implications. One of the crucial implications was felt in the partial collapse of the healthcare system in the state. Major part of the infrastructure was either destroyed or made non-functional. The working mechanism characterised of health centre or institution was destroyed seriously.

(ii) In this chaotic and insecure situation, a significant number of medicos and para medicos, especially those working in rural/hilly areas preferred to leave the valley. As a result, there were neither specialised/expert doctors available nor could all medical facilities/services be provided. The healthcare system collapsed in such a way that there was no regular supply of drugs to healthcare centres at district and sub district levels, so the patients in all areas especially in far flung mountainous areas could not get the needed medicines.

(iii) In this abnormal situation, gender healthcare suffered equally. The infrastructure services and practices in this highly specialised area were destroyed or damaged and it could not function effectively and could not even fulfil minimum needs of the concerned women. It was essentially in that situation that a poor woman died because of not getting the required medical treatment at the village, sub-district and district levels. due to extreme damage to hospitals, buildings and institutions.

2. GHC Areas and Needs

(i) The GHC referred to certain particular specialised medical areas directly related to GH. So, most of the women are fully aware about it. The respondents during study identified clearly the GHC areas as mentioned below:

1. Gynaecology
2. Reproductive Child Health and Maternal Child Health
3. Pre/post-delivery and Natal Care
4. Cardiology
5. Child Healthcare
6. Issues Pertaining to Adolescent Health
7. Mental Health
8. Nutritional Care
9. Social and Preventive Medicine
10. Oncology
11. Reproductive Endocrinology
12. Anamic Care
13. Gastroenterology
14. Immunology
15. Nephrology
16. Clinical Biochemistry
17. Caesarian
18. Orthopaedics
19. Paediatrics

(ii) In the background of GHC facilities available in J&K and the disastrous impact of conflict situation in last two decades the women have developed specific health needs in order to keep their health medically fit. Some of these health, needs are mentioned below:

1. Separate Hospitals for Women
2. Specialised Female staff
3. Health Education
4. Equipped Referral Transport
5. Awareness Programmes
6. Improved Facilities and Infrastructure
7. Attention to Fitness and Regular Exercise
8. Regular Health Check-ups
9. Immunisation
10. Healthy Stress-free/Environment
11. Remove Gender Disparity
12. Pre and Post-marital Counselling
13. Family Care
14. Nutrition
15. Maternity Care
16. Adequate Supply of Medicines
17. Blood Banks of PHC's

18. Women Empowerment
19. Pre and post-delivery care
20. Familial Support to Women
21. Early Diagnosis of Disease
22. Night Services
23. Mobile Medical Units
24. Night Services
25. Mobile Medical Units

3. GHC: Government Policy and Programmes

(i) In general, there is a prevalent policy of the government to take full care of and fulfil all basic needs of gender health care. The concerned government institutions, agencies and healthcare centres are conscious and committed to the implementation of these policy and related programmes. But there seems not sufficient awareness about this among common people. They don't have exact knowledge and requisite information in this regard. The government attempts to uphold and implement these policy ideas and ideals within the financial resources and medical infrastructure and facilities/services available. Though the government of J&K faces the same types of restrictions, its performance towards healthcare in general and GHC system in particular can be characterised as 'passive' or 'apathic' which it adopted due to chronic political instability in the state from 1947 onwards.

(ii) In this ustable and uncertain political condition, no proper planning could be carried out, no programmes could be implemented and no scheme could be implemented in the field of HC and GHC in particular. The politicians, planners and bureaucrats had no time to invest in sectors like health and education. In this situation, the schemes and programmes formulated and adopted by the Central Government could be adopted and implemented in the state, that helped the suffering lot in the health sector. In the recent past, the ideal example in this regard can be cited of NRHM which proved very effective in helping the needy in all concerned health fields and sub-fields.

(iii) Thus, common people and the professionals involved in health sector gave these views. While medicos and paramedics are more concerned about the suffering of common people, the health administration was not seriously concerned about it. Thus, the former themselves felt unable to perform the ideal role and the latter took least interest in the implementation of health ideals.

4. GHC and its Major Health Problems

(i) It has been observed that GHC faces lot of problems and multidimensional diseases. In fact, this field and sub-field has been conventionally associated with several diseases and this list has been added with other chronic and dangerous diseases. Our investigation in this regard revealed the names of diseases mentioned below:

1. UTI
2. Hysterectomy
3. Leucorroea and Other Infections
4. Anaemia
5. Arthritis
6. Thyroid
7. Osteoporosis
8. PCOD
9. Menstrual Irregularity
10. Infertility
11. Abortion
12. Dysmenorrhoea
13. Gestational Diabetes
14. Breast Cancer
15. Menorrhagia
16. Female Sexual Dysfunction
17. Depression/Hypertension
18. Gonorrhoea
19. Gout
20. Fibroids
21. Backache/pain
22. Malnutrition
23. Pre and post-delivery Complications
24. UTI and STD
25. Cervical Cancer
26. Jaundice
27. Polymorgia
28. Gynecological Disorders
29. Ovarian Cancer
30. Genital Herpes
31. Hepatitis A/B
32. Syphilis
33. Menstrual Disorders
34. Endometriosis
35. Pelvic Pain
36. Heart Problems
37. Hormonal Imbalances

(ii) Further investigation in the field of major health problems diagnosed revealed other major crucial problems related to the GHC. These other problems of woman included the following:

1. Late Marriages
2. Communication Gap
3. Illiteracy
4. Hygiene
5. Lack of Funding Schemes
6. Lack of Facilities
7. Gender Bias
8. Negligence by Women
9. Less Preventive Education
10. Females (specialists) not Available
11. Less Educated
12. Expensive Treatment
13. Too Many Children
14. Hectic Work Schedule
15. Less Family Support
16. Cultural Restrictions
17. Unhygienic Environment
18. Negligence by Doctors
19. Poverty
20. Self medication
21. Programmes not Implemented Properly
22. Lack of Supervision and Accountability
23. Noacceptance to Modern Healthcare
24. Lack of Adolescent Health Education
25. Violence Against Women
26. Complications During and After Pregnancy
27. Shyness Among Women
28. Drug Abuse
29. Non-Accessibility
30. Transportation
31. Affordability
32. Awareness Issues

(iii.) This investigation also led us to the preposition that GHC is directly as well as indirectly related to the CHC. These sub-fields of healthcare are intrinsically inversely related and are tied in reciprocal relations. While the entirety of CHC depends upon the GHC, the reverse is equally correct. This social and health reality has been associated with the GHC in Kashmir.

5. GHC: Major Issues

In the recent past, the GHC has been discussed, evaluated and analysed by official as well as non-official agencies such as health institutions, healthcare centers, and NGOs. In this background, various issues of GHC in Kashmir at presen were discussed. Five major issues were highlighted as major issues which include the following:

(i) Family Planning: It was felt by the largest section of woman that this practice goes in the ultimate interest of woman. So, its adoption may be considered as positive step towards women emancipation. So, they put forth their view that while this practice helps women to attain positive health gains, it also helps in the social progress of the concerned family. They also present an objective critique of cultural limitations and positive view of religious guidelines. In this way, this issue helps in the care of GHC assessment.

(ii)Sex Ratio: This issue arose d in recent decades when the decadal census records revealed the declining sex ratio, i.e., number of woman per 1,000 male population in the state. Since the sex ratio was found declining constantly, it was felt that this trend stands dangerous for women, it may involve even their survival. With this declining trend among children of less than six years of age, it was felt highly dangerous and alarming as this was done only after knowing the female sex of the baby followed by female foeticde. There was a unanimity in upholding the human dignity of the girl child. There was a common view that the illegal practice of abortion of female foeticide must be strictly opposed and all centers/clinics of sex determination tests must be closed immediately. Following this preventive and reformative measures, the perpetrators of this crime must be punished through legal measures.

(iii) Reducing the Maternal Mortality Rates

(a) One of the great concerns expressed by common people and professionals with equal intensity was the increasing trend of maternal mortality which has been caused in J&K due to various factors. Thus, the increasing number of illegal abortions, increasing IMR, least facilities/ services available at the time of delivery and so on have constibuted to heavy increase in the maternal mortality which stands higher than the national average.

(b) In this context, there must be organised and systematic efforts on the part of governmental and non-governmental health organisations and the health centers to follow the grand objective of decreasing MM rate, in all sections of the Kashmiri society. This has got a significant degree of support from the centrally sponsored schemes and programmes which have strong financial allocations. These measures will not only improve the status of GHC but the general improvement and empowerment of women in Kashmir.

(iv) Cultural Restrictions: The other issue of grave concern was:

(a) that of the impact of cultural restrictions of GHC which has all proved negative and counter productive in a traditional situation of Kashmiri culture, partly determined by religion. The gender healthcare has been at the receiving end. Consequently, while many women have not consulted the expert/specialised doctor in the absence of concerned female doctor, neither they intend to consult the male doctors in future. Even, in the family context, they are not allowed to treat themselves medically independently and they are not permitted to take any initiative in this regard. This tradition-determined cultural restriction have had completely negative impact on women health in Kashmir. Though a lot of general information has been revealed in the Kashmiri society in the recent decades, the women health sector in rural and hilly areas has not been affected radically.

(b) In the preceding context, it was upheld that strong, modern and organised formal initiatives are needed for making the cultural environment pro-gender. In actuality, the tradition and culture must be made in tone with the changing trends in contemporary times. So, culture in the present context must be utilised to serve the cause of gender, development and change.

(iv) GHC System: the Positive Views

The investigation in this study clearly revealed that common people and professionals and semi-professionals had developed positive views regarding GHC system. These views included the following:

(i) The HC system in the state lack a clear and independent policy and consequent plans and programmes. On the part of the government the most needed services demand these measures regarding GHC which must be initiated so that it can be institutionalised.

(ii) The second positive view was that state must play its positive role in the establishment of this system. It is only the state which can highlight broader network of GHC services and facilities. It can especially contribute to infrastructure i.e. latest technology and all necessary facilities and services, in addition to various necessary actions to fulfil demands and make this service satisfactory.

(iii) In this situation, the GHC in all areas must be an effective system fulfilling all its objectives. The private sector can also play very positive role. In reality, the private corporate sector has already established its roots in the health sector. Now, it has to be diverted towards a particular objective that is related to GHC system. Moreover, it is sure that it will contribute in terms of expertise, new and high level technology, infrastructure and various facilities and services.

(iv) Another dominant view related to the establishment of GHC system is that in addition to formal measures like infrastructure and latest technology, the entire community of medicos and paramedics have to be trained in the GHC ethos and GH services and facilities have to be provided to them necessarily during their service tenure. It means two types of efforts on the part of doctors, paramedics, health administrators and health authorities. In the first stage, all sections of this health fraternity have to evolve the gender sensitive ethos which will take care of all basic needs of women especially at the time of delivery and pregnancy. At the second stage, these sections of health fraternity have to work together in consideration and co-operation to provide necessary basic infrastructure, technological knowledge, facilities and services. Most important is that all sections feel conscious as well as committed to the gender health ideas and ideals.

6. The Suggestions Framework

During our investigation, suggestions were also presented for the established, betterment and improvement in the GHC system. The responses came in the shape of suggestions at three levels, in other words, directed to different institutional organisational entities. These suggestions in brief are mentioned below:

(i) For the Government of J&K

(a) Formulation, enactment and implementation of GH Policy in J&K.
(b) Expansion and Improvement in GH services.
(c) Increase in the number of female medical staff in all hospitals.
(d) Increase in the level of infrastructure.
(e) Coordination between various institutions of GHC sector.
(f) Carrying out mass awareness programme for GHC.
(g) Investigation about GHC in various sub-fields of health.
(h) Relevant GHC training to all medical and paramedical staff.
(i) Establishment of blood banks in every hospital for gender needs.
(j) Availability of funds for purchase of medicines.
(k) Root out the practice of corruption.
(l) Taking care of doctors service conditions.
(m) Proper and intensive care of pregnancy and delivery.
(n) Establishment of women's separate hospitals.
(o) Opening of fair price medical shops in hospitals.
(p) Special treatment of women mental healthcare.
(q) GH services to all far-flung areas.
(r) Availability of ambulances in every HCs.

(s) Efforts towards popularising health education within and outside family.

(ii) For NGOs

(a) Very active role of NGOs in all fields.
(b) Highlighting the importance of GHC problems.
(c) Follow the health policy like a mission.
(d) Organisation of GH camps, events and *melas*.
(e) Necessary family counselling must be carried out.
(f) Health survey among women must be carried out for knowing and assessing the enormity of Gender Health Problems.
(g) Helping the poor women in financial and non-financial terms.
(h) Promote the ideas and ideals of GH Culture.
(i) Carry out awareness programs about GHC.
(j) Create the environment of cooperation with the government,
(k) Utilisation of all formal and non-formal resources for GHC.

(iii) For Civil Society

(a) Check the corruption practice in hospitals.
(b) Paying attention towards preventive care in GHC.
(c) Attempts to stop self-medication.
(d) Asking scople to follow seriously doctors' advice.
(e) Highlight GHC issues.
(f) Organising conferences for raising Gender healthcare consciousness.
(g) Helping the adoption of GHC culture.
(h) Co-operate with governmental programmes and schemes.

APPENDICES

1. Gender Health Statics at large
2. Questionnaire of the Gender Health Study

Gender Healthcare Areas APPENDICES

Q. No. 1(a) S. No.	*FIELDS*	*SRI (D1) G*	*P*	*BUD (D2) G*	*P*	*ANA (D3) G*	*P*	*BAR (D4) G*	*P*	*General*	*Responses Professional*	*Total*
1.	Gynaecology	81	46	70	20	82	33	88	48	321	147	468
2.	Obesterics	30	23	70	21	63	20	77	50	240	114	354
3.	Maternal Healthcare											
	Pre and Post-Natal	25	15	0	0	0	1	0	0	25	16	41
4.	Healthcare	18	3	0	0	7	10	3	4	28	17	45
5.	Cardiology	4	5	0	0	1	1	0	0	5	6	11
6.	Child Health Ca:e											
	Issues/Care of	4		0	0	0	0	0	0	4	3	7
7.	Adolescent Girls	23	20	0	0	0	0	0	0	23	20	43
8.	Mental Health	18	13	0	4	0	0	1	1	19	18	37
9.	Nutritional Care											
	Child and Mater.ıal	9	11	0	0	0	0	0	0	9	11	20
10.	Health Care Soc.al											
	and Preventive	21	0	0	0	0	0	0	0	21	0	21
11.	Medicine	0	0	4	9	0	0	0	6	4	15	19
12.	Oncology	0	0	15	4	0	0	13	16	18	20	38
13.	R. Endocrinology	0	0	11	8	9	9	9	6	29	23	52
14.	RCH and MCH											
	Pre/post-dellivery	0	0	6	20	61	20	33	8	100	48	148
15.	Care	0	0	0	0	2	0	0	0	2	0	2
16.	Anaemic Care	0	0	0	1	0	0	0	0	0	1	1
17.	Gastroentrology	0	0	0	2	0	0	0	0	0	2	2
18.	Immunology	0	0	2	2	0	0	0	0	2	2	4
19.	Nephrology	0	0	0	2	0	0	0	0	0	2	2
20.	Female mortality	0	0	0	2	0	0	0	0	0	2	2
21.	Clinical Biochemistry											
	Issues of Adolesent	0	0	0	2	0	0	0	0	0	2	2
22.	Girls	0	0	0	0	2	0	0	0	2	0	2
23.	Child Care	0	0	0	0	3	0	0	0	3	0.	3
24.	Paediatrics	0	0	0	0	2	0	0	0	2	0	2
25.	Infertility	0	0	0	0	1	0	0	0	I	0	1
26.	Osteoporosis	0	0	0	0	I	0	0	0	1	0	1
27.	Ceasarian	0	0	0	0	0	2	0	0	0	2	2
28.	Orthopaedics	0	0	0	0	0	3	0	0	0	3	3
29.	Endocrinology	0	0	0	0	0	0	0	12	0	12	12
30.	Community Medicine	0	0	0	0	0	0	1	2	1	2	3

1 b 2. Gender Healthcare Needs

Q. No. 1(b) S. No.	*NEEDS*	*SRI (D1) G*	*P*	*BUD (D2) G*	*P*	*ANA (D3) G*	*P*	*BAR (D4) G*	*P*	*General*	*Responses Professional*	*Total*
1.	Separate Hospita.s for Woman	0	0	0	0	0	0	29	20	29	20	49
2.	Female Staff		0	0	0	0	0	9	2	9	2	11
3.	Health Educators/ Health Education	14	16	0	0	12	3	57	34	83	53	136

4.	Referral Transportation	0	0	0	2	5	5	26	12	31	19	50
5.	Awareness Programmes	3	8	26	30	44	26	6	15	79	158	
6.	Accessible Hospitals	0	0	0	0	0	0	8	11	8	11	19
7.	Female Doctors	0	0	0	1	0	0	43	7	43	8	51
8.	Female Paramadical Staff	0	0	0	0	0	1	8	5	8	6	14
9.	Separate and Accessible Hospitals	0	0	0	3	10	2	24	21	34	26	60
10.	All Facilites and Infrastructure	0	0	10	1	0	0	34	13	44	14	58
11.	Fitness	4	6	0	0	0	0	0	0	4	6	10
12.	Health checkup	29	1	0	0	0	0	0	0	29	1	30
13.	Infrastructure	2	0	0	0	0	0	0	0	2	0	2
14.	Immunisation	3	1	17	6	27	5	0	0	47	12	59
15.	Sex Education	12	3	9	1	1	0	0	0	22	4	26
16.	Sufficient manpower	0	0	0	0	0	0	0	0	0	0	0
17.	Healthy environment /Stress free	42	9	0	0	0	0	0	0	42	9	51
18.	Remove Gender Disparity	6	4	1	1	0	0	0	0	7	5	12
19.	Pre/post-marital Counselling	9	0	0	2	0	0	0	0	9	2	11
20.	Family Care	6	4	0	0	0	0	0	0	6	4	10
21.	Clinical Haematology	0	1	0	0	0	0	0	0	0	1	1
22.	Nutrition	69	0	65	12	45	13	0	0	179	25	204
23.	Maternity care	0	0	1	3	0	0	0	0	1	3	4
24.	Decision Making	0	3	0	0	0	0	0	0	0	3	3
25.	Prof. Female Staff	0	1	0	0	0	0	0	0	0	1	1
26.	Adequate Supply of Medicines	0	0	0	0	3	13	0	0	3	13	16
27.	Blood Banks in PHC's	0	0	0	2	3	5	0	0	3	7	10
28.	IFA Tablets	0	0	0	0	11	0	0	0	11	0	11
29.	Free Supply of Medicines	0	0	0	0	3	0	0	0	3	0	3
30.	Hygeinic Environment	0	0	0	0	7	10	0	0	7	10	17
31.	Health Counselling	0	0	4	1	0	1	0	0	4	2	6
32.	Female Gynaecologists and Staff	0	0	0	0	10	4	0	0	10	4	14
33.	Women Empowerment	0	0			2		0	0	3	2	5
34.	Separate OPD's for Woman	0	0	0	0	7	2	0	0	2	2	4
35.	Paediatric Care	0	0	0	1	0	2	0	0	0	3	3
36.	Nephrologist	0	0	0	0	0	1	0	0	0	1	1
37.	Cardiac Care	0	0	0	0	0	1	0	0	0	1	1
38.	Pre and Post-delivery Care	0	0	18	11	3	0	0	0	21	11	32
39.	Free Medical Checkup's	0	0	4	1	1	0	0	0	5	1	6
40.	Familial Support to Woman	0	0	0	0	1	0	0	0	1	0	1
41.	Adequate Facilities and Infrastructure	0	0	0	0	2	0	0	0	2	0	2
42.	Neo-Natal Care in	0	0	0	0	1	0	0	0	1	0	1

	Hospitals											
43.	Early Diagnosis of Diseases	0	0	0	1	0	0	0	0	0	1	1
44.	Preventive education	0	0	2	6	0	0	0	0	2	6	8
45.	Hygenic Environment	0	0	18	22	0	0	0	0	18	22	40
46.	Descision-making authority to women	0	0	0	1	0	0	0	0	0	1	1
47.	Night services	0	0	1	1	0	0	0	0	1	1	2
48.	Mobile medical units	0	0	0	1	0	0	0	0	0	1	1
49.	Regular Exercise and fitness	0	0	9	0	0	0	0	0	9	0	9
50.	Familial Support to Woman	0	0	9	8	0	0	0	0	9	8	17
51.	Good food	0	0	3	0	0	0	0	0	3	0	3
52.	Mental fitness	0	0	1	0	0	0	0	0	1	0	1

(2a 3. Gender Healthcare Polieces

Q. No.		*SRI*		*BUD*		*ANA*		*BAR*				
2(a)		*(D1)*		*(D2)*		*(D3)*		*(D4)*			*Responses*	
S. No.	*Policy*	*G*	*P*	*G*	*P*	*G*	*P*	*G*	*P*	*General*	*Professional*	*Total*
1.	No Health Policy of the State	29	23	6	8	18	5	0	0	53	36	89
2.	Don't Know	9	4	22	10	53	16	11	7	95	37	132
3.	No response	58	20	70	16	1	3	10	0	139	39	178
4.	Centrally Sponsored Schemes	3	3	0	0	27	21	67	32	97	56	153
5.	Defunct Health Policy	1	0	0	0	1	5	12	11	14	16	30
6.	Health *Melas*	0	0	0	1	0	0	0	0	0	1	1
7.	NRHM	0	0	0	9	0	0	0	0	0	9	9
8.	No Gender Health Policy	0	0	0	8	0	0	0	0	0	8	8
9.	Free Services To Pregnant Ladies	0	0	5	4	0	0	0	0	5	4	9
10.	Population Control Awareness	0	0	0	1	0	0	0	0	0	1	1

(2b 4. Gender Healthcare Programmes

Q. No.		*SRI*		*BUD*		*ANA*		*BAR*				
2(b)		*(D1)*		*(D2)*		*(D3)*		*(D4)*			*Responses*	
S. No.	*Reflection*	*G*	*P*	*G*	*P*	*G*	*P*	*G*	*P*	*General*	*Professional*	*Total*
1.	NO Response	93	47	92	45	81	30	0	0	266	122	388
2.	JSY, JSSK, RCH, MCTS, ICDS	0	2	0	0	0	15	0	0	0	17	17
3.	IMR, MMR	0	0	0	0	4	5	0	0	4	5	9

	Decreased											
4.	Don't Know any Health Policy of the State	7	0	0	0	6	0	34	4	47	4	51
5.	NRHM	0	1	0	0	4	0	0	0	4	1	5
6.	Inadequate Medicine and Facilities	0	0	0	0	5	0	0	0	5	0	5
7.	Yes	0	0	2	5	0		54	43	56	48	104
8.	NO	0	0	6	0	0		12	3	18	3	21

2c 4. Gender Healthcare Attitudes

Q. No. 2(c) S. No.	*Attitude*	*SRI (D1) G*	*P*	*BUD (D2) G*	*P*	*ANA (D3) G*	*P*	*BAR (D4) G*	*P*	*Responses General*	*Professional*	*Total*
1.	Positive (Appropriate) Following Guidelines	0	3	0	0	0	10	18	18	18	31	49
2.	Negative We Lack Best Health Administrators	0	0	0	0	11	3	72	31	83	34	117
3.	No Response	93	43	78	46	75	28	10	1	256	118	374
4.	MCTS has made Everyone Accountable	0	0	0	0	0	2	0	0	0	2	2
5.	Corrupted Administrators	0	0	0	0	0	4	0	0	0	4	4
6.	They Lack Administrative Skills	0	0	0	0	14	3	0	0	14	3	17
7.	Don't Know	7	4	0	0	0	0	0	0	7	4	11
8.	Many Programmes have been Started	0	0	0	2	0	0	0	0	0	2	2
9.	Proper Planning is Needed	0	0	0	2	0	0	0	0	0	2	2
10.	Just Relying on Central Level Programmes	0	0	0	1	0	0	0	0	0	1	1
11.	More Attention towards Women Health	0	0	3	1	0	0	0	0	3	1	4
12.	Resources are Diverted towards Amarnath *Yatris*	0	0	0	1	0	0	0	0	0	1	1

13.	Programmes by Central Government	0	0	0	1	0	0	0	0	0	1	1
14.	No Programme by State	0	0	0	1	0	0	0	0	0	1	1
15.	Proper Implementation is Needed	0	0	4	2	0	0	0	0	4	2	6
16.	Less Attention and more Corruption	0	0	22	4	0	0	0	0	22	4	26

3a 5. Gender Healthcare Diseases

Q. No 3a S. No.	*DISEASES*	*SRI (D1)*		*BUD (D2)*		*ANA (D3)*		*BAR (D4)*			*Responses*	
		G	*P*	*G*	*P*	*G*	*P*	*G*	*P*	*General*	*Professional*	*Total*
1.	UTI	36	17	0	0	0	0	0	0	36	17	53
2.	Hysterectomy	7	0	4	2	0	0	0	0	11	2	13
3.	Leucohorrea	28	15	44	19	2	2		0	74	36	110
4.	Anaemia	39	16	71	39	40	27	67	50	217	132	349
5.	Arthritis	17	0	5	4	0	0	0	0	16	4	20
6.	Thyroid	11	10	18	19	17	16	45	34	91	79	170
7.	Osteoporosis	14	3	3	10	1	5	0	0	18	18	36
8.	PCOD	5	9	9	11	0	0	0	0	14	20	34
9.	Menstrual Irregularity	0	0	0	0	0	0	23	6	23	6	29
10.	Infertility	10	3	9	1	0	0	0	0	19	4	23
11.	Abortion	0	0	0	1	0	0	0	0	0	1	1
12.	Dysmenhorrhea	6	2	7	1	0	2	0	0	13	5	18
13.	Gestational Diabetes	5	0	1	1	0	0	0	0	6	1	7
14.	Breast Cancer	1	4	10	3	0	0	5	0	16	7	23
15.	Uterus Related Issues	0	0	0	0	0	0	0	0	0	0	0
16.	Menorrhagia	4	0	5	2	0	1	0	0	9	3	12
17.	Post-Delivery Issues	0	0	C	0	0	0	0	0	0	0	0
18.	Vaginitis	2	6	6	4	1	3	0	0	9	13	22
19.	Female Sexual Dysfunction	3	1	0	0	0	0	0	0	3	1	4
20.	Depression	1	1	0	0	6	4	0	0	7	5	12
21.	Gonorrhea	0	1	0	0	0	0	0	0	0	1	1
22.	Gout	0	1	0	0	0	0	0	0	0	1	1
23.	Fibroids	2	0	3	5	0	5	0	0	5	10	15
24.	Backache/pain	13	0	12	1	2	0	0	0	27	1	28
25.	Malnutrition	0	0	2	1	30	7	7	4	39	12	51
26.	Pre and Post-Delivery Complications	0	0	11	6	7	0	0	0	18	6	24

27.	Infectious Diseases	0	0	0	2	0	0	0	0	0	2	2
28.	UTI and STDs	0	0	26	40	8	17	68	39	102	96	198
29.	Hypertension during pregnancy	0	0	3	0	0	0	0	0	3	0	3
30.	Blood Pressure	0	0	0	0	1	0	0	0	1	0	1
31.	Hypertension	0	0	0	0	2	0	0	0	2	0	2
32.	Cervical Cancer	0	0	0	0	1	0	0	0	1	0	1
33.	Jaundice	0	0	0	0	0	1	0	0	0	1	1
34.	Polymorghia	0	0	0	0	0	1	0	0	0	1	1
35.	Gynaecological Disorder	0	0	0	0	0	2	0	0	0	2	2
36.	Ovarian Cancer	0	0	0	0	0	1	0	0	0	1	1
37.	Gental Herpes	0	0	0	0	0	1	0	0	0	1	1
38.	Breast Cancer	0	0	0	0	0	11	0	0	0	11	11
39.	Hapititis A & E	0	0	0	0	0	2	0	0	0	2	2
40.	Syphilis	0	0	0	0	0	2	0	0	0	2	2
41.	Diabetics	0	0	0	0	1	1	0	0	1	1	2
42.	Menstural Disorders	0	0	0	0	1	6	0	0	1	6	7
43.	Heart Diseases	0	0	0	0	4	1	0	0	4	1	5
44.	Tension/Stress /Hypertension	0	0	0	0	0		33	19	33	19	52
45.	Endometriosis	0	0	0	0	0	2	0	0	0	2	2
46.	Pelvic Pain	0	0	0	0	0	2	0	0	0	2	2
47.	Heart Problems	0	0	0	0	0	0	23	17	23	17	40
48.	Hormonal Imbalances	0	0	0	0	0	0	10	4	10	4	14

3b 6. Gender Healthcare Treatment

Q. No.		*SRI*		*BUD*		*ANA*		*BAR*				
3b	*Do they get*	*(D1)*		*(D2)*		*(D3)*		*(D4)*			*Responses*	
S. No.	*Proper Treatment*	*G*	*P*	*G*	*P*	*G*	*P*	*G*	*P*	*General*	*Professional*	*Total*
1.	***YES***	82	22	50	35	43	23	97	46	272	126	398
2.	Private Clinics	35	6	17	3	10	2	61	19	123	30	153
3.	Govt. Hospitals	34	9	14	27	30	**9**	3	5	81	50	131
4.	Both Private and Public Hospitals	10	5	18	5	3	12	36	17	67	39	106
5.	Dispensaries	3	2	0	0	0	0	0	0	3	2	5
6.	Private Preffered	0	0	0	0	0	0	0	9	0	9	9
7.	Only Consultation no Free Drugs	0	0	1	0	0	0	0	0	1	0	1
		0	0	0	0	0	0	0	0	0	0	0
	NO	16	26	47	15	57	27	3	4	123	72	195
1.	Expensive Treatment	5	3	10	2	2	4	0	0	17	9	26
2.	Lack of Prof. Female Staff	4	1	16	2	4	1	0	0	24	4	28

3.	Unawareness	2	3	0	0	0	0	0	0	2	3	5
4.	Lack of Supplies	1	1	0	0	0	0	0	0	1	1	2
5.	Lack of Infrastructure and Manpower	1	10	0	0	0	0	0	0	1	10	11
6.	Lack of Facilities	1	4	6	3	51	22	0	0	58	29	87
7.	Shyness to Come Forward	2	4	0	0	0	0	0	0	2	4	6
8.	Free and Effective Treatment not Available	0	0	9	3	0	0	0	0	9	3	12
9.	Drugs Not Available	0	0	3	5	0	0	0	0	3	5	8
10.	Negligent Behaviour of Doctors	0	0	2	0	0	0	0	0	2	0	2
11.	Poverty	0	0	1	0	0	0	0	0	1	0	1
		0	0	0	0	0	0	0	0	0	0	0
	NO RESPONSE	2	2	3	0	0	0	0	0	5	2	7

3c 7. Gender Healthcare Means and Ways

Q. No. 3(c) S. No.	*Ways and Means*	*SRI (D1)*		*BUD (D2)*		*ANA (D3)*		*BAR (D4)*		*Responses*		
		G	*P*	*G*	*P*	*G*	*P*	*G*	*P*	*General*	*Professional*	*Total*
1.	Health Education	8	10	0	0	30	19	33	1	71	30	101
2.	Counselling	20	3	7	12	6	3	0	0	33	18	51
3.	Awareness	23	34	13	11	12	1	25	35	73	81	154
4.	Remove Gender Bias	0	0	9	1	0	0	11	0	20	1	21
5.	Specific Gender Health Policy	0	3	2	2	0	0	0	0	2	5	7
6.	Improve Infrastructure	4	0	0	0	11	4	0	0	15	4	19
8.	Sufficient Workforce	5	0	0	0	0	0	0	0	5	0	5
9.	Provision of Facilities	5	0	0	0	0	0	0	0	5	0	5
10.	Workshops	1	0	0	0	0	0	0	0	1	0	1
11.	Empower Women	1	0	5	1	13	9	17	11	36	21	57
12.	Social Mobilisation	3	0	0	0	0	0	0	0	3	0	3
13.	Education	19	0	32	7	0	0	0	0	51	17	68
14.	*NO RESPONSIE*	11	0	0	1	0	0	0	0	11	1	12
15.	Motivation	0	0	0	1	0	0	0	0	0	1	1
16.	Recruit Female staff	0	0	2	2	0	3	0	0		5	7

17.	Proper planning	0	0	8	1	0	0	0	0		1	9
18.	Specialized Treatment	0	0	0	1	0	0	0	0	0	1	1
19.	Pre & post marital counselling	0	0	1	0	0	0	0	0	1	0	1
20.	Family support	0	0	1	0	0	0	0	0	1	0	1
21.	Remove Cultural Barriers and Restrictions	0	0	0	0	3	1	3	0	6	1	7
22.	Health Administration Should Function Properly	0	0	0	0	0	1	0	0	0	1	1
23.	Separate OPD's for Woman	0	0	0	0	1	2	0	0	1	2	3
24.	Separate Hospital's for Woman	0	0	0	0	7	1	0	0	7	1	8
25.	Proper Utilization of Funds	0	0	0	0	0	1	0	0	0	1	1
26.	Health Facilities at ICDS Centers	0	0	0	0	0	1	0	0	0	1	1
27.	Centrally Sponsored Schemes Properly Implemented	0	0	0	0	5	2	0	0	5	2	7
28.	State Specific Schemes	0	0	0	0	4	1	0	0	4	1	5
29.	More Allocation of Funds for Gender Health	0	0	0	0	0	1	0	0	0	1	1
30.	Free Health Care to Woman	0	0	0	0	6	0	0	0	6	0	6
31.	Woman Themselves Should take on Stand	0	0	0	0	1	0	0	0	1	0	1
32.	Health Administrator's Should Function Properly	0	0	0	0	1	0	0	0	1	0	1
33.	Participation of Women in Decision Making	0	0	0	0	0	0	11	3	11	3	14

Q. No. 3(d) S. No.	*Problems*	*SRI (D1) G*	*P*	*BUD (D2) G*	*P*	*ANA (D3) G*	*P*	*BAR (D4) G*	*P*	*Responses General*	*Professional*	*Total*
1.	Late Marriages	15	7	0	0	0	1	0	0	15	8	23
2.	Communication Gap	0	2	0	0	6	4	56	44	62	50	112
3.	Leucohorrea	9	3	0	0	0	0	0	0	9	3	12
4.	Anaemia	25	7	0	0	0	0	0	0	25	7	32

5.	PCOD	16	2	0	0	0	0	0	0	16	2	18
6.	Osteoporosis	20	4	0	0	0	0	0	0	20	4	24
7.	Thyroid	25	15	0	0	0	0	0	0	25	15	40
8.	Illiteracy	0	2	0	0	3	2	0	0	3	4	7
9.	Hypertension	9	2	0	0	0	0	0	0	9	2	11
10.	Infertility	24	9	0	0	0	0	0	0	24	9	33
11.	Women Cancers	10	5	0	0	0	0	0	0	10	5	15
12.	Hysterectomy	10	7	0	0	0	0	0	0	10	7	17
13.	Hygiene	5	1	0	0	0	0	0	0	5	1	6
14.	Fibroids	3	3	0	0	0	0	0	0	3	3	6
15.	Gestational Diabetes	4	3	0	0	0	0	0	0	4	3	7
16.	Vaginitis	0	2	0	0	0	0	0	0	0	2	2
17.	Gout	3	3	0	0	0	0	0	0	3	3	6
18.	Lack of Funding Schemes	11	1	0	0	1	0	0	0	12	1	13
19.	Lack of Facilities	12	2	27	1	0	0	0	0	39	3	42
20.	Gender Bias	10	4	16	9	8	1	0	0	34	14	48
21.	Stress/Strain /Backache	29	0	0	0	0	0	0	0	29	0	29
22.	Negligence by Women	0	0	15	10	2	4	0	0	17	14	31
23.	Less Preventive Education	0	0	2	0	0	0	0	0	2	0	
24.	Female Doctors Not Available	0	0	36	4	0	0	0	0	36	4	16
25.	Facilities not Available	0	0	3	2	7	4	0	0	10	6	
26.	Less Education	0	0	4	7	0	0	0	0	4	7	11
27.	Expensive Treatment	0	0	4	0	1	0	0	0	5	0	5
28.	Too Many Children	0	0	1	5	0	0	0	0	1	5	6
29.	Hectic Work Schedule	0	0	1	0	0	0	0	0	1	0	1
30.	Less Family Support	0	0	10	1	2	0	0	0	12	1	13
31.	Cultural Restrictions	0	0	15	7	16	6	68	38	99	51	150
32.	Financial Dependency of Women	0	0	3	0	0	1	0	0	3	1	4
33.	Weak Referral System	0	0	2	1	0	0	0	0	2	1	3
34.	Over burden on Women	0	0	12	20	0	0	0	0	12	20	32
35.	Unhygienic Environment	0	0	3	7	3	0	0	0	6	7	13
36.	Increase Awareness	0	0	6	3	0	0	0	0	6	3	9
37.	Negligence by Doctors	0	0	9	0		0	0	0	9	0	9
38.	Poverty	0	0	4	3	4	2	0	0	8	5	13
39.	Unavailability of Specialists	0	0	2	0	0	0	0	0	2	0	2
40.	Malnutrition	0	0	3	0	13	0	0	0	16	0	16
41.	Self-medication	0	0	3	0	1	0	0	0	4	0	4

42.	Programmes not Properly Implemented	0	0	2	0	0	0	0	0	2	0	2
43.	Spurious Drug Supply	0	0	3	1	0	4	0	0	3	5	8
44.	Lack of Supervision and Accountability	0	0	1	1	0	0	0	0	1	1	2
45.	Overcrowdedness of Hospitals	0	0	5	0	0	0	0	0	5	0	5
46.	Patrarchial Society	0	0	1	0	0	0	0	0	1	0	1
47.	Corruption	0	0	0	3	2	1	0	0	2	4	6
48.	Unacceptance to Modern Health Care	0	0	0	1	5	11	0	0	5	12	17
49.	Lack of Adolescent Health Education	0	0	0	2	0	0	0	0	0	2	2
50.	24×7 services not Available	0	0	0	1	0	0	0	0	0	1	1
51.	Blood Banks not Available	0	0	0	1	0	0	0	0	0	1	1
52.	Violence against Women	0	0	0	1	1	0	0	0	1	1	2
53.	Complications during and after Pregnancy	0	0	0	2	0	0	0	0	0	2	2
54.	Shyness Among Women	0	0	0	3	0	0	0	0	0	3	3
55.	Un-accessibilty	0	0	0	0	8	2	0	0	8	2	10
56.	Medicines Expensive	0	0	0	0	0	2	0	0	0	2	2
57.	Unawareness	0	0	0	0	0	4	0	0	0	4	4
58.	Woman Overburdened	0	0	0	0	2	1	0	0	2	1	3
59.	Drug Abuse	0	0	0	0	1	0	0	0	1	0	1
60.	No Response	0	0	0	0	14	0	0	0	14	0	14
61.	Accessibility	0	0	0	0	0	0	44	27	44	27	71
62.	Transportation	0	0	0	0	0	0	34	22	34	22	56
63.	Affordability	0	0	0	0	0	0	24	2	24	2	26
64.	Awareness Issues	0	0	0	0	0	0	20	1	20	1	21

3e 9. Gender Healthcare Issues

Q. No. 3(e) S. No.	*ISSUES*	*SRI (D1)*		*BUD (D2)*		*ANA (D3)*		*BAR (D4)*		*Responses General*	*Professional*	*Total*
1.	Family Planning	G	P	G	P	G	P	G	P			
2.	Prefered	50	0	0	0	0	0	0	0	50	0	50
3.	Less Preffered	40	0	0	0	0	0	0	0	40	0	40
4.	After Three Children	10	0	0	0	0	0	0	0	10	0	10

	NO RESPONSE	0	50	34	9	25	4	0	0	59	63	122
6.	Contraceptive Pills Mainly Used	0	0	0	4	0	0	0	0	0	4	4
7.	Improve Education about it	0	0	10	2	0	0	0	0	10	2	12
8.	Counselling is Needed	0	0	0	1	0	0	0	0	0	1	1
9.	Mainly Tubcclomy	0	0	8	7	12	11	0	0	20	18	38
10.	Burden on Females	0	0	0	1	0	0	0	0	0	1	1
11.	Lack of Awareness	0	0	0	7	0	0	0	0	0	7	7
12.	Less Prevalent in Rural Areas	0	0	0	8	0	0	0	0	0	8	8
13.	Low Acceptance in Rural Areas	0	0	2	1	2	4	19	4	23	9	32
14.	Child Spacing Methods should be Used	0	0	0	3	13	0	0	0	13	3	16
15.	Excessive Use of Contraceptives Create Problems	0	0	0	2	0	0	0	0	0	2	2
16.	Less Practised	0	0	30	2	0	0	0	0	30	2	32
17.	Due to Conflict People Prefer More Children	0	0	1	3	0	0	0	0	1	3	4
18.	Don't Know	0	0	11	0	0	0	0	0	11	0	11
19.	Not Allowed in Islam	0	0	4	0	9	11	0	0	13	11	24
20.	Accepted Norm Now for Better Standard of Living	0	0	0	0	18	13	81	46	99	59	158
21.	Still Need Awareness in Far Flung Areas	0	0	0	0	16	2	0	0	16	2	18
22.	Accepted Because of Incentives	0	0	0	0	0	4	0	0	0	4	4
23.	Promoted because of NRHM	0	0	0	0	0	1	0	0	0	1	1
24.	Use of Improper Methods	0	0	0	0	3	0	0	0	3	0	3
25.	Education can Promote it	0	0	0	0	2	0	0	0	2	0	2

Q.No. 3(f). *S. No.*	*SEX RATIO*	*SRI (D1)* *G*	*P*	*BUD (D2)* *G*	*P*	*ANA (D3)* *G*	*P*	*BAR (D4)* *G*	*P*	*Responses* *General*	*Professional*	*Total*
1.	Declined	20	0	0	0	0	0	0	0	20	0	20
2.	Normal	60	0	58	10	4	0	0	0	122	10	132
3.	Any Other	5	0	0	0	0	0	0	0	5	0	5

4.	*NO RESPONSE*	15	50	25	32	20	16	13	1	60	99	159
5.	Female Sex Decreasing	0	0	5	1	0	0	0	0	5	1	6
6.	Don't Know	0	0	12	7	0	0	0	0	12	7	19
7.	Needs Awareness /Counselling	0	0	0	0	15	7	87	44	15	51	66
8.	Strict Laws Needed against the Culprits of Female Foeticide	0	0	0	0	12	1	0	0	12	1	13
9.	MCTS has Controlled it Now	0	0	0	0	2	4	0	0	2	4	6
10.	Moral and Religious Education can Curb this Menace	0	0	0	0	16	4	0	0	16	4	20
11.	Declining is a Concern	0	0	0	0	4	4	0	0	4	4	8
12.	Empower the Woman	0	0	0	0	1	0	0	0	1	0	1
13.	Dowry is the Actual Culprit	0	0	0	0	1	0	0	0	1	0	1
14.	Illegal Abortions Responsible	0	0	0	0	10	3	0	0	10	3	13
15.	Gender Bias Responsible	0	0	0	0	1	0	0	0	1	0	1
16.	Need is to Highlight its Consequences	0	0	0	0	0	4	0	0	0	4	4
17.	Needs to be Balanced	0	0	0	0	1	2	0	0	1	2	3
18.	Promote Education	0	0	0	0	5	4	0	0	5	4	9
19.	Illiteracy Responsible	0	0	0	0	1	0	0	0	1	0	1
20.	NRHM Aimed to Curb This	0	0	0	0	0	1	0	0	0	1	1
21.	Inadequate Facilities Responsible	0	0	0	0	1	0	0	0	1	0	1
22.	Our Society is Dominateci by Male/Less Preferance to Female	0	0	0	0	6	0	0	0	6	0	6
23.	Awareness is Going on	0	0	0	0	0	0	0	4	0	4	4
24.	Emerging Issue	0	0	0	0	0	0	0	1	0	1	1

3g 11. Female Foeticide

Q.No. 3(g)	*Female Foeticide*	*SRI (D1)*		*BUD (D2)*		*ANA (D3)*		*BAR (D4)*		*Responses*		
		G	*P*	*G*	*P*	*G*	*P*	*G*	*P*	*General*	*Professional*	*Total*
1.	Done Illegally	30	0	0	0	22	14	57	29	109	43	152
2.	any other	20	0	0	0	0	0	0	0	0	0	0
3.	No Response	50	50	35	21	21	5	0	2	56	78	134
4.	Private Clinics	0	0	10	5	0	0	0	0	10	5	15
5.	Unregistered Clinics	0	0	1	4	0	0	0	0	1	4	5

6.	Strict Law Enforcement	0	0	0	6	0	0	0	0	0	6	6
7.	Improve Awareness	0	0	0	1	11	12	0	0	11	13	24
8.	Not Common	0	0	0	4	0	0	0	0	0	4	4
9.	Moral and Religious Education	0	0	0	2	5	4	0	0	5	6	11
10.	Don't Know	0	0	29	3	0	0	0	0	29	3	32
11.	Un Wanted Pregnancies	0	0	1	1	0	0	0	0	1	1	2
12.	Not Reportec	0	0	13	2	0	0	0	0	13	2	15
13.	Supervision	0	0	11	1	0	0	0	0	11	1	12
14.	Now Controlled to a large extent	0	0	0	0	5	7	0	0	5	7	12
15.	Need to be Tackled With the Help of Law	0	0	0	0	5	3	0	0	5	3	8
16.	MCTS has Controlled it	0	0	0	0	7	4	0	0	7	4	11
17.	NRHM Aimed to Curb this Menace	0	0	0	0	5	1	0	0	5	1	6
18.	Gender Bias Responsible	0	0	0	0	8	0	0	0	8	0	8
19.	Dowry Actual Culprit	0	0	0	0	1	0	0	0	1	0	1
20.	Illitracy Responsible	0	0	0	0	7	0	0	0	7	0	7
21.	Quite Illegal and Needs to be Curbed	0	0	0	0	1	0	0	0	1	0	1
22.	Empower the Woman	0	0	0	0	2	0	0	0	2	0	2
23.	Banned	0	0	0	0	0	0	43	19	43	19	62

3h 12. Maternal Mostality

Q.No 3(h) S.No.	*Maternal Mortality*	*SRI (D1) G*	*P*	*BUD (D2) G*	*P*	*ANA (D3) G*	*P*	*BAR (D4) G*	*P*	*Responses General*	*Professional*	*Total*
1.	REDUCED	40	0	15	14	10	10	0	0	65	24	89
2.	NO RESPONSE	60	50	13	16	29	9	0	0	102	75	177
3.	Institutional Deliveries can Reduce it	0	0	0	2	0	0	0	0	0	2	2
4.	Weak Referral System	0	0	17	3	0	0	0	0	17	3	20
5.	Mainly In Far Flung Areas	0	0	8	3	0	0	0	0	8	3	11
6.	24×7 Services Not Available	0	0	0	2	0	0	0	0	0	2	2
7.	High due to Lack of Maternity Hospitals	0	0	0	3	0	0	0	0	0	3	3
8.	Inequipped Ambulance Services	0	0	0	3	0	0	0	0	0	3	3
9.	Lack Of Facilities	0	0	31	1	0	0	0	0	31	1	32
10.	Unavailability of Blood Banks	0	0	0	1	0	0	0	0	0	1	1
11.	Decreased due to JSY	0	0	5	1	0	0	0	0	5	1	6
12.	Negligence of Doctors	0	0	11	1	0	0	0	0	11	1	12
13.	IMR/MMR Cases Increasing (Case of	0	0	0	0	1	1	15	8	16	9	25

	G.B Panth)											
14.	Moral and Religious Education Needed	0	0	0	0	5	4	0	0	5	4	1
15.	MCTS has Controlled it Now	0	0	0	0	0	5	0	0	0	5	5
16.	Still Eases Reported from for Flung Areas	0	0	0	0	0	2	0	0	0	2	2
17.	Nadequate Facilities /Referral System Responsible	0	0	0	0	15	7	0	0	15	7	2
18.	NRHM Aimed to Curb this Menace	0	0	0	0	3	3	0	0	3	3	e
19.	Woman's Themselves Ignorant	0	0	0	0	0	1	0	0	0	1	1
20.	Empower the Woman	0	0	0	0	1	0	0	0	1	0	1
21.	Our Society is dominated by Male/Less Preferance to Female	0	0	0	0	4	0	0	0	4	0	4
22.	Female Counsellors can Curb This Menace	0	0	0	0	0	4	0	0	0	4	4
23.	Dowry Actual Culprit	0	0	0	0	7	0	0	0	7	0	7
24.	Strict Laws can only Curb This Menace	0	0	0	0	2	0	0	0	2	0	2
25.	Illitracy Responsible	0	0	0	0	1	0	0	0	1	0	1
26.	Woman's are not Treated Equally	0	0	0	0	13	0	0	0	13	0	13
27.	Awareness Needed	0	0	0	0	9	4	0	0	9	4	13
28.	Decreasing IMR/MMR due to Centrally Schemes	0	0	0	0	0	0	85	42	85	42	127

Q.No. 3(i).		*SRI (D1)*		*BUD (D2)*		*ANA (D3)*		*BAR (D4)*		*Responses*		
S. No.	*Cultural Restrictions*	*G*	*P*	*G*	*P*	*G*	*P*	*G*	*P*	*General*	*Professional*	*Total*
1.	EXISTS	98	0	0	0	0	0	0	0	98	0	98
2.	NO RESPONSE	2	50	37	31	42	11	0	0	81	92	173
3.	In some Families	0	0	15	3	0	0	0	0	15	3	18
4.	Female Doctors Needed	0	0	0	1	7	9	22	15	29	25	54
5.	Male Dominance	0	0	2	3	0	5	0	0	2	8	10
6.	Less care to Women	0	0	13	5	0	0	0	0	13	5	18
7.	More Prevalent in Far Flung Areas	0	0	15	7	0	0	0	0	15	7	22
8.	Gender Bias	0	0	12	0	0	0	0	0	12	0	12
9.	Reduced Now	0	0	3	0	0	0	0	0	3	0	3
10.	Less Education	0	0	2	0	0	0	0	0	2	0	2
11.	Less Facilities	0	0	1	0	0	0	0	0	1	0	1
12.	It is a Problem for Gender Health Care	0	0	0	0	4	8	0	0	4	8	12
13.	Still our Culture Prefer	0	0	0	0	11	8	0	0	11	8	19

	Male Child											
14.	Illitracy Responsible	0	0	0	0	11	0	0	0	11	0	11
15.	Now We Treate Male and Female Equally	0	0	0	0	2	0	0	0	2	0	2
16.	It is a Barrier for Gender Empowerment	0	0	0	0	11	0	0	0	11	0	11
17.	Woman's Health is not Given Consideration	0	0	0	0	8	2	0	0	8	2	10
18.	Woman's Feel shy for Consultation from Male Doctor's	0	0	0	0	4	7	0	0	4	7	11
19.	Yes Still a Problem and Need is for:	0	0	0	0	0	0	100	50	100	50	150
20.	Provision of Separate Hospitals	0	0	0	0	0	0	72	35	72	35	107

4a 14. Gender Health-Limitations

Q. NO. 4(a) S. No.	*Lacking in the Present Health care*	*SRI (D1) G*	*P*	*BUD (D2) G*	*P*	*ANA (D3) G*	*P*	*BAR (D4) G*	*P*
1.	Female Gynaecologists /Doctor's	61	25	75	19	66	32	78	39
2.	Insufficient Facilities and Infrastructure	97	35	80	34	54	13	32	25
4.	Separate Hospitals for Woman	0	2	0	0	14	6	40	15
5.	Policies and Programmes	32	0	0	0	0	0	0	0
6.	Medical attention	49	7	0	0	0	0	0	0
7.	Unadultered drugs /Medicines	55	1	0	0	0	0	0	0
8.	Funds	4	0	0	0	0	0	0	0
9.	Facilities in PHC's	0	1	0	0	0	0	0	0
10.	Health Education /Educators and Awareness	0	1	0	0	12	5	0	0
11.	Special Gender Treatement	0	2	0	0	0	0	48	29
12.	Privacy	0	1	0	0	0	0	0	0
13.	NO RESPONSE	0	2	11	0	0	0	0	0
14.	24×7 Services	0	0	1	1	0	0	0	0
15.	Drug Quality	0	0	10	0	0	0	0	0
16.	Inadeuate Supply of Medicines	0	0	11	12	34	14	0	0
17.	No Policy for Gender Health	0	0	1	2	0	1	0	0
18.	Fair Price Medical Shops	0	0	4	2	0	0	0	0
19.	Blood Banks at PHc's	0	0	10	4	7	7	0	0
20.	Well Equiped Ambulances	0	0	6	4	28	7	0	0
21.	Referral Service	0	0	8	1	12	10	0	0
22.	Policy for Poor People	0	0	9	0	0	0	0	0

23.	Less Health Education	0	0	8	0	0	0	0	0
24.	Negligence of Doctors	0	0	9	0	0	0	0	0
25.	Treatment is Expensive	0	0	1	0	0	0	0	0
26.	Programme not properly Implemented	0	0	4	0	0	0	0	0
27.	Supervision and Motivation	0	0	5	2	0	0	0	0
28.	Remove Gender Disparity	0	0	1	0	0	0	0	0
29.	Counselling Centres	0	0	2	0	10	7	0	0
30.	Lack of staff Both Doctors and Paramedics	0	0	0	18	25	14	20	10
31.	Screening Programmes	0	0	0	1	0	0	0	0
32.	No Proper Allocation of Funds	0	0	0	0	4	2	0	0
33.	No Incentives to Work in Far Flung Areas	0	0	0	0	0	1	0	0
34.	Specialised lab for Tests	0	0	0	0	2	1	0	0
35.	No Heating System in Winters	0	0	0	0	4	0	0	0
36.	No Provision of Free Drugs	0	0	0	0	2	0	0	0
37.	Less Accessibility to Healthcare	0	0	0	0	2	0	10	3
38.	No Check on Spurious Drugs	0	0	0	0	1	0	0	0
39.	No PHC's on 24×7 Basis	0	0	0	0	2	0	0	0

4b 15. Gender Healthcare:

Q.No. 4b S. No.	*Role of State Bar*	*SRI (D1)*		*BUD (D2)*		*ANA (D3)*		*BAR (D4)*		*Responses*		
		G	*P*	*G*	*P*	*G*	*P*	*G*	*P*	*General*	*Professional*	*Total*
1.	Provision of Female Doctor	2	0	0	0	18	17	36	20	.56	37	93
2.	Strengthen Infrastructure	25	9	7	15	28	9	0	0	60	33	93
3.	Supervision/ Inspections	33	14	47	5	2	2	0	0	82	21	103
4.	Improve Facilities	12	23	17	0	0	0	15	7	44	30	74
5.	Make Strict Drug Laws	10	3	0	1	0	0	0	0	10	4	14
6.	Maintain Doctor Patient Ratio	6	5	14	5	0	0	0	0	20	10	30
7.	Well Trained and Adequate Staff	4	6	30	9	0	0	0	0	34	15	49
8.	Ban on Private Practice	0	2	0	2	0	4	0	0	0	8	8
9.	Check Adulteration	12	8	0	1	0	0	0	0	12	9	21
10.	Check Corruption	4	3	0	3	0	0	0	0	4	6	10

11.	Mission Based Planning	0	2	0	0	0	0	0	0	0	2	2
12.	Prof. Female Staff	2	2	0	0	0	0	15	8	17	10	27
13.	Check Doctors Stagnation	6	4	0	0	0	0	0	0	6	4	10
14.	Provide Medical Supplies	22	2	0	0	0	0	0	0	22	2	24
15.	NO RESPONSE	3	4	6	9	0	0	0	0	9	13	22
16.	Improve Services	0	0	41	9	0	0	0	0	41	9	50
17.	Stress on Preventive Care	0	0	2	0	0	0	0	0	2	0	2
18.	Early Diagonosis	0	0	1	1	0	0	0	0	1	1	2
19.	Free Drug Supply	0	0	2	3	11	2	0	0	13	5	18
20.	Check on Doctors	0	0	10	0	0	0	0	0	10	0	10
21.	Proper Planning	0	0	27	0	0	0	0	0	27	0	27
22.	Increase Health Education	0	0	10	0	0	0	0	0	10	0	10
23.	24×7 Services	0	0	4	4	4	5	0	0	8	9	17
24.	Fair Price Medical Shops	0	0	8	4	0	0	0	0	8	4	12
25.	Proper Referral System	0	0	4	3	3	0	0	0	7	3	10
26.	Policy for poor people	0	0	17	1		0	0	0	17	1	18
27.	Check on Drug Quality	0	0	14	5	4	0	0	0	18	5	23
28.	Overcrowdedness	0	0	4	0	0	0	0	0	4	0	4
29.	Blood Banks at PHC's	0	0	2	1	0	0	0	0	2	1	3
30.	Proper Implementation	0	0	15	5	1	3	0	0	16	8	24
31.	Attention towards other Needs o Women	0	0	0	0	0	0	0	0	0	0	0
32.	More Maternity Hospitals	0	0	0	1	0	0	0	0	0	1	1
33.	Strang thinning PHC's	0	0	0	2	0	4	0	0	0	6	6
34.	Check on Private Institutions	0	0	0	1	0	0	0	0	0	1	1
35.	Ambulances Services	0	0	0	2	0	0	5	5	5	7	12
36.	Proper Use of Funds	0	0	0	3	0	2			0	5	5
37.	Educate the Woman	0	0	0	0	12	1	35	9	47	10	57
38.	Promote Awareness	0	0	0	0	3	3	25	2	28	5	33
39.	Incentives to Work in Far Flung Areas	0	0	0	0	0	1			0	1	1
40.	Gender Health Policy of the State	0	0	0	0	8	1	30	12	38	13	51
41.	Accessible Hospitals lo Far Flung Areas	0	0	0	0	1	4	40	27	41	31	72
42.	Free Healthcare to Woman	0	0	0	0	6	0	0	0	6	0	6
43.	Heating Arrangement in Winters	0	0	0	0	1	0	0	0	1	0	1
44.	Operation Theatre for Woman	0	0	0	0	1	0	0	0	1	0	1

45.	Separate Hospitals for Woman	0	0	0	0	4	0	0	0	4	0	4
46.	Bottom Level Work be Clone	0	0	0	0	2	0	0	0	2	0	2
47.	Separate OPD's for Woman	0	0	0	0	1	0	0	0	1	0	1
48.	Empower The Woman	0	0	0	0	1	0	0	0	1	0	1
49.	Autonomous Monitoring Cell	0	0	0	0	6	0	0	0	6	0	6
50.	Politics and Health be Seperated	0	0	0	0	0	3	0	0	0	3	3
51.	Short Term Courses for Paramadical Staff	0	0	0	0	0	0	15	4	15	4	19
52.	Provision of Well Trained Paramedical Staff	0	0	0	0	0	0	20	4	20	4	24
53.	Provision of New Hospitals	0	0	0	0	0	0	4	1	4	1	5
54.	Provision of Female Gynaecologists	0	0	0	0	0	0	10	3	10	3	13

Role of Private Sector

Q. No. 4c		*SRI (D1)*		*BUD (D2)*		*ANA (D3)*		*BAR (D4)*		*Responses*		
S. No.	*Role of peniate Sector*	*G*	*P*	*G*	*P*	*G*	*P*	*G*	*P*	*General*	*Professional*	*Total*
1.	*YES*	63	35	44	26	44	23	100	50	251	134	385
2.	Private Clinics and Hospitals	47	10	26	18	20	13			93	41	134
3.	Encourage PPPs	4	11							4	11	15
4.	No-Response	12	14	0	1					12	15	27
5.	NGO's Counsellors			1	3	22	10	60	30	83	43	126
6.	Nursing Homes			11	1					11	1	12
7.	Doctors not Working in Govt Sector			5	3					5	3	8
8.	Mobile Medical Units			1	0					1	0	1
9.	Educational Institutions					2	0	25	11	27	11	38
10.	Private Business Organisation							15	9	15	9	24
										0	0	0
	NO	37	9	56	24	56	27	0	0	149	60	209
1.	Strengthen Govt Hospital	15	3	13	9	6	6			34	18	52
2.	Inadequate Manpower in Govt	17	3							17	3	20
3.	Limited Resources	5	3							5	3	8
4.	Poor People cannot Afford			27	11	35	13			62	24	86
5.	Expensive			9	4	13	5			22	9	31

6.	Private Clinics only Making Money			7	0	2	3			9	3	12
	NO RESPONSE	0	6							0	6	6

4d 16. Awareness about Gender Healthcare

Q.No. 4d S.No.	*Satisfactory Level of Awareness*	*SRI (D1) G*	*P*	*BUD (D2) G*	*P*	*ANA (D3) G*	*P*	*BAR (D4) G*	*P*	*Responses General*	*Professional*	*Total*
1.	YES	59	15	18	8	6	4	0	0	83	27	110
2.	NO	41	25	82	42	94	46	100	50	317	163	480
3.	IF NO What IS Needed	0	0	0	0	0	0	0	0	0	0	0
4.	Planned Programme	0	3	0	0	0	0	0	0	0	3	3
5.	Counselling	20	2	0	0	2	0	0	0	22	2	24
6.	Education	2	6	8	12	0	0	0	0	10	18	28
7.	Awareness	12	13	2	2	0	0	0	0	14	15	29
8.	Preventive Measures	7	1	0	0	0	0	0	0	7	1	8
9.	awareness in Far Flung Areas	0	0	14	24	0	0	0	0	14	24	38
10.	Health Camps	0	0	7	2	0	0	0	0	7	2	9
11.	Counsellors in Hospitals	0	0	4	2	0	0	0	0	4	2	6
12.	Health Education	0	0	7	6	4	0	10	1	21	7	28
13.	Awareness through Mass Media	0	0	45	1	26	13	0	0	71	14	85
14.	Health *Melas*	0	0	3	3	15	4	0	0	18	7	25
15.	Medical Camps	0	0	1	1	0	0	0	0	1	1	2
16.	Don't Know	0	0	1	0	0	0	0	0	1	0	1
17.	Sex Education	0	0	0	2	0	0	0	0	0	2	2
18.	Health Education to Adolescent Girls	0	0	0	1	3	0	0	0	3	1	4
19.	NGOS	0	0	0	0	7	9	10	3	17	12	29
20.	ICDS workers and ASHA's	0	0	0	0	11	1	0	0	11	1	12
21.	Co-operation of Various Agencies	0	0	0	0	3	3	35	17	38	20	58
22.	Religious Scholars Involved	0	0	0	0	4	2	0	0	4	2	6
23.	Proper Utilisation of Funds Meant for Awareness	0	0	0	0	2	0	45	29	47	29	76
24.	Panchayat Has a Role	0	0	0	0	2	0	0	0	2	0	2
25.	Seminars and Workshops	0	0	0	0	5	0	0	0	5	0	5
26.	NO RESPONSE	0	15	0	0	0	0	0	0	0	15	15

4e 17. Training to Meolieor and Para-mediess

Q.NO. 4e S. No.	Training to Medicos and Paramedics	SRI (D1) G	SRI (D1) P	BUD (D2) G	BUD (D2) P	ANA (D3) G	ANA (D3) P	BAR (D4) G	BAR (D4) P	General	Responses Professional	Total
1.	Documentaries	0	1	0	0	0	0	0	0	0	1	1
2.	Short Training Courses	43	6	4	2	35	4	30	24	112	36	148
3.	Workshops	23	14	5	16	18	19	23	3	69	52	121
4.	Refresher Courses	11	13	21	14	7	2	0	0	39	29	68
5.	Supervision	7	4	9	1	0	0	0	0	16	5	21
6.	Awareness	1	2	0	0	0	0	0	0	1	2	3
7.	Active Participation	0	2	0	0	0	0	0	0	0	2	2
8.	Add on Courses	7	1	0	0	0	0	0	0	7	1	8
9.	Seminars	6	0	0	0	0	0	0	0	6	0	6
10.	NO RESPONSE	2	7	11	2	2	0	0	0	15	9	24
11.	As per new Technology	0	0	21	5	0	0	0	0	21	5	26
12.	Moral Education	0	0	13	0	4	3	0	0	17	3	20
13.	Inservice Trainings	0	0	9	9	29	18	0	0	38	27	65
14.	As per Gender Needs	0	0	7	1	0	0	0	0	7	1	8
15.	Expert Trainings	0	0	0	0	2	2	0	0	2	2	4
16.	Behavioural Trainings	0	0	0	0	1	1	47	23	48	24	72
17.	Cultural Trainings	0	0	0	0	2	1	0	0	2	1	3

Q.NO. 4f S. No.	SOCIAL ENVIRONMENT	SRI (D1) G	SRI (D1) P	BUD (D2) G	BUD (D2) P	ANA (D3) G	ANA (D3) P	BAR (D4) G	BAR (D4) P	General	Responses Professional	Total
1.	Women Empowerment	0	1	11	7	8	7	25	19	44	34	78
2.	Social Mobilisation	4	17	0	7	0	0	0	0	4	24	28
3.	Awareness	4	7	21	7	32	11	27	13	84	38	122
4.	Social and Preventive Medicine	0	1	0	0	0	0	0	0	0	1	1
5.	Counselling	28	6	5	7	0	0	0	0	33	13	46
6.	Media, Seminars	1	1	0	0	0	0	0	0	1	1	2
7.	Public Participation	1	1	0	1	0	0	0	0	1	2	3
8.	Education	34	8	26	5	27	6	0	0	87	19	106
9.	Any Other	14	0	0	0	0	0	0		14	0	14
10.	NO RESPONSE	14	8	4	3	0	0	0	0	18	11	29
11.	Develop Infrastructure	0	0	3	0	8	7	0	0	11	7	18

12.	Develop Patient Doctor Relationship	0	0	2	0	0	0	0	0	2	0	2
13.	Maintain Doctor Patient Ratio	0	0	1	0	1	0	0	0	2	0	2
14.	Health education	0	0	17	8	2	4	0	0	19	12	31
15.	Women Should Took Stand	0	0	2	1	0	3	0	0	2	4	6
16.	Equal Attention	0	0	7	0	0	0	0	0	7	0	7
17.	Family Support	0	0	1	0	3	0	0	0	4	0	4
18.	Sex Education	0	0	0	1	0	0	0	0	0	1	1
19.	Remove Gender Bias	0	0	0	2	7	0	0	0	7	2	9
20.	Co-operation Between Govt. and Civil Society	0	0	0	1	0	0	0	0	0	1	1
21.	Separate Politics and Health	0	0	0	0	0	1	0	0	0	1	1
22.	Create Proper Link Between Government and Civil Society	0	0	0	0	2	4	0	0	2	4	6
23.	Implement Schemes in Letter And Spirit	0	0	0	0	0	1	0	0	0	1	1
24.	Recruit Female Staff	0	0	0	0	4	2	0	0	4	2	6
25.	Separate Healthcare for woman	0	0	0	0	2	2	0	0	2	2	4
26.	Equal attention towards Women's Health	0	0	0	0	0	2	0	0	0	2	2
27.	Create Environment that Woman will Feel Secure	0	0	0	0	2	0	0	0	2	0	2
28.	Healthcare Accessible to Masses	0	0	0	0	2	0	0	0	2	0	2
29.	Space of Gender Health in the Primarly Level Curriculum	0	0	0	0	0	0	15	11	15	11	26
30.	Participation of Women in Decision Making	0	0	0	0	0	0	33	7	33	7	40

4g 19. Relationship Between GHC and CH

Q.NO. 4g S. No.	*RELATIONSHIP BETWEEN CHC & GHC*	*SRI (D1)*		*BUD (D2)*		*ANA (D3)*		*BAR (D4)*		*Responses*		
		G	*P*	*G*	*P*	*G*	*P*	*G*	*P*	*General*	*Professional*	*Total*
1.	Interrelated	8	17	39	6	10	5	0	0	57	28	85
2.	Interdependent	82	28	19	8	72	31	0	0	173	67	240
3.	Any Other	7	0	0	0	0	0	0	0	7	0	7
4.	No Response	3	5	0	4	1	0	0	0	4	9	13

5.	Totally Dependent	0	0	17	31	0	0	45	19	62	50	112
6.	A Healthy Mother Can Produce a Healthy Child	0	0	25	0	7	7	0	0	32	7	39
7.	Post-marital Counselling is Important	0	0	0	1	0	0	0	0	0	1	1
8.	Breast Feeding	0	0	0	0	2	2	19	11	21	13	34
9.	Mutual Relationships	0	0	0	0	2	1	0	0	2	1	3
10.	Close and Intimate	0	0	0	0	3	4	0	0	3	4	7
11.	Nutritional	0	0	0	0	3	0	25	13	28	13	41
12.	Survival	0	0	0	0	0	0	11	7	11	7	18

5a 20. Features of traditional Health Culture

Q.NO. 5(a) S. No.	*Features of Traditional Health Culture*	*SRI (D1)*		*BUD (D2)*		*ANA (D3)*		*BAR (D4)*		*Responses*		
		G	*P*	*G*	*P*	*G*	*P*	*G*	*P*	*General*	*Professional*	*Total*
1.	Simple	17	4	0	0	0	0	0	0	17	4	21
2.	Healthy Lifestyle	15	6	8	3	0	0	0	0	23	9	32
3.	Stress Free	0	3	0	0	0	0	0	0	0	3	3
4.	Belief Based / Folk Treatment	42	17	9	11	0	0	0	0	51	28	79
5.	Not Health Conscious	3	1	0	0	0	0	0	0	3	1	4
6.	No Health Conscious	9	1	9	5	0	0	0	0	18	6	24
7.	Effective and Less Deterious	2	1	0	0	0	0	0	0	2	1	3
8.	Don't Know	0	4	2	5	0	0	0	0	2	9	11
9.	Any Other	7	0	0	0	0	0	0	0	7	0	7
10.	No Response	5	13	8	0	0	0	0	0	13	13	26
11.	Irrelevant Response	0	0	4	0	0	0	0	0	4	0	4
12.	Herbal Medicines Mainly Used	0	0	9	4	0	0	0	0	9	4	13
13.	Unawareness and ignorance	0	0	11	3	0	0	0	0	11	3	14
14.	Less Scientific Knowledge	0	0	4	3	0	0	0	0	4	3	7
15.	Less Acceptance to Allopathy	0	0	7	3	0	0	0	0	7	3	10
16.	Hakims & Pirs Were Consulted	0	0	9	0	29	12	0	0	38	12	50
17.	Home Deliveries were Common	0	0	8	5	0	0	0	0	8	5	13
18.	Diagonosis was not Clear	0	0	5	3	0	0	0	0	5	3	8
19.	Self-Medication	0	0	3	2	1	2	0	0	4	4	8
20.	MMR and IMR on Rise	0	0	1	0	0	0	0	0	1	0	1

21.	Less Prevalence of Diseases	0	0	3	1	0	0	0	0	3	1	4
22.	Depends on Family	0	0	0	1	0	0	0	0	0	1	1
23.	More Restrictions on Women	0	0	0	1	0	0	0	0	0	1	1
24.	People Were Unhealthy and Unhygeinic	0	0	0	0	7	4	65	10	72	14	86
25.	No Health Awareness	0	0	0	0	7	2	20	11	27	13	40
26.	People were Healthy due to Climate	0	0	0	0	3	2	0	0	3	2	5
27.	Unscientific/ Informal Means of Treatment	0	0	0	0	2	3	0	0	2	3	5
28.	Less Health Conscious	0	0	0	0	7	3	0	0	7	3	10
29.	Dai's were Catering to the Pregnant	0	0	0	0	9	3	0	0	9	3	12
30.	Woman's Health was Neglected	0	0	0	0	4	2	10	14	14	16	30
31.	Complications Attributed to *Jins Kochun* etc.,	0	0	0	0	2	1	0	0	2	1	3
32.	Reluctance towards Modern Care	0	0	0	0	1	4	0	0	1	4	5
33.	Less Diagnostic Techniques Prevalent	0	0	0	0	1	2	0	0	1	2	3
34.	Simple Life Style/ Depression, Stress was Less	0	0	0	0	4	1	0	0	4	1	5
35.	No Follow. ups and Tracking System	0	0	0	0	0	3	0	0	0	3	3
36.	Male Dominance	0	0	0	0	3	1	5	15	8	16	24
37.	Less Concern for Health	0	0	0	0	7	5	0	0	7	5	12
38.	Ayurvedic Medicines Preferred	0	0	0	0	7	0	0	0	7	0	7
39.	Institutional Deliveries were least preferred	0	0	0	0	1	0	0	0	1	0	1
40.	Home Based Care	0	0	0	0	2	0	0	0	2	0	2
41.	Ignorant about Health Needs	0	0	0	0	2	0	0	0	2	0	2
42.	Belief Based Care *'Yezband Zalon'*	0	0	0	0	1	0	0	0	1	0	1

5b 21. Changes observed in Gender Health Culture

Q.NO. 5(a) S. No.	*Changes Occurred*	*SRI (D1)*		*BUD (D2)*		*ANA (D3)*		*BAR (D4)*		*Responses*		
		G	*P*	*G*	*P*	*G*	*P*	*G*	*P*	*General*	*Professional*	*Total*
1.	YES	37	87	97	37	91	50	100	50			
2.	Stressful Life	15	47	0	0	0	0	0	0	15	47	62
3.	Scientific System in Demand	11	20	0	0	0	0	0	0	11	20	31
4.	Conflict Changed Life	7	10	0	0	0	0	0	0	7	10	17
5.	Indiscriminate Use of Drugs	4	10	0	0	0	0	0	0	4	10	14
6.	Increase in life threatening Diseases	0	0	6	1	0	0	0	0	6	1	7
7.	Specialised Treatment Available	0	0	5	5	0	0	0	0	5	5	10
8.	Acceptance to Allopathic System	0	0	16	15	0	0	0	0	16	15	31
9.	Awareness has Increased	0	0	15	0	0	0	0	0	15	0	15
10.	Specialised Treatment Preferred	0	0	13	0	0	0	0	0	13	0	13
11.	Institutional Deliveries Preferred	0	0	7	2	0	0	0	0	7	2	9
12.	Consciousness has Increased	0	0	5	4	0	0	0	0	5	4	9
13.	Modern Techniques Used	0	0	5	7	0	0	0	0	5	7	12
14.	More life style Disesses	0	0	9	2	0	0	0	0	9	2	11
15.	Complex lifestyle	0	0	13	0	0	0	0	0	13	0	13
16.	No response	0	0	3	0	0	0	0	0	3	0	3
17.	Self-Medication	0	0	0	1	0	0	0	0	0	1	1
18.	Formal Means of Consultations Preferred	0	0	17	18	0	0	0	0	17	18	35
19.	Woman's Health is now Given Consideration (Schemes)	0	0	2	5	0	0	0	0	2	5	7
20.	Mother Child Tracking System	0	0	4	3	0	0	0	0	4	3	7
21.	People remain Hygeinic	0	0	3	2	0	0	0	0	3	2	5
22.	Increasing number of Diseases	0	0	0	1	0	0	0	0	0	1	1
23.	Education has Changed the Health Culture	0	0	7	4	92	47	0	0	99	51	150
24.	Awareness is improved	0	0	13	6	0	0	0	0	13	6	19

25.	Busy life Schedule	0	0	0	1	0	0	0	0	0	1	1
26.	Early Diagnosis of Diseases	0	0	0	2	0	0	0	0	0	2	2
27.	People are now Health concious	0	0	11	6	0	0	0	0	11	6	17
28.	Scientific Treatement Available	0	0	0	2	0	0	0	0	0	2	2
29.	Equal Preferance to Both the Genders	0	0	2	0	0	0	0	0	2	0	2
30.	English Medicines Preferred	0	0	11	0	0	0	0	0	11	0	11
31.	Institutional Health care preferred	0	0	6	0	0	0	0	0	6	0	5
32.	No Further Explanation Provided	0	0	0	0	0	0	8	3	8	3	11
33.	Acceptance to Modern Healthcare	0	0	15	0	0	0	0	0	15	0	15
34.	No Response	9	9	3	13	0	0	0	0	12	22	34
35.	NO	4	4	0	0	p	0	0	0	4	4	8
36.	Strong religious beliefs	0	0	2	0	0	0	0	0	2	0	2
37.	Less Awareness	0	0	4	0	0	0	0	0	4	0	4
38.	Situation Worsening	0	0	1	0	0	0	0	0	1	0	1
39.	Number of Tension Patients Increased	0	0	2	0	0	0	0	0	2	0	2

Health Culture

Q. No. 5(c) S. No	*Prevailing Health Culture*	*SRI (D1)*		*BUD (D2)*		*ANA (D3)*		*BAR (D4)*		*Responses*		
		G	*P*	*G*	*P*	*G*	*P*	*G*	*P*	*General*	*Professional*	*Total*
1.	Allopathic Treatement	17	13	0	0	0	0	0	0	17	13	30
2.	Lifestyle Diseases on Rise	19	10	0	0	0	0	0	0	19	10	29
3.	Health Cautious but not Healthy	23	9	0	0	0	0	0	0	23	9	32
4.	Negligence	2	2	0	1	0	0	0	0	2	3	5
5.	Doctor's Preffered	17	1	0	0	14	9	0	0	31	10	41
6.	Unhealthy Culture	11	1	0	0	0	0	0	0	11	1	12
7.	Lack of Mission Based Planning	0	2	0	0	0	0	0	0	0	2	2
8.	Improved than Before	1	1	8	5	0	0	46	17	55	23	78
9.	Don't Know	0	2	0	0	0	0	0	0	0	2	2
10.	No Response	10	9	1	7	0	0	0	0	11	16	27
11.	Not Good	0	0	3	0	0	0	0	0	3	0	3
12.	Satisfactory	0	0	27	10	0	0	0	0	27	10	37
13.	More Diseases	0	0	15	1	0	0	0	0	15	1	16
14.	Not Upto Mark	0	0	2	0	0	0	0	0	2	0	2

15.	Inadequate Facilities	0	0	12	4	4	1	0	0	16	5	21
16.	Due to Poverty People Ignore	0	0	2	0	0	0	0	0	2	0	2
17.	Awareness Increased	0	0	9		0	0	0	0	9	3	12
18.	Good	0	0	8	2	0		19	4	27	6	33
19.	Self-Medication	0	0	2	0	6	0	0	0	8	0	8
20.	Life Expectancy Increased	0	0	1	0	0	0	0	0	1	0	1
21.	Acceptance to Modern Health System	0	0	6	5	25	19	0	0	31	24	55
22.	Gender Health Less improved	0	0	2	0	0	0	0	0	2	0	2
23.	Male Dominance	0	0	2	0	0	0	0	0	2	0	2
24.	MMR and IMR has decreased	0	0	0	2	0	0	0	0	0	2	2
25.	Specialised has increased	0	0	0	2	0	0	0	0	0	2	2
26.	Endemie and Epidemics Decreased	0	0	0	1	0	0	0	0	0	1	1
27.	Life Style Diseases Increased	0	0	0	6	0	0	0	0	0	6	6
28.	Availibility and Acessibility Increased	0	0	0	1	1	2	0	0	1	3	4
29.	In Between Tradition and modernity	0	0	0	0	1	5	0	0	1	5	6
30.	Tension and stress are Common Issues now	0	0	0	0	7	2	0	0	7	2	9
31.	Tracking the Health Records	0	0	0	0	9	1	0	0	9	1	10
32.	Woman's Health Ignored	0	0	0	0	2	1	0	0	2	1	3
33.	People are now Health Concious	0	0	0	0	7	2	0	0	7	2	9
34.	Formal System of Medicines Accepted	0	0	0	0	1	2	0	0	1	2	3
35.	Neglected and Ignored	0	0	0	0	0	0	35	29	35	29	64
36.	Stressful life	0	0	0	0	4	0	0	0	4	0	4
37.	People Consult Local Chemists	0	0	0	0	2	0	0	0	2	0	2
38.	Negligence towards Health Issues	0	0	0	0	4	0	0	0	4	0	4
39.	Improving Health Status	0	0	0	0	1	0	0	0	1	0	1
40.	Less Acceptance to Modem Healthcare	0	0	0	0	1	0	0	0	1	0	1

41.	Women's are now Careful about Health Issues	0	0	0	0	4	0	0	0	4	0	4
42.	Our Health Culture is not so Developed	0	0	0	0	2	0	0	0	2	0	2
43.	Our Health Culture is Improving	0	0	0	0	3	0	0	0	3	0	
44.	More Side Effects due to Modern Medicines	0	0	0	0	1	0	0	0	1	0	1

5d 23. Reason, for Gender Health

Q. No. 5(d) S. No	*Reasons*	*SRI(D1) G*	*P*	*BUD(D2) G*	*P*	*ANA(D3) G*	*P*	*EAR(D4, G*	*P*
1.	Lifestyle Changed	41	20	15	0	0	0	0	0
2.	Modernity	9	2	0	0	0	0	0	0
3.	Illitracy and Unawareness	6	1	2	1	7	2	16	1
4.	Lack of Knowledge	0	1	0	0	0	0	0	0
5.	Education	19	4	43	16	21	11	50	7
6.	Globalisation	13	6	0	0	0	0	0	0
7.	Technological Developments	0	2	0	5	0	0	0	0
8.	Don't Know	0	3	0	0	0	0	0	0
9.	Any Other	17	0	0	0	0	0	0	0
10.	No Response	24	11	0	0	0	0	4	1
11.	Conflict	0	0	8	0	2	1	0	0
12.	Free healthcare	0	0	0	0	0	1	0	0
13.	Food Habits	0	0	10	5	0	0	0	0
14.	Govt not Paying Full Attention	0	0	4	1	0	0	0	0
15.	Non Serious Approach of State	0	0	0	0	0	2	8	16
16.	Awareness	0	0	5	2	45	17	0	0
17.	Facilities not Available	0	0	2	0	0	0	0	0
18.	Lifestyle Diseases on Rise	0	0	3	0	0	0	0	0
19.	Corruption	0	0	5	2	2	0	12	5
20.	Improper Planning	0	0	4	4	1	2	0	0
21.	Negligence of Doctors	0	0	2	0	0	0	0	0
22.	Stress of life	0	0	3	0	0	0	0	0
23.	Centrally	0	0	1	4	0	0	40	14

	Sponsored Programmes								
24.	Gender Bias	0	0	2	0	0	0	0	0
25.	Cultural Restrictions	0	0	1	0	8	10	16	6
26.	No Response	0	0	1	9	0	0	0	0
27.	Accessibility	0	0	0	0	10	6	0	0
28.	Institutional deliveries	0	0	0	1	0	0	0	0
29.	Over burdeness on women	0	0	0	2	0	0	0	0
30.	Adulteration in Food Items	0	0	0	1	0	0	0	0
31.	Cultural Change	0	0	0	1	0	0	0	0
32.	Spurious Drug	0	0	0	1	5	0	0	0
33.	No Separate Gender Health Policy	0	0	0	0	1	0	15	8
34.	Ignorance	0	0	0	0	3	0	0	0
35.	State has Ignored This Area	0	0	0	0	1	0	0	0
36.	Inadequate Funding	0	0	0	0	4	0	8	3
37.	Avaliability	0	0	0	0	1	0	0	0
38.	New Schemes and Serivces (Incentives)	0	0	0	0	6	9	0	0

5e 24. Features of Gender Healthcare in Kashmir

Q. No. 5(e) S. No.	*GH ignorance in past*	*SRI(D1)*		*BUD(D2)*		*ANA(D3)*		*BAR(D4)*	
		G	*P*	*G*	*P*	*G*	*P*	*G*	*P*
1.	Illitracy	13	6	31	12	33	29	75	47
2.	Ignorance	34	14	68	25	21	8	69	43
3.	Poverty	29	16	0	0	0	0	0	0
4.	Unawareness	26	19	0	0	31	12	0	0
5.	Lack of Manpower	0	2	0	0	0	0	0	0
6.	Prevailing Conditions	4	1	0	0	0	0	0	0
7.	No Facilities	0	2	0	0	0	0	0	0
8.	Orthodox attitude	5	0	0	0	0	0	0	0
9.	No Response	10	9	4	8	0	0	0	0
10.	Not Ignored Needs were Less	0	0	4	3	2	2	0	0
11.	Unavailibility	0	0	7	4	12	4	0	0
12.	Male Dominance	0	0	4	0	3	0	20	0
13.	Supersititious Behaviour	1	0	9	1	0	0	0	0
14.	Poverty	0	0	12	6	2	0	0	0
15.	Conflict	0	0	1	4	2	0	0	0
16.	Lack of Health Education	0	0	1	0	0	0	0	0

17.	Gender Bias	0	0	1	0	0	0	0	0
18.	Less Intervention of State	0	0	0	0	0	1	6	10
19.	Religiousity	0	0	0	0	0	0	10	4
20.	Lower Status to Women	0	0	0	0	3	0	0	0
21.	Cultural Restrictions	0	0	0	0	4	0	20	16
22.	Under-developed	0	0	0	0	1	0	0	0

Q. No. 5(f) S. NO.	*GH ignorance in Present Situation?*	*SRI(D1) G*	*P*	*BUD(D2) G*	*P*	*ANA(D3) G*	*P*	*BAR(D4) G*	*P*
1.	Unawareness	20	11	0	0	19	7	0	0
2.	Poverty	29	9	47	11	3	1	0	0
3.	Ignorance	21	9	2	7	0	0	0	0
4.	Busy Life Style	0	2	0	0	0	0	0	0
5.	Modernisation	0	1	0	0	0	0	0	0
6.	Tension in Valley/Restrictions	3	1	0	0	0	0	0	0
7.	Expensive Treatement	8	1	9	0	3	31	0	0
8.	Negligence/Woman themselves responsible	1	2	2	14	19	7	0	0
9.	Limited resources	11	2	0	0	0	0	0	0
10.	No Response	7	12	0	0	0	0	0	0
11.	Unavailibility	0	0	24	8	0	0	0	0
12.	Noseperate Facilities for Women	0	0	0	0	0	1	0	0
13.	Illiteracy	0	0	2	0	5	3	0	0
14.	Cultural Restrictions	0	0	3	0	2	1	0	0
15.	Inadequate facilities	0	0	0	0	28	15	0	0
16.	Lack of Infrastructure	0	0	3	1	0	0	0	0
18.	Gender Bias	0	0	1	0	4	2	0	0
19.	Low Status of Women	0	0	1	3	0	0	0	0
20.	No Response	0	0	6	3	0	0	0	0
21.	Conflict	0	0	0	1	2	1	34	25
22.	Not Ignored now	0	0	0	2	2	1	0	0
23.	No Proper Fund Implementation	0	0	0	0	3	0	27	11
24.	No Proper Implementation of Policies	0	0	0	0	1	0	0	0
25.	Negligence of Government and Doctors	0	0	0	0	1	0	0	0
26.	Diversion of Funds for Defence	0	0	0	0	3	0	0	0
27.	No Proper Health Education and Awareness	0	0	0	0	0	1	0	0

28.	Corruption	0	0	0	0	1	2	0	0
29.	Busy work schedule of Woman	0	0	0	0	0	2	0	0
30.	No Sound Gender Health Policy	0	0	0	0	0	2	24	7
31.	Inadequate Female Staff	0	0	0	0	4	3	0	0
32.	Not in the Priority List	0	0	0	0	0	0	4	1
33.	Lack of Funds due to Conflict (Diversion)	0	0	0	0	0	0	6	5
34.	Ignored Sector	0	0	0	0	0	0	5	1

5g 26. Gender Health 5: Valaes and Noroo

Q. No. 5(g)		*SRI (D1)*		*BUD (D2)*		*ANA (D3)*		*BAR (D4)*			*Responses*	
S. NO.	*Values and Norms*	*G*	*P*	*G*	*P*	*G*	*P*	*G*	*P*	*General*	*Professional*	*Total*
1.	Yes	86	38	100	50	100	50	95	37	381	175	556
2.	No	8	3	0	0	0	0	5	13	13	16	29
3.	To Some Extent	0	2	0	0	0	0	0	0	0	2	2
4.	No Response	6	7	0	0	0	0	0	0	6	7	13

5h 27. Gender Health: Domestic Contaet

Q. No. 5(h)	*Health in*	*SRI (D1)*		*BUD (D2)*		*ANA (D3)*		*BAR (D4)*			*Responses*	
S. NO.	*Domestic Context*	*G*	*P*	*G*	*P*	*G*	*P*	*G*	*P*	*General*	*Professional*	*Total*
1.	Very Good	2	5	0	0	0	0	0	0	2	5	7
2.	Good	31	66	15	6	14	7	20	3	80	82	162
3.	Better	4	9	23	0	0	0	0	0	27	9	36
4.	Deteriorating	2	8	0	0	0	0	0	0	2	8	10
5.	Not so good	2	0	32	26	28	13	0	0	62	39	101
6.	Stressful	3	0	0	0	4	0	0	0	7	0	7
7.	No Response	6	12	0	0	1	0	0	0	7	12	19
8.	Pathetic	0	0	25	0	0	0	0	0	25	0	25
9.	Improved Than Before	0	0	4	6	0	0	0	0	4	6	10
10.	Good if Educated	0	0	1	0	0	0	0	0	1	0	1
11.	UnHealthy and Unhygeinic	0	0	0	3	39	22	80	47	119	72	191
12.	Less Awareness	0	0	0	3	0	0	0	0	0	3	3
13.	Less Accessibility	0	0	0	1	0	0	0	0	0	1	1
14.	Satisfactory	0	0	0	2	4	3	0	0	4	5	9
15.	Overburdened	0	0	0	1	0	0	0	0	0	1	2
16.	Depends on Family	0	0	0	2	0	0	0	0	0	2	2
17.	Un Hygienic	0	0	0	0	0	0	0	0	0	0	0
18.	Worst	0	0	0	0	7	5	0	0	7	5	12
19.	Good in Urban Areas	0	0	0	0	3	0	0	0	3	0	3

5i 28. Working Contect of Gender Health

Q. No. 5(i) S. NO.	HEALTH IN WORKING CONTEXT	SRI (D1) G	P	BUD (D2) G	P	ANA (D3) G	P	BAR (D4) G	P	Responses General	Professional	Total
1.	Good	16	18	57	17	0	0	20	3	93	38	131
2.	Betteer	44	13	5	16	2	4	0	0	51	33	84
3.	Very Good	14	10	0	0	0	0	0	0	14	10	24
4.	Overburdened	19	1	11	3	7	0	0	0	37	4	41
5.	Keeping Pace with Life	0	1	0	0	0	0	0	0	0	1	1
6.	No Response	7	7	5	2	0	0	0	0	12	9	21
7.	Not Good	0	0	19	1	24	4	0	0	43	5	48
8.	Satisfactory	0	0	0	3	33	7	0	0	33	10	43
9.	More Caring	0	0	0	1	0	0	0	0	0	1	1
10.	Stressfull but Active and Awared	0	0	0	5	0	0	0	0	0	5	5
11.	Stressful	0	0	3	2	23	28	0	0	26	30	56
12.	Unhealthy	0	0	0	0	3	3	80	47	83	50	133
13.	Disturbed	0	0	0	0	5	3	0	0	5	3	8
14.	Not Satisfactory	0	0	0	0	3	1	0	0	3	1	4

Q. No. 5 (j) S. NO.	Has Working Context Changed Health Status	SRI(D1) G	P	BUD(D2) G	P	ANA(D3) G	P	BAR(D4) G	P
1.	YES	70	32	90	46	47	13	17	25
2.	Financial Security	55	19	0	0	17	5	0	0
3.	Ventilation with Friends/Colleagues etc.,	6	4	0	0	0	0	0	0
4.	Work Motivation	4	4	0	0	0	0	0	0
5.	No Response	5	5	0	0	0	0	0	0
6.	Accessibility to healthcare	0	0	0	0	5	2	0	0
7.	Financial Independence	0	0	21	10	0	0	0	0
8.	Freedom	0	0	9	2	0	0	0	0
9.	Change in Outlook	0	0	3	1	0	0	0	0
10.	More Active	0	0	10	14	0	0	0	0
11.	More Caring	0	0	5	2	0	0	0	0
12.	Financially Secure	0	0	8	0	0	0	0	0
13.	Peer Pressure	0	0	7	3	0	0	0	0
14.	Change in life style	0	0	8	2	0	0	0	0
15.	More Awareness and Knowledge	0	0	6	0	22	5	0	0
16.	Overburdened	0	0	7	7	0	0	0	0
17.	Healthy life style	0	0	0	0	4	2	0	0
18.	No Response	0	0	9	5	0	0	0	0
19.	Education	0	0	0	0	0	4	0	0
20.	Empowered	0	0	0	0	2	0	0	0
21.	Hygienic Environment	0	0	0	0	4	0	0	0

22.	Busy Work Schedule so less Diabetes	0	0	0	0	2	0	0	0
23.	No	30	18	7	4	53	37	83	25
24.	Stress	0	5	0	0	8	2	0	0
25.	Overburdened	24	6	4	3	43	33	0	0
26.	No Response	6	4	0	1	0	0	0	0
27.	Brain drain	0	1	0	0	0	0	0	0
28.	Unawareness	0	2	0	0	0	0	0	0
29.	Busy work schedule	0	0	0	0	2	2	0	0
30.	Still dependent due to Male Dominance	0	0	3	0	0	0	0	0
31.	No Response	0	0	3	0	0	0	0	0

6a 30. Impast on Gender Health

Q. No. 6(a) S. NO.	*Impact Experienced on GH During Last Two Decades*	*SRI(D1)*		*BUD(D2)*		*ANA(D3)*		*BAR(D4)*	
		G	*P*	*G*	*P*	*G*	*P*	*G*	*P*
1.	Late Marriages and Other Social Problems	8	3	0	0	0	0	0	0
2.	Mental Health Diseases on Rise	21	19	0	0	0	0	0	0
3.	Infrastructure damaged	39	9	0	0	0	0	0	0
4.	Limited Physical Movement	0	2	0	0	0	0	0	0
5.	Stressful	3	1	0	0	0	0	0	0
6.	Increase in Health Issues	11	5	0	0	0	0	0	0
7.	Brain drain/Negative Effect	18	6	0	2	0	0	0	0
8.	No Response	0	5	0	0	0	0	7	3
9.	No Impact	0	0	6	1	0	0	0	0
10.	Negative Effect	0	0	12	13	75	32	0	0
11.	Women's Mainly Effected	0	0	19	4	0	0	0	0
12.	More Psychological problems	0	0	15	11	1	2	0	0
13.	Increase in MMR	0	0	6	2	0	1	0	0
14.	Worst Hit	0	0	16	8	0	0	0	0
15.	Don't Know	0	0	1	3	0	0	0	0
16.	Destruction to Whole System	0	0	11	1	0	0	0	0
17.	Rise in Diseases	0	0	9	1	0	0	0	0
18.	Problems to Health Care Providers	0	0	3	1	0	0	0	0
19.	Funds Diverted	0	0	2	0	1	0	0	0
20.	Negligence towards Health Sector	0	0	0	2	23	15	77	44
21.	Good Impact Increase in Hospitals	0	0	0	1	0	0	0	0

22.	Not in the Planning List Because of Diversion of Funds to Conflict	0	0	0	0	0	0	8	3
23.	No Maintenance	0	0	0	0	0	0	5	0
24.	No Improvement due to Conflict	0	0	0	0	0	0	2	0
25.	No Utlization of Funds	0	0	0	0	0	0	5	0
26.	No New Construction of Infrastructure	0	0	0	0	0	0	3	0

6b 31. Infrasteueture damaged in urban and rural Areas

Q. No. 6(b) S. NO.	*Infrastructure in rural & urbea areas*	*SRI (D1)*		*BUD (D2)*		*ANA (D3)*		*BAR (D4)*			*Responses*	
		G	*P*	*G*	*P*	*G*	*P*	*G*	*P*	*General*	*Professional*	*Total*
1.	Destruction/ Destroyed Infrastructure	24	20	0	0	0	0	8	0	32	21	53
2.	Damaged	9	6	0	0	0	0	0	0	9	6	15
3.	Broken	7	2	0	0	0	0	0	0	7	2	9
4.	Ambulances Burnt	6	4	8	6	13	2	0	0	27	12	39
5.	Good	0	1	0	0	0	0	0	0	0	1	1
6.	Less Developed	10	0	15	0	0	0	0	0	25	0	25
7.	No Response	44	17	33	11	2	0	2	8	81	36	117
8.	Negligence towards this Sector	0	0	3	0	0	0	0	0	3	0	3
9.	Destruction in both Areas	0	0	14	8	0	0	0	0	14	8	22
10.	Rural Areas Effected More	0	0	6	4	0	0	67	28	73	32	105
11.	Don't Know	0	0	4	0	0	0	0	0	4	0	4
12.	Loss of both Infrastructure and Manpower	0	0	7	7	0	0	40	17	47	24	71
13.	Patient Number Increased	0	0	3	0	0	0	0	0	3	0	3
14.	Less Attention to Improve it	0	0	4	3	2	3	0	0	6	6	12
15.	Funds Diverted	0	0	3	2	2	3	25	3	30	8	38
16.	Develepment Movement	0	0	0	5	4	10	0	0	4	15	19
17.	Increase in MMR and IMR	0	0	0	1	0	0	0	0	0	1	1
18.	Increase in Patient no Infrastrucure is Same	0	0	0	3	0	0	0	0	0	3	3

19.	Construction of new Hospitals was Least Possible	0	0	0	0	4	3	0	0	4	3	7
20.	Overburdened and Overcrowded Hospitals in both the areas	0	0	0	0	5	6	40	21	45	27	72
21.	No Proper Concern for Infrastructure as Conflict Remained the Vital Focus	0	0	0	0	2	15	0	0	2	15	17
22.	Infrastructure Destroyed during Cross Firing in Many Areas	0	0	0	0	9	0	0	0	9	0	9
23.	Much of Infrastructure Occupied by Army Personnal during Conflict	0	0	0	0	3	0	0	0	3	0	3
24.	Unavaliabilty of Referral Transport	0	0	0	0	7	0	0	0	7	0	7
25.	Much of the Funds Remained Un-utilised	0	0	0	0	9	0	0	0	9	0	9
26.	Roads Underdeveloped	0	0	0	0	1	0	45	1	46	1	47
27.	We still have Many Hospitals Operating from Rented Building	0	0	0	0	3	1	0	0	3	1	4
28.	On an Average a Doctor Cater's to about 50 Patients in One Hour in District Hospital Anantnag/ Understaffed	0	0	0	0		1	0	0	0	1	1
29.	Hospitals Few in Comparison to Needs	0	0	0	0	4	0	0	0	4	0	4
30.	Couldn't be Developed Because of Curfews in Urban Areas	0	0	0	0		0	0	0	3	0	3
31.	Slow Construction of New Hospitals	0	0	0	0	0	0	12	17	12	17	29
32.	Projects Stopped for New Constructions	0	0	0	0	0	0	33	3	33	3	36

33.	Insufficient Numbers of Hospitals	0	0	0	0	0	0	37	24	37	24	61
34.	Maintenance of Hospitals	0	0	0	0	0	0	18	2	18	2	20

	Facilities in Urban and Rural Areas	*G*	*P*	*G*	*P*	*G*	*P*	*G*	*P*	*G*	*P*	*Total*
1.	Imbalance	0	15	0	0	0	0	0	0	0	15	15
2.	Impaired	0	7	0	0	0	0	0	0	0	7	7
3.	Destroyed	24	12	0	0	0	0	0	0	24	12	36
4.	Malfunctioned	0	0	0	0	0	0	0	0	0	1	1
5.	Inadequate	37	3	19	14	8	7	45	14	109	24	133
6.	No Response	39	12	40	19	16	10	0	0	95	41	136
7.	Underdeveloped Facilities in Rural Areas	0	0	8	2	0	0	0	0	8	2	10
8.	Facilities not Improved as per Requirement	0	0	7	1	0	0	0	0	7	1	8
9.	Doctors and Paramedics Left State	0	0	7	2	0	0	0	0	7	2	9
10.	Supply of Medicine not Adequate	0	0	5	0	12	11	60	34	77	11	88
11.	Sudden Rise in Patient Number	0	0	3	5	0	0	0	0	3	5	8
12.	Don't Know	0	0	2	0	0	0	0	0	2	0	2
13.	Diversion of Resources for Conflict Resolution	0	0	6	1	0	0	0	0	6	1	7
14.	Facilities Improved in both Areas	0	0	3	6	0	0	0	0	3	6	9
15.	Healthcare was Least Available	0	0	0	0	1	16	0	0	1	16	17
16.	Insufficient Staff	0	0	0	0	2	6	0	0	2	6	8
17.	Medicines Meant for Common Masses Supplied to the Army Personnel	0	0	0	0	0	1	0	0	0	1	1
18.	Availing Facilities was not Easy due to Crackdowns and Curfews	0	0	0	0	8	3	0	0	8	3	11
19.	Inadequate Female Staff	0	0	0	0	0	2	55	5	55	2	57
20.	Doctors Unavailable	0	0	0	0	6	0	0	0	6	0	6

21.	Still Inadequate Because of Corruption	0	0	0	0	8	0	0	0	8	0	8
22.	Not Yet Adequate	0	0	0	0	14	0	0	0	14	0	14
23.	Because of Pandit Migration Many Specialised Doctors were Lost by Us	0	0	0	0	3	0	0	0	3	0	3
24.	Private Clinics Now Preferred	0	0	0	0	1	0	0	0	1	0	1
25.	For Want of Facilities People Prefer Other States For Consultancy	0	0	0	0	4	0	0	0	4	0	4
26.	Highly Qualified Doctors Still Move to Other States Because of Conflict	0	0	0	0	2	0	35	2	37	0	37
27.	Still Private Clinics Cater to Rural Populace Because of Inadequate Facilities in Government Hospitals	0	0	0	0	6	0	0	0	6	0	6
28.	Understaffed Hospitals	0	0	0	0	4	0	0	0	4	0	4
29.	Medicines not Available	0	0	0	0	4	0	0	0	4	0	4
30.	Many a Woman Died at Home during Pregnancy in Conflict (Crackdown's and Curfews)	0	0	0	0	3	0	0	0	3	0	3
31.	More Suffered	0	0	0	0	5	0	0	0	5	0	5

6d 33. Gender Health Suffrings

Q. No. 6(c) S. NO.	*Women Suffer Due to Collapse of Health System*	*SRI (D1)*		*BUD (D2)*		*ANA (D3)*		*BAR (D4)*			*Responses*	
		G	*P*	*G*	*P*	*G*	*P*	*G*	*P*	*General*	*Professional*	*Total*
1.	YES	80	40	82	50	100	50	100	50	362	190	552
2.	RCH and MCH	36	18	0	0	14	7	0	0	50	25	75
3.	Overall Health	23	13	0	0	38	20	9	7	70	40	110
4.	Gynae and Obesterics	13	5	0	0	0	0	13	8	26	13	39

5.	Depression, Trauma Stress and Mental Health etc.	8	4	58	39	39	17	35	21	140	81	221
6.	MMR Increased	0	0	11	2	0	0	0	0	11	2	13
7.	Cardiological	0	0	0	0	9	6	43	14	52	20	72
8.	PTSD	7	3	0	0	0	0	0	0	7	3	10
9.	Don't Know	6	1	0	0	0	0	0	0	6	1	7
10.	Late Marriages	0	2	0	0	0	0	0	0	0	2	2
11.	Physical Violence	0	3	0	0	0	0	0	0	0	3	3
12.	NO	6	3	6	0	0	0	0	0	12	3	15
13.	No Response	14	7	12	0	0	0	0	0	26	7	33

6e 34. Medical Losees during conflict

Q. No.	*How Medical Losses*	*SRI*		*BUD*		*ANA*		*BAR*			*6(e)*	
Due to Collapse		*(D1)*		*(D2)*		*(D3)*		*(D4)*			*Responses*	
S. NO.	*Be Fulfilled*	*G*	*P*	*G*	*P*	*G*	*P*	*G*	*P*	*General*	*Professional*	*Total*
1.	Mission based Planning	0	2	0	0	0	0	0	0	0	2	2
2.	Improve Facilities	47	29	8	0	4	3	0	0	59	32	91
3.	Improve Infrastructure	21	7	8	4	4	2	0	0	33	13	46
4.	Improve Professional Female staff	24	5	0	0	1	14	0	0	25	19	44
5.	Counselling	0	2	0	0	0	0	0	0	0	2	2
6.	Improved hospitals	0	5	0	0	0	0	0	0	0	5	5
7.	No Response	7	4	0	0	0	0	0	0	7	4	11
8.	Primary focus is needed	0	0	28	9	0	0	0	0	28	9	37
9.	Proper use of Resources	0	0	3	3	0	0	0	0	3	3	6
10.	Effective use of Money	0	0	3	0	0	0	0	0	3	0	3
11.	Proper Implementation	0	0	5	3	2	1	0	0	7	4	11
12.	Frame Policies	0	0	5	0	0	0	0	0	5	0	5
13.	Resolve Conflict	0	0	3	2	26	7	77	44	106	53	159
14.	Health Policy for J&K	0	0	6	3	3	6	0	0	9	9	18
15.	Proper Planning	0	0	6	10	0	0	0	0	6	10	16
16.	Both Govt and Private should join Hands	0	0	1	3	0	0	0	0	11	3	14

17.	Attention to Mental Health	0	0	1	1	0	0	0	0	1	1	2
18.	Proper Training	0	0	1	0	0	0	0	0	1	0	1
19.	Centre State NGO'S Co-operation	0	0	3	5	3	0	0	0	6	5	11
20.	Gender Specific Schemes	0	0	2	3	0	0	23	6	25	9	34
21.	More Allocation of Funds	0	0	0	0	15	5	0	0	15	5	20
22.	No Response	8	0	7	4	0	0	0	0	15	4	19
23.	Prioritise Gender Health Than-Defence and Wars	0	0	0	0	0	1	0	0	0	1	1
24.	Separate Hospitals For Woman	0	0	0	0	1	0	0	0	1	0	1
25.	Educate the Woman	0	0	0	0	1	0	0	0	1	0	1
26.	Empower The Woman	0	0	0	0	3	0	0	0	3	0	3
27.	Health Administrators Should Work with Dedication	0	0	0	0	1	0	0	0	1	0	1
28.	Free Healthcare to Woman	0	0	0	0	13	0	0	0	13	0	13
29.	Proper Monitoring and Evaluation	0	0	0	0	8	0	0	0	8	0	8
30.	Call Back Pandits and Work for their Rehabilitation	0	0	0	0	3	0	0	0	3	0	3

7e. 35. Gender Healthcare: Suggestions

Q.NO. 7 S.NO.	*Suggestions For GHC*	*SRI(DI)* G	P	*BUD(D2)* G	P	*ANA(D3)* G	P	*BAR(D4)* G	P	*Responses* *General*	*Professional*	*Total*
1.	Supervision	23	10	0	0	0	0	2	0	25	10	35
2.	Check Stagnation of Doctors	5	4	0	0	0	0	0	0	5	4	9
3.	Maintain Doctor Patient Ratio	4	0	7	3	1	0	0	0	12	3	15
4.	Formulate and Implement GH Policies and Schemes	13	0	0	0	3	0	0	0	16	0	16
5.	Improve Quality of Drugs/Food	0	2	2	0	0	0	0	0	2	2	4
6.	Check Corruption And Adulteration	7	6	9	1	0	0	0	0	16	7	23

7.	Improve Facilities	9	8	7	6	0	0	0	0	16	14	30
8.	Mission based Planning	1	6	5	4	0	0	0	0	6	10	16
9.	Inspections	5	2	0	0	0	0	0	0	5	2	7
10.	Increase Female Staff	3	3	0	0	2	7	16	0	21	10	31
11.	Improve Infrastructure	15	4	19	7	25	12	0	0	59	23	82
12.	Co-ordination	2	0	0	0	0	0	0	0	2	0	2
13.	Gender Health policy	1	0	1	1	4	4	35	15	41	20	61
14.	Aware People, Conduct Health Surveys	11	0	0	0	0	0	0	0	11	0	11
15.	No Response	1	5	0	0	0	0	0	0	1	5	6
16.	Proper Supervision on Doctors	0	0	23	0	0	0	0	0	23	0	23
17.	Proper Implementation	0	0	7	7	2	3	1	0	10	10	20
18.	24×7 Services	0	0	1	4	0	0	0	0	1	4	5
19.	Supervision and Accountability	0	0	7	7	1	0	0	0	8	7	15
20.	Training Medical Professionals	0	0	4	0	0	0	1	0	5	0	5
21.	Free Supply of Drugs	0	0	3	1	0	0	0	0	3	1	4
22.	Increase Blood Banks	0	0	1	1	0	0	0	0	1	1	2
23.	Increase Funds	0	0	2	0	1	0	0	0	3	0	3
24.	Mass Awareness	0	0	2	1	0	0	0	0	2	1	3
25.	Proper Tracking on deliveries and Pregnancies	0	0	0	1	0	0	0	0	0	1	1
26.	More Maternity Hospitals	0	0	0	2	5	4	12	8	17	14	31
27.	Free Health Camps and Investigations	0	0	0	2	0	0	0	0	0	2	2
28.	Proper Attention Authorities	0	0	0	1	0	0	0	0	0	1	1
29.	Fair Price Medical Shops	0	0	0	1	0	0	0	0	0	1	1
30.	Work for the Resolution of Conflict	0	0	0	0	1	0	0	0	1	0	1
31.	Special Policy for the Mental Health of Woman	0	0	0	0	1	0	0	0	1	0	1

32.	Provide Accessible Healthcare in Far Flung Areas	0	0	0	0	7	0	6	6	13	6	19
33.	Provision of Well Equiped Ambulances	0	0	0	0	0	0	12	2	12	2	14
34.	Provision of Specialised Doctors Round the Clock	0	0	0	0	0	0	3	3	3	3	6
35.	Provision of health Education	0	0	0	0	0	0	4	0	4	0	4
36.	Construction of New Hospitals	0	0	0	0	0	0	3	0	3	0	3

7b 36. Suggestion for NGO

		SRI (D1)		BUD (D2)		ANA (D3)		BAR (D4)		Responses		
S. NO.	SUGGESTION FOR NGO'S	G	P	G	P	G	P	G	P	General	Professional	Total
1.	Awareness	59	27	33	18	0	0	50	33	142	78	220
2.	Health Investigalion Camps	17	1	0	0	0	0	0	0	17	1	18
3.	Health Melas	2	1	0	0	11	1	0	0	13	2	15
4.	Highlight Critical Issues	4	3	0	0	8	7	0	0	12	10	22
5.	Follow Based Mission Progravmmes	0	5	0	0	0	0	0	0	0	5	5
6.	Work in Coordination	0	1	0	0	0	0	0	0	0	1	1
7.	Preventive Measures	4	0	0	0	0	0	0	0	4	0	4
8.	Health Education	8	0	19	14	29	28	0	0	56	42	98
9.	No Response	6	12	17	4	0	0	0	0	23	16	39
10.	Aware People about their Rights	0	0	1	0	0	0	45	17	46	17	63
11.	Help Poor People	0	0	5	4	0	0	0	0	5	4	0
12.	Create Awareness	0	0	16	1	0	0	0	0	16	1	17
13.	Don't Know	0	0	1	0	0	0	0	0	1	0	1
14.	Family Counselling	0	0	5	1	10	1	0	0	15	2	17

15.	Highlight Gender Sesitive Issues	0	0	2	0	0	0	0	0	2	0	2
16.	Marital Counselling	0	0	1	1	0	0	0	0	1	1	2
17.	Cooperation with Government	0	0	0	6	7	7	5	0	12	13	25
18.	Promote Health Culture	0	0	0	1	0	0	0	0	0	1	1

7c 37. Suggestion for Civil Society

		SRI	*BUD*	*ANA*		*B.AR*						
	Suggestions For	*(D1)*		*(D2)*		*(D3)*		*(D4)*			*Responses*	
S.NO.	*Civil Society*	*G*	*P*	*G*	*P*	*G*	*P*	*G*	*P*	*General*	*Professional*	*Total*
1.	Cooperation	82	35	45	21	4	3	0	0	131	59	190
2.	Responsibly demand their rights	3	4	0	0	0	0	0	0	3	4	7
3.	Awareness	9	2	0	1	27	7	0	0	36	10	46
4.	Health Education	1	0	0	0	0	0	0	0	1	0	1
5.	Utilise Facilities Responsibly	1	0	0	0	4	8	17	5	22	13	35
6.	Check Corruption	1	0	0	0	0	0	0	0	1	0	1
7.	No Response	3	9	17	6	0	0	0	0	20	15	35
8.	Should take Care of Themselves	0	0	14	5	0	0	0	0	14	5	19
9.	Make Better Use of Resources	0	0	13	4	0	0	0	0	13	4	17
10.	Demand for Their Rights	0	0	9	2	0	0	0	0	9	2	11
11.	Understand Their Role and Responsibility	0	0	1	0	0	0	0	0	1	0	1
12.	Attention Towards Preventive Care	0	0	0	1	0	0	0	0	0	1	1
13.	Stop Self Medication	0	0	1	2	0	0	0	0	1	2	3
14.	Should Adhere to Doctors Advice	0	0	0	4	0	0	0	0	0	4	4

15.	Should Get Conscious About Health Needs	0	0	0	2	0	0	0	0	0	2	2
16.	Promote Preventive Care	0	0	0	2	0	0	0	0	0	2	2
17.	Highlight the Issues	0	0	0	0	8	11	37	35	45	46	91
18.	Help the Needy by Counselling	0	0	0	0	13	2	0	0	13	2	15
19.	Work in Co-ordination with Government	0	0	0	0	3	3	0	0	3	3	6
20.	Follow ups	0	0	0	0	0	3	0	0	0	3	3
21.	Demand for their Rights	0	0	0	0	0	7	0	0	0	7	7
22.	Should Take Care of Themselves	0	0	0	0	6	0	0	0	6	0	6
23.	Vigil at the Services Provided the Govt Health Centres	0	0	0	0	0	0	15	8	15	8	23
24.	Criticism of Gender Health Issues in a Demorcatic Manner	0	0	0	0	0	0	23	2	23	2	25
25.	Creating Pressure Groups for Policy Making	0	0	0	0	0	0	8	0	8	0	8

7d 38. Suggestion for all

	Q No For All	*SRI(DI)*	*BUD(D2)*		*ANA(D3)*			*B.AR(D4)*		*Responses*		
S. NO.	*One Suggestion*	*G*	*P*	*G*	*P*	*G*	*P*	*G*	*P*	*General*	*Professional*	*Total*
1.	Awareness	0	0	0	0	11	3	0	0	0	0	14
2.	Work in Co-ordination to Curb Corruption	0	0	0	0	3	3	0	0	0	0	6
3.	Work in Co-ordination to Resolve the Conflict of Kashmir	0	0	0	0	17	0	0	0	0	0	17

4.	Promote Education and Counselling to Woman	0	0	0	0	4	0	0	0	0	0	4

8a 39. Background Information of Respondents

Q. NO.	*BACKGROUND INFORMATION*											
(8) (a)		*SRI(D1)*		*BUD(D2)*		*ANA(D3)*		*BAR(D4)*			*RESPONSES*	
S. NO.	*Background*	*G*	*P*	*G*	*P*	*G*	*P*	*G*	*P*	*General*	*Professional*	*Total*
1.	***AGE***											
	14-30	38	19	44	26	30	8	31	11	143	64	207
	40-45	33	22	44	22	52	36	56	34	185	114	299
	45 AND ABOVE	29	9	12	2	18	6	13	5	72	22	94
	Total									400	200	600
2.	***SEX***											
	MALE	20	24	26	30	48	29	65	28	159	111	270
	FEMALE	80	26	74	20	52	21	35	22	241	89	330
	Total									400	200	600
3.	***RESIDENCE***											
	RURAL	17	12	86	42	50	27	65	23	218	104	322
	URBAN	83	38	14	8	50	23	35	27	182	96	278
	Total									400	200	600
4.	***MARITAL STATUS***											
	MARRIED	56	30	71	26	46	29	64	37	237	122	359
	UNMARRIED	42	20	21	24	51	19	34	11	148	74	222
	WIDOWED	2	0	8	0	2	1	0	0	12	1	13
	DIVORCED	0	0	0	0	1	1	2	2	3	3	6
	Total									400	200	600
5.	***INCOME***											
	BELOW 50000	98	44	89	35	65	10	86	29	338	118	456
	50000-I LAC	2	6	8	15	30	35	13	21	53	77	130
	I LAC-2LAC	0	0	3	0	5	5	1	0	9	5	14
	ABOVE	0	0	0	0	0	0	0	0	0	0	0
	Total									400	200	600
6.	***WORKING STATUS***											
	DOMESTIC	43	0	66	0	50	36	7	0	166	36	202
	WORKING	57	50	34	50	50	14	93	50	234	164	398
	Total									400	200	600
7.	***LANGUAGE***											
	KASHMIRI	100	48	100	48	100	50	100	50	400	196	596
	URDU	0	2	0	2	0	0	100	50	100	54	154
	ENGLISH	0	0	0	0	0	0	70	50	70	50	120

	GOJIRI	0	0	0	0	0	0	0	0	0	0	0
	PAHAR1	0	0	0	0	0	0	2	1	2	1	3
	PUNJABI	0	0	0	0	0	0	2	2	2	2	4
	OTHERS	0	0	0	0	0	0	3	2	3	2	5
8.	***FAMILY TYPE***											
	NUCLEAR	86	43	34	20	58	44	52	27	230	134	364
	JOINT	14	7	66	30	42	6	48	23	170	66	236
	Total									400	200	600
9.	***FAMILY OCCUPATION***											
	AGRICULTURE	6	4	34	4	47	0	28	9	115	17	132
	SERVICES	66	28	38	46	48	50	42	32	194	156	350
	TRADE AND COMMERCE	15	11	0	0	3	0	10	0	28	11	39
	BUSINESS	13	7	28	0	2	0	20	9	63	16	79
	Total									400	200	600
10.	***LITERACY***											
	LITERATE	79	50	53	50	83	50	100	50	315	200	515
	ILLITERATE	21	0	47	0	17	0	0	0	85	0	85
	MATRIC	20	0	28	4	16	0	5	0	69	4	73
	12TH	17	2	11	6	16	0	11	6	55	14	69
	B.A	15	0	10	9	22	0	15	3	62	12	74
	ABOVE	27	48	4	31	29	50	69	41	129	170	299

QUESTIONNAIRE OF THE GENDER HEALTHCARE STUDY

QUESTIONNAIRE

FROM 'GENDER NEGATIVE TO GENDER POSITIVE' HEALTH CARE SYSTEM: A STUDY OF GENDER HEALTH CARE AND CONFLICT IN J&K

Q.No. (1) Gender Healthcare Fields and Needs

(1.a) Identify the major fields of Gender Healthcare in Kashmir

•

•

•

(1.b) Identify the Gender Health Needs in Kashmir.

•

•

•

Q.No. (2) Gender Health and Government Policy and Programmes

(2.a) What are the major features of gender health policy in J&K?

•

•

•

(2.b) Does this policy reflect in the planning and programmes, Yes, No?

•

•

•

If yes, Give details

(2.c) What is the general attitude about the Gender Health Policy and programmes among the health administrators?

Q.No. (3) Gender Health Diseases Problems and Issues in J&K

(3.a) What are the common gender diseases prevailing in Kashmir

•

•

•

(3.b) Do they get proper treatment- Yes/No

If Yes, Where from?

If No, Why?

(3.c) Identify the ways and means through which the gender differentiation: In healthcare can be removed.

(3.d) What are the major Gender Health Problems in Kashmir?

-
-
-

(3.e) Comment on these Gender Health issues in J&K: Family Planning:

- Gender Sex ratio:
- Female foeticide (Abortion):
- Maternal Mortality:
- Cultural Restrictions:

Q.No. (4) Gender Healthcare System from Gender Point of View

(4.a) What is lacking in the present healthcare system from the gender point of view?

-
-
-

(4.b) What do you feel about the role of state in Gender Healthcare (Identify the measures to be taken).

-
-
-

(4.c) Do you feel there is the role of Private Sector in Gender Healthcare in J&K? Yes/No

-
-
-

If Yes, Identify the agencies and institutions

If No, Give reasons

(4.d) Do you feel there is satisfactory level of awareness about Gender Health in Kashmir? Yes, No

If no, what is needed in this regard?

(4.e) How can we train the medical and paramedical staff in Gender Healthcare?

(4.f) How can we develop and maintain the Gender Health Care social environment in Kashmir?

(4.g) What is the relationship between child Healthcare and gender healthcare?

Q.No. (5) Gender Health Culture in Kashmir

(5.a) What are the General features of Traditional Health Culture in Kashmir?

(5.b) Has any change occurred in these conditions Yes, No?

If yes, Cite Examples

If No, Why?

(5.c) Give an assessment of the prevailing (existing) Gender health culture in Kashmir?

(5.d) What are the reasons for these conditions?

(5.e) Why Gender Health was ignored in the past in Kashmir?

(5.f) Why the Gender Health is ignored in the present situation?

(5.g) Do values and norms support the attitude of Ignorance towards Gender Health?

(5.h) What is the condition of Health of Women in domestic Context?

(5.i) What is the Condition of Health of Women in working Context?

(5.j) Has the Working status changed her health status? Yes/No.

If yes, Give examples

If No, cite reasons

Q.No. (6) Gender Health and Conflict

(6.a) What Kind of impact was experienced on Gender health in Kashmir during last two decades?

(6.b) What Kind of impact conflict-had on the existing healthcare system particularly?

Infrastructure:

In Urban areas

In Ruralareas

(6c)Facilities:

In Urban areas

In Rural areas

(6.d) Did Women suffer because of the collapse of health system in Kashmir? Yes, No.

If- yes mention about areas (Medical areas):

(6.d) How can these medical losses due to conflict be fulfilled?

Q.No. (7) Suggestions

What are your suggestions about Gender Health Care in Kashmir for?

(7.a) Government

(7.b) N.G.Os

(7.c) Civil Society

Index

N